SPANISH GOLDEN AGE TEXTS IN THE TWENTY-FIRST CENTURY

SPANISH GOLDEN AGE STUDIES

Series Editor:
Professor Duncan Wheeler (University of Leeds)

Editorial Advisory Board:
Dr Jonathan Bradbury (University of Exeter)
Professor Peter Evans (Queen Mary, University of London)
Professor Barbara Fuchs (UCLA)
Professor Enrique García Santo-Tomás (University of Michigan)
Dr Stuart Green (University of Leeds)
Professor Javier Huerta Calvo (Universidad Complutense de Madrid)
Dr Melanie Henry (University of Durham)
Dr Anne Holloway (Queen's University, Belfast)
Professor Rosa Navarro Durán (Universidad de Barcelona)
Dr John Rutherford (The Queen's College, University of Oxford)

SPANISH GOLDEN AGE TEXTS IN THE
TWENTY-FIRST CENTURY
TEACHING THE OLD THROUGH THE NEW

Idoya Puig and Karl McLaughlin (eds)

Peter Lang
Oxford • Bern • Berlin • Bruxelles • New York • Wien

Bibliographic information published by Die Deutsche Nationalbibliothek
Die Deutsche Nationalbibliothek lists this publication in the Deutsche
Nationalbibliografie; detailed bibliographic data is available on the Internet at
http://dnb.d-nb.de.

A catalogue record for this book is available from the British Library.

A CIP catalog record for this book has been applied for at the Library of Congress.

ISSN 2297-5225
ISBN 978-1-78874-635-9 (print) • ISBN 978-1-78874-636-6 (ePDF)
ISBN 978-1-78874-637-3 (ePub) • ISBN 978-1-78874-638-0 (mobi)

Cover design by Peter Lang Ltd.
Cover image by David Rodríguez Suárez.

© Peter Lang AG 2019
Published by Peter Lang Ltd, International Academic Publishers,
52 St Giles, Oxford, OX1 3LU, United Kingdom
oxford@peterlang.com, www.peterlang.com

Idoya Puig and Karl McLaughlin have asserted their right under the Copyright,
Designs and Patent Act, 1988, to be identified as Editors of this Work.

All rights reserved.
All parts of this publication are protected by copyright.
Any utilisation outside the strict limits of the copyright law, without the
permission of the publisher, is forbidden and liable to prosecution.
This applies in particular to reproductions, translations, microfilming,
and storage and processing in electronic retrieval systems.

This publication has been peer reviewed.

Contents

List of Figures ix

List of Tables xi

Acknowledgements xiii

Introduction 1

PART I Setting the context 9

JEREMY LAWRANCE
1 Why Golden Age? 11

STUART DAVIS
2 The Golden Age in the Hispanic Studies classroom:
   The changing shape of what we teach our undergraduates
   in the UK 31

PART II Teaching the old through the new 55

ALMUDENA GARCÍA GONZÁLEZ
3 El estudio del mundo literario de la España del siglo diecisiete
   desde la ficción televisiva del siglo ventiuno: autores, obras y
   contexto presentes en *El Ministerio del Tiempo* 57

TED BERGMAN
4 What 50 Cent can teach us about Quevedo: The case for
   using analogy and video clips 71

COLLIN McKINNEY
5 The next best thing?: Introducing *Don Quijote* as a
   graphic novel   87

IDOYA PUIG
6 Teaching literature and language using a multiliteracies
   framework: Exploring intercultural skills with Cervantes's
   La española inglesa   105

JULES WHICKER
7 Technologically assisted translational activity: An approach
   to teaching Spanish Golden Age literature   123

PART III Teaching poetry   139

KARL McLAUGHLIN
8 Meaningful parallels for students: Golden Age poetic
   production as examples of talent shows and celebrity spats 141

ANTONIO CARREÑO-RODRÍGUEZ
9 Golden Age 'diss tracks': Teaching Baroque poetry and
   polemic through rap   159

RUBÉN CRISTÓBAL HORNILLOS
10 La poesía clásica a través de canciones actuales   177

PART IV Teaching theatre   191

AROA ALGABA GRANERO AND SARA SÁNCHEZ-HERNÁNDEZ
11 El proyecto de innovación docente *TAAULA. El teatro áureo
   en el aula de Filología*   193

GEMA CIENFUEGOS ANTELO

12 Escenas para el aula de E/LE: el personaje femenino en el
    teatro del Siglo de Oro   211

DUNCAN WHEELER

13 The pedagogic potential (and limitations) of
    cinematic adaptations   227

Notes on contributors   249

Index   255

Figures

Figure 5.1.	Don Quijote recovers at home (Davis, *The Complete Don Quixote*, 25)	94
Figure 5.2.	Alonso Quijano and his grandson come upon the windmills (Flix, *Don Quijote*, 95)	97
Figure 5.3.	Maritornes, 'La criada malencarada de cuerpo gallardo' (Davis, *The Complete Don Quixote*, 63)	99
Figure 5.4.	Don Quijote drinks the 'bálsamo de Fierabrás' (Davis, *The Complete Don Quixote*, 78)	100
Figure 5.5.	Title page (Davis, *The Complete Don Quixote*, 5)	102
Figure 5.6.	Tale of the 'Curioso impertinente' (Davis, *The Complete Don Quixote*, 124)	103
Figura 10.1.	Portada ilustrativa del material didáctico. Fuente: elaboración propia	182
Figura 10.2.	Índice de la propuesta didáctica. Fuente: elaboración propia	183
Figura 10.3.	Secuenciación de una unidad didáctica. Fuente: elaboración propia	184
Figura 10.4.	Comienzo de la unidad 8 con los textos encarados. Fuente: elaboración propia	186
Figura 10.5.	Comienzo de la unidad 15 con los textos encarados. Fuente: elaboración propia	187

Tables

Table 2.1.	Authors and directors taught in at least 25 per cent of surveyed departments in 2015–16 data collection	44
Table 2.2.	Texts taught in at least 20 per cent of surveyed departments in 2015–16 data collection	45
Table 2.3.	Golden Age authors or anonymous texts taught in at least 13 per cent of surveyed departments in 2015–16 data collection	46
Table 2.4.	Golden Age texts taught in at least 35 per cent of surveyed departments in 2015–16 data collection	47
Table 2.5.	Authors taught in at least 10 per cent of surveyed departments in at least one of the three data collections	49
Table 2.6.	Texts taught in at least 10 per cent of surveyed departments in at least one of the three data collections	50
Table 2.7.	The presence of Golden Age material in each data collection	51
Tabla 11.1.	Recursos empleados en *TAAULA*	197
Tabla 11.2.	Asignaturas de *TAAULA*	199
Tabla 11.3.	Temario de la asignatura	200
Tabla 11.4.	Grupos de trabajo	202
Tabla 11.5.	Preguntas y resultados de la encuesta	203
Tabla 11.6.	Preguntas y resultados de la encuesta	207

Acknowledgements

This book would not have been possible without the help and support of numerous individuals and institutions, whom the editors would like to acknowledge here. Firstly, to Peter Lang Publishing, in particular series editor Duncan Wheeler, for their receptiveness to our initial proposal to explore innovative pedagogical practices in Golden Age Studies across several countries, as well as for their constant encouragement and advice during the past year as this volume was put together. We are indebted to the Department of Languages, Linguistics and TESOL at Manchester Metropolitan University, particularly its head, Derek Bousfield, for the financial and other support provided both for this publication and for the earlier academic events from which it emanated. Carmen Herrero, head of Spanish, deserves our gratitude for the understanding and flexibility that allowed us the time to produce the manuscript. We would also like to express our appreciation to Helen Darby and staff at Research in Art and the Humanities (RAH!) at the university for their long-standing support. We are grateful to the Instituto Cervantes in Manchester for the assistance provided for the symposium that led to this volume and to Margaret Vaudrey for her invaluable contribution to the editing process. Finally, our heartfelt gratitude goes to all the authors, particularly Jeremy Lawrance, who answered our call for papers and demonstrated an inspirational willingness to contribute their expertise and enthusiasm to the project.

Introduction

Few would dispute that the Golden Age represented the high point of Spain's cultural flowering, an unprecedented demonstration of a nation's talent in prose fiction, poetry and theatre. The sixteenth and seventeenth centuries spawned a plethora of innovative and creative literary minds that placed Spain on the global literary map. For that very reason, the study of literature, not just Spanish but world, would be incomplete without reference to authors of the stature of Cervantes, Quevedo, Calderón or Lope de Vega, just as it would be inconceivable without mention of Shakespeare. This height of achievement has been rightly reflected down the years in the presence of many canonical Golden Age authors on university and pre-university Spanish courses worldwide.

However, changing interests and contexts in education have caused this prominent presence to wane notably in countries such as the United Kingdom and the United States. Spain enjoys a more fortunate position in that the aforementioned canonical writers continue to feature very visibly on the curriculum at secondary and tertiary level. However, as will become apparent in this volume, this does not mean that teachers in Spain do not share the growing concern voiced by their international colleagues at the disappearance of Golden Age from the curriculum for reasons ranging from the perceived difficulty of the texts of the period to the greater demand for (and, in some cases, imposition of) less specialized teaching in many higher education institutions.

Even if the precise motives underlying the decline have still to be fully established, there is clear agreement that the Golden Age – as an invaluable manifestation of Spanish culture and history – must continue to be studied. In the light of the rapid decline in the number of universities offering specialist modules in the period, it is becoming increasingly obvious that new approaches are required to preserve or rekindle interest in topics which many of today's learners, products perhaps of a results-oriented and surface (as opposed to a deep) learning culture, consider outmoded and of little relevance to their needs and interests.

These and similar concerns prompted the co-editors of the present volume to organize an event which, although they did not know it at the time, was to prove the more immediate genesis of the collection of papers included here. Among the commemorations held in 2016 to mark the 400th anniversary of the deaths of Cervantes and Shakespeare, Karl McLaughlin and Idoya Puig organized a celebration at Manchester Metropolitan University to bring together students from the university's Languages Department and its renowned School of Theatre. 'Tilting at Windmills: Cervantes "meets" Shakespeare 400 years on' consisted of readings of Cervantes by undergraduate students of Spanish from various years, followed by performances by drama students of excerpts from some of Shakespeare's best-known plays. It concluded with a dramatized fictional meeting between the two writers, who engaged in a humorous philosophical reflection on their world, one that – as it turned out – was not too dissimilar to that of today in terms of its pressing issues, including the state of universities, Britain's place in Europe, and immigration.

The success of the event exceeded all expectations and the organizers subsequently discovered, to their great satisfaction, that one parent had taken to reading *Don Quijote* in full after seeing his relatively shy daughter blossom as she delivered an inspirational reading of a lengthy passage in Spanish to a packed audience. The overwhelmingly positive outcome led to an invitation to repeat the unusual commemoration for the general public at Manchester Central Library. The success was particularly gratifying given that, as occurs in many universities today, neither of the two organizers – holders of PhDs on this period of Spanish literature – teaches their subject on programmes which focus largely on twentieth-century culture and the use of film. Both have observed with concern the progressive disappearance of literature courses in favour of content perceived to be more popular with, and accessible to, present-day students.

Almost exactly one year later, in April 2017, as part of the annual Association of Hispanists of Great Britain and Ireland (AHGBI) conference in Cardiff, Stuart Davis organized a panel entitled 'From Canon to Cultural Studies?: Hispanic Literature and Film in UK Spanish Degrees', which reviewed current trends in the teaching of canonical texts in universities. Although the scope of the panel covered literature in the broad sense,

Introduction

the responses confirmed growing fears for the fate of Golden Age texts in university teaching and prompted the co-editors of this volume to organize a one-day symposium in the spring of 2018 at Manchester Metropolitan University. The aim of the symposium was to bring together academics to examine the current state of Golden Age teaching and provide a platform to share good practice and explore creative approaches in order to ensure the continued presence of sixteenth- and seventeenth-century Spanish authors in the classroom.

It was immediately apparent from the papers and the ensuing debates at the symposium, which attracted participants from the United Kingdom, Spain and the United States, that it was not just a similar problem that was shared across different countries: equally importantly, there was a shared willingness to address, as a matter of some urgency, the protection, preservation and transmission of the literary classics of the Spanish Golden Age, along with lesser-known works and authors of the period. Broad consensus existed among contributors that the opportunity should be seized to reimagine the teaching of these texts in ways that would complement rather than replace traditional approaches. Ways that would speak creatively to students and enable them to access literary content for which they feel little or no affinity. In an ideal educational world, students – precisely because they are students – would possess the requisite intrinsic motivation to want to learn as much as possible, in their original format, about the writings of authors whose ideas helped shape Spanish literary culture. However, there is no escaping the fact that, to borrow and adapt Friedrich Schleiermacher's much-quoted statement on the dilemma faced by translators, teachers of Golden Age literature often have little choice but to 'move' the author towards the student, in this case adapting context and content to facilitate understanding by learners for whom such works prove highly challenging in terms of language and cultural relevance.

The need for a creative approach is aptly summed up by Sidney Donnell, who – referring to the author of *Don Quijote* – advocated that 'professors of Cervantes must get ahead of the curve and contribute to the creation of programs of study that make sense to students before they take a seat on the first day of classes. The academic road ahead is more and more interdisciplinary, and early modern literary works have a crucial role to play in the teaching of language, of culture, and of genres as acts of communication'.[1] While far from new, endeavours to adapt and update teaching methodologies have been stepped up noticeably in the current millennium, with Cervantes inevitably occupying a prominent position in such approaches.[2] Drama and poetry have not been neglected, however, and it is worth underlining the important contributions made by authors such as Bass and Greer, Thacker and Wheeler, in addition to the special edition of *Calíope* devoted to the teaching of Golden Age poetry.[3]

For all the undeniable attraction it holds for academic research, Golden Age cannot evade the modern-day reality of higher education, which includes the near-permanent prospect of closures of Languages departments due to falling student numbers and the risk of the disappearance of modules deemed excessively demanding on the intellectual level. The luxury of small tutorials with a handful of committed students who read a different work for each weekly seminar is one enjoyed by the fortunate few among academics today. Growing competition for students and the need to ensure a continuous stream of tuition fee revenue have transformed the way universities operate, forcing many to respond by providing products demanded by students who increasingly expect delivery tailored to their requirements and interests. There is no ignoring either that, as an inescapable part of this process, teaching and learning have evolved to embrace a more student-centred focus,

---

1 Sidney Donnell, '*Don Quixote* in the Balance: Early Modern Studies and the Undergraduate Curriculum', in James A. Parr and Lisa Vollendorf, eds, *Approaches to Teaching Cervantes's Don Quixote* (New York: Modern Language Association of America, 2015), 197–205, 204.

2 In addition to the collection of articles of Parr and Vollendorf, quoted above, noteworthy contributions include Edward H. Friedman, 'Quixotic Pedagogy; Or, Putting the Teacher to the Test', *Hispania*, 88/1 (2005), 20–31, and Margaret Boyle, 'Teaching Don Quixote in the Digital Age: Page and Screen, Visual and Tactile', *Hispania* 99/4 (2016), 600–14.

3 See, respectively, Laura R. Bass and Margaret R. Greer, eds, *Approaches to Teaching Early Modern Spanish Drama* (New York: Modern Language Association of America, 2006); Jonathan Thacker, ed., *A Companion to Golden Age Theatre* (Woodbridge: Tamesis, 2007); Duncan Wheeler, 'Las adaptaciones cinematográficas como (posible) herramienta pedagógica', *Anuario Lope de Vega* 24 (2018), 260–8; and 'Teaching Golden Age Poetry', Edward Friedman, ed., *Calíope* 11/2 (2005).

including communicative and task-based learning approaches and the necessary integration of new technologies in the teaching of the literary classics.

The present volume brings together Hispanist expertise from the United Kingdom, United States and Spain with the aim of offering not further lamentation on the state of Golden Age today but studies and suggestions covering different authors, along with approaches which have the potential to be applied across poetic, prose and dramatic texts by Cervantes, Quevedo, Góngora, Lope de Vega and a host of other sixteenth- and seventeenth-century authors.

As evidenced by the aforementioned symposium and the subsequent contacts among academics who were, in many cases, unaware of each other's existence let alone their common lines of pedagogical endeavour, shared problems call for shared solutions and deeper integration of approaches, not work in isolation within departments, universities and even countries. In this regard, the proposed holding of a joint conference between the Cervantes Society of America (CSA) and the Asociación de Cervantistas (AC) in 2021 is welcome news and a step in the right direction.

Likewise, the volume offered here aims to be a step in an urgently needed direction, uniting as it does under one roof a valuable range of carefully thought pedagogical ideas and initiatives from different countries to increase the attraction of Golden Age to students. It has a four-part structure. Part I provides relevant context and the rationale for the publication, including reasons why Golden Age literature and culture merit our permanent attention. It commences with a compelling case made by Jeremy Lawrance, one of British Hispanism's foremost authorities on the early modern period, as to why Spanish Golden Age texts must continue to be studied not solely for their intrinsic value and pleasure, but also for their undisputed relevance and unique unrepeatability. Further contextualizing the need for new approaches, Stuart Davis examines the changing shape of undergraduate provision in Hispanic Studies in the United Kingdom and offers an illuminating comparison of data for the range of peninsular literature taught on courses across a period of two decades (1998–2016), identifying key authors and texts and how their fortunes have fared of late. The overview of the current situation in British universities evidences, in the vast majority of cases, the worrying decline in interest in this crucial period of Spanish literature and culture.

Part II sets out a number of general and specific proposals for the successful integration of old and new in teaching across a broad range of Golden Age topics. It commences with a study by Almudena García González of the presence of Golden Age literature in one of Spain's most popular television series, *El Ministerio del Tiempo*, which the author forcefully contends should be used as a tool to introduce students to the period and help them develop critical thinking around its most renowned literary figures. Ted Bergman then demonstrates how an intriguingly entitled module ('Action Heroes and Anti-Heroes in Early Modern Spain') taught at the University of St Andrews stimulates analytical imagination through cross-medium comparisons and thematic parallels that offer a modern perspective on works that might otherwise appear inaccessible to today's visual-culture learners, helping attenuate apprehension at the prospect of tackling a Golden Age text. Collin McKinney continues the emphasis on new classroom approaches to teaching classical texts in a style more suited to the tastes and habits of millennials by assessing the advantages and shortcomings of using alternate versions of the single most important literary work produced during the Golden Age, *Don Quijote*, including Rob Davis's graphic-novel adaptation of Cervantes's masterpiece. Taking one of Cervantes's *Novelas ejemplares* (*La española inglesa*) as an example, Idoya Puig illustrates the benefits of applying a multiliteracies approach combining different channels of communication and multimodal forms of linguistic expression to the study of literary texts in order to foster traditional reading skills and raise intercultural awareness. The part concludes with an analysis by Jules Whicker of the benefits of translational activity (both individual and collaborative) for stimulating a deeper understanding of and more active engagement with the linguistic, cultural and intellectual dimensions of Golden Age texts.

Part III focuses specifically on poetry and offers detailed proposals for creative engagement by students with the genre. It opens with a suggestions by Karl McLaughlin for establishing contextual parallels, for example between seventeenth-century literary academies and the ubiquitous TV talent shows of today, that might speak meaningfully to modern-day students and help them engage more willingly and successfully with Golden Age texts and literary culture. Antonio Carreño-Rodríguez then explores how the perspective of contemporary popular music, in particular the antagonism conveyed in so-called 'diss tracks', can prove useful for introducing students to the poetic rivalries and feuds that characterized much of the literary debate of the period. For his part, Rubén Cristóbal Hornillos outlines an initiative, trialled with learners of Spanish in Poland, in which present-day songs from a variety of genres such as pop, rock, reggae and reggaeton helped bring early modern poetry closer to the students' cultural and aesthetic universe, while also facilitating the teaching of aspects such as thematic content, metre and rhyme.

Finally, Part IV focuses on the theatre of the Golden Age and offers further examples of how new approaches might be incorporated to stimulate learner interest. Aroa Algaba Granero and Sara Sánchez-Hernández present a new pedagogical approach at the University of Salamanca which centres on the use of modern-day performances of Golden Age drama as a classroom tool to facilitate competency in the reading of Spanish plays from the period. Gema Cienfuegos Antelo reviews the current state of the teaching of literature in Spain and outlines a proposal for helping students of Spanish as a Foreign Language better experience the emotions of Golden Age theatre through dramatized readings, voice coaching, acting, and a focus on female characters in scenes from canonical dramatic works. Duncan Wheeler brings the volume to a close by reiterating our collective responsibility to seek solutions to the decline of Golden Age in the context of a post-literary culture, including by harnessing the possibilities offered by audiovisual productions to safeguard the continued presence of Spanish classical theatre as part of a holistic education both in Spain and beyond.

As will become clear in the pages that follow, there is widespread agreement among many at the coalface of Golden Age teaching – it is worth recalling that, as the title makes clear, the volume addresses teaching as opposed to the purely research strand of Golden Age, which may well remain beyond all but the keenest of present-day students – as to the need to bring authors and texts closer to the interests and styles of twenty-first-century learners. There will, perhaps inevitably, be criticism that such methodologies run the risk of devaluing or diluting the richness and complexity of Spain's most impressive literary and cultural epoch.[4] However, as the contributions collected

---

4   In a carefully reasoned but somewhat scathing review of a book on the teaching of Latin American *boom* novels, Dominic Moran describes 'a series of largely depressing snapshots of current teaching methodologies and practices employed in Hispanic

here aim to show, the teaching context is changing rapidly and, with appropriate thought and method, these approaches have the potential to encourage students to subsequently take the plunge and explore authors, times and works in greater depth once they have been coaxed into dipping a foot in the waters of Golden Age.

Idoya Puig and Karl McLaughlin

Studies departments across the United States'. However, the Oxford don makes an exception for one chapter, 'so radical (or so hopelessly démodé – it amounts to the same thing) that I was surprised it was included: rather than reaching for the Lego or DVD collection, he recommends that students majoring in Spanish acquire some books'. See Dominic Moran, 'Teaching the Latin American Boom', *Modern Language Review* 122/3 (2017), 730–1.

PART I

Setting the context

JEREMY LAWRANCE

1 Why Golden Age?

ABSTRACT
This introductory paper explores the intrinsic value and pleasure offered by the reading and study of Spanish Golden Age texts. Why Golden Age? Not only because these implicitly universal texts are among the most celebrated of any literature, not just Spanish. That celebrity is itself a sufficient source of interest to justify teaching them. More than that, however, they deserve students' attention today because of their undisputed relevance, their immeasurable difference, and unique unrepeatability. To these reasons, one must add the essential aspect of otherness they contain, their potential to open up perspectives on the world that are not the same as ours. Exploring an unfamiliar vision of humanity is a challenge, one that involves not just appropriating the texts to our concerns but also *being* appropriated by them as we engage with the task of fusing the details of their material content with their truth content.

Our aim is to describe a range of exciting new ways to teach Golden Age literature. I am conscious, however, that one aspect of the following preface may seem out of key. Our concert is in A-major, allegro, but I shall touch one down-beat B♭-minor note: namely, what we might call a crisis in our subject.

The reason I shall do so is that it broaches my chief conviction on the topic of reading and studying Golden Age texts, which is the *intrinsic* value and pleasure they offer. This is no doubt an unscholarly way of putting the matter, and for sure it does not admit of rigorous critical discussion – though that will not stop me trying to discuss it. But if there is a keynote to my essay, it is this. Why Golden Age? We are often exhorted, for the purpose of upholding our subject, to seek ways of showing it to be 'relevant'. It is salutary to meditate on the question of relevance and I shall do so, obliquely, but I am of the opinion that we must never lose sight of a more elemental and overwhelming reason for defending it. In the end, it is not the 'relevance' of *Don Quijote* or *Lazarillo de Tormes* that justifies what we do, but almost the opposite: it is these great texts' immeasurable *difference*, their unique unrepeatability, their potential to open up perspectives on the world that are not the same as ours ... and by that token are implicitly universal. I shall argue that, as we rightly seek to find new ways of presenting the works to modern readers, we should keep in view this vital aspect of otherness. In other words, that we should strive from time to time to let students know that what they are engaged with is a profoundly unfamiliar vision of humanity and that exploring it is a challenge: one that involves not just appropriating the texts to our concerns but also *being* appropriated by them.

To explain what I mean, I invoke the only critical theorist I propose to discuss, Walter Benjamin. He begins his seminal essay on 'The task of the translator' – that is, on the role of translatability (*Übersetzbarkeit*) in the *Fortleben* or afterlife of great works – with the statement, '*Nowhere* in relation to a work of art or an art form does consideration of the audience prove fruitful'.[1] This is a decidedly provocative manner of expressing my point about the primacy of intrinsic literary values over 'relevance'. However, he goes on to theorize it in a positive way. To suppose that our task in teaching texts is to translate the 'information' in them is a fundamental error. The 'information' in literary works is of little significance, since their essence is everything that is *not* information:

> Is a translation meant for readers who do not understand the original? That seems [...] the only conceivable reason for saying 'the same thing' over again. What, then, does a literary work 'say'? What information does it convey? Very little, to those who understand it. Its essential quality is not information, not communication. The sort of

---

[1] Walter Benjamin, 'The Task of the Translator', trans. Harry Zohn, in Marcus Bullock and Michael W. Jennings, eds, *Selected Writings*, I: *1913–26* (Cambridge, MA: Belknap Press of Harvard University, 1996), 253–63, 253, from 'Die Aufgabe des Übersetzers', in Charles Baudelaire, '*Tableaux parisiens*': *Deutsche Übertragung, mit einem Vorwort über die Aufgabe des Übersetzers*, trans. Walter Benjamin, Drucke des Argonautenkreises 5 (Heidelberg: Weissbach, 1923), vii–xvii, cited from the Rolf Tiedemann and Hermann Schweppenhäuser with Theodor W. Adorno and Gershom Scholem, eds, in *Gesammelte Schriften*, 7 vols in 13 tomes + 3 Supplements (Frankfurt: Suhrkamp, 1972–89), IV: *Kleine Prosa. Baudelaire-Übertragungen*, ed. Tillman Rexroth, 2 vols consecutively paginated (1972), I, 9–21, 9. Henceforth page references are given to both English and German, separated by a slash. At certain points I modify the translations, as here, to bring out more clearly the relevant point in the original.

> translation that seeks to convey the meaning could convey nothing but information – hence, the inessential. [...] But isn't what a literary work contains *besides* information – [...] the essential – defined as the unfathomable, the mysterious, the 'poetic'? (253/9)

Interpretation, then, is not translation in the commonplace sense, for that renders only the 'inessential'. Good interpretation 'recreates' the original:

> Translations that are more than paraphrases of content arise when, in the course of its afterlife, [...] the life of the original work attains its always renewed, latest, and most complete unfolding. (255/11)

This notion of the work's *afterlife* bears directly upon our topic: for translation in Benjamin's sense means the 'unfolding' (*Entfaltung*) of the original in a different time and place. Hence 'the history of the great works of art tells us about their descent from prior models, their realization in the age of the artist, *and* what in principle should be their *eternal afterlife* in succeeding generations' (255/11). He adds further – and this is the crux of the matter and the reason for my bringing him up:

> In the work's afterlife – which would not have this name if it were not a transformation and renewal of something *living* – the original is changed. [...] [But] to attribute the essence of such transformations [...] to *the subjectivity of posterity* rather than to the *special living quality of language and its works* [...] would mean to deny, through weak thinking, one of the most powerful and fruitful historical processes. (256/12–13, my emphases)

Thus, against the notion that it is for modern readers to invent new subjective interpretations of great works, Benjamin interposes the retort that the text's multiple levels of meaning are all already encoded in its form and language. Hence the tug-of-war between 'reconstruing' and 'being reconstructed' to which I referred above. In this sense translation/interpretation/recreation is a provisional way, not of reading new meanings into texts, but of coming to terms with their foreignness, their alterity. The original is changed, but so are we. Benjamin's term *Übersetzung* thus directly relates to *our* task in teaching Golden Age. 'Any final solution', he says, 'remains out of reach' (257/14); but if what is important is 'the element that transcends relaying subject matter', then 'fidelity' takes on a new sense: not faithfulness to the text's inessential 'information', but 'loving and detailed attention to incorporating the original's *way* of meaning'. 'Interpretation', he concludes, 'must *let itself go*, so as to voice the intention of the original not as *reproduction* but as *harmony*' (260/18). Our reading 'catches fire from the eternal life of the works *and* the perpetually renewed life of language' (257/14, my emphases).[2]

This incendiary metaphor may not sound too practical an approach to new methodologies for 'Teaching the old through the new'. However, a year later in his essay on Goethe's *Elective Affinities*, Benjamin returned to the topic with a point that, as I hope to show below, does suggest ways of directly informing practice. He opens up a distinction between commentary and critique. The former concentrates on explaining the vanishing *realia*, the material content (*Sachgehalt*) of the work; the latter seeks its truth content (*Wahrheitsgehalt*). But paradoxically, as the work's material content disappears from the world, its truth content stands ever more clear and apart. Hence later critics are granted 'an invaluable criterion' denied to the writer and his contemporaries: for them 'the existence of the *realia* was clear but their meaning mostly hidden', whereas for us 'historical distance enables the work's critique'.[3] Take, for instance, Calderón's *La vida es sueño* – not Benjamin's example, but a text he was to illuminate four years later in a study directly relevant to the Golden Age and well known to critics of its drama. Modern commentators, starting with the Romantics in the nineteenth century, have surrounded every line with an immense apparatus of

---

2   Benjamin coined the expression *immanente Kritik* to denote this process. As John McCole explains, 'Immanent criticism regards the work as essentially incomplete; it unfolds the work by making its potential qualities actual, its implicit features explicit. The result is to "reflect" the work [...] at a higher level of clarity and explicitness. [...] therefore, criticism changes the work, goes beyond it, in a sense even completes it', *Walter Benjamin and the Antinomies of Tradition* (Ithaca, NY: Cornell University Press, 1993), 90. Taken up by thinkers like Adorno, Lyotard, etc., the term has acquired a distinct, though still relevant sense. See Robert J. Antonio, 'Immanent Critique as the Core of Critical Theory: Its Origins and Developments in Hegel, Marx and Contemporary Thought', *British Journal of Sociology* 32 (1981), 330–45.

3   'Goethe's *Elective Affinities*', in his *Selected Writings*, I: *1913–26*, 297–360, 297–8; from 'Goethes Wahlverwandtschaften', in Hugo von Hofmannsthal, ed., *Neue deutsche Beiträge*, Folge ii (1924–25), Heft 1, 38–138 and Heft 2, 134–68, cited from in Rolf Tiedemann and Hermann Schweppenhäuser, eds, *Gesammelte Schriften*, I: *Abhandlungen*, 3 vols (Frankfurt: Suhrkamp, 1974), I, 125–201, 125–6.

explanations of its early modern religious, political and psychological ideologies, its Baroque metaphysic of *desengaño* and allegorical style, its fantastical setting in an imaginary Poland, the complex textual problems of its author's two versions for stage and press, its later reworking as an *auto sacramental*, etc. Yet for modern spectators these antiquarian *realia* fall away, leaving the play's astounding dramatic images to work their magic and communicate all the more powerfully their deeply unsettling message about the tendency of *desengaño* to end not so much in uplifting 'dis-illusion' as in scary disillusionment.[4] 'If the work is fire,' concludes Benjamin's passage, 'the commentator analyses it as chemist, the critic as alchemist'.

To suggest what this notion of a work's critique as alchemical re-creation might mean, and how 'voicing the intention of the original as harmony' could serve our end, which is to further what Benjamin called the *Nachreife* or endlessly fruitful 'after-ripening' of great works, I propose to give below two brief examples. But before doing so, permit me to return, in order to make one further theoretical point, to what at the outset I called the 'crisis' in our subject.

If there is one Spanish work of which every English-speaker has heard – and not just English, for statistics show that after the Bible we are talking of the most translated text in history, not even excepting *Harry Potter* – it is *Don Quijote*. On the face of it, then, it seems strange – or would seem strange to an alien from another planet – that not only our masters in management but even Spanish departments themselves appear to have agreed that it is acceptable to offer degrees in Spanish that include no course on Cervantes because they have no staff conversant with the Golden Age. I have not researched the statistics, but the facts are patent. When I was a student

---

4   As I try to suggest in '*La vida es sueño*', in Jonathan Thacker and Roy Norton, eds, *A Companion to Calderón de la Barca* (Woodbridge: Tamesis, forthcoming 2019); and likewise for Góngora, in '"El yugo de ambos sexos sacudido" (*Soledad* I. 237–83): Góngora's *Serranas* and Nympholepsy', in Oliver Noble Wood and Nigel Griffin, eds, *A Poet for All Seasons: Eight Commentaries on Góngora*, Spanish Series 156 (New York: Hispanic Seminary of Medieval Studies, 2013), 111–36. Benjamin's remarks on Calderón's play as the supreme Baroque tragedy are in his *The Origin of German Tragic Drama*, trans. John Osborne, intro. by George Steiner, 2nd edn (London: Verso, 1998), 81; from *Ursprung des deutschen Trauerspiels* [1928], in *Gesammelte Schriften*, I: *Abhandlungen*, I, 203–430, 260.

such a situation would have been unimaginable. Golden Age was a mainstay of our subject, both in numbers of teachers and in prestige. But then, in the ten years from 1975 to 1985, there was only one pre-modern university post advertised in England (at Manchester). After 1985 matters became even more alarming as the crowd of retiring Golden Age specialists, many among the most eminent and respected in the world, were not replaced, so that by 2005 there were even fewer lecturers in our subject than in medieval Spanish. There has been no decline in the quality and quantity of up-and-coming researchers and aspirants to posts, but our subject itself appears to be waning. I recently returned from a stay at the École normale supérieure in France, where I listened to jeremiads on the same theme. Even in Spain I hear similar stories and everywhere there is a palpable sense of doom.

It is worth reflecting for a moment on the reasons for this state of affairs. Hispanic studies have grown immensely in the last five decades. They now embrace world-wide literatures, cultures, and histories, new disciplines such as gender studies, post-colonialism, cinema, and new methodologies in critical and cultural theory, while numbers of students have quadrupled. This is an entirely positive development, one by which we are all enriched and from which Golden Age studies have notably benefitted. Yes, to some extent the explosion has crowded out early modern studies. However, a moment's reflexion dispels any notion that this can be the root cause of the predicament. There is no causal reason why broadening approaches should endanger our subject; exactly the reverse. We must look to more profound structural changes. Chief among them, I submit, and the one that provides theoretical lessons, is the demise of the canon.

We know that, in the wake of Deconstruction, post-Structuralism, then feminism and post-colonialism, influential voices have challenged the validity of the very notion of a 'canon'. It was created by Romantic nationalists of the nineteenth century, for whom language embodied the unquenchable 'spirit of the nation', expressed in the refined works of the canonical authors. However, as Rey Chow observed in 1995, the motor of recent comparative literature studies is precisely *not* the universality of national canons, but a 'fundamental questioning of the limits of Western discourse'.[5] There is little need to list the political avatars of this reversal, although I would merely

---

[5] In her 'In the Name of Comparative Literature', in Charles Bernheimer, ed., *Comparative Literature in the Age of Multiculturalism* (Baltimore, MD: Johns Hopkins University Press, 1995), 107–16, 112.

draw your attention to the memorable opening of Srinivas Aravamudan's essay on the rise and fall of the realist novel as the dominant canonic form of literary mimesis of the last 150 years:

> A small dugout canoe named the *Novel* was sighted off the coast of San Juan Fernandez island, in the balmy waters of the Caribbean, during the year 1719. Brought back by intrepid English explorers, it was a *machine* and an *organism*; in fact, an alien creature that grew in size and scope, reproducing itself promiscuously through the next few centuries. [...] However, while the Novel's descendants have become capacious, carrying much of humankind in their bellies, these iron dragons have also become long in the tooth, weak in the jaw, and dull of claw.[6]

Aravamudan goes on to give an Eastern perspective on this tale. He notes that the story of the discovery of the canoe *Novel* by English imperialists has been 'dismissed by some as rampant mythmaking, and older rumours concerning make-believe knights charging windmills [...] are brought forward in Robinson Crusoe's stead'. No doubt we happily concur that Cervantes, not Defoe, 'discovered' realism, but Aravamudan's fable is prologue to a fundamental questioning of the genre, proposing the alternative model of oriental 'free' or 'unbound' forms of non-realist mimesis, or what we call romance.[7] Other approaches have tended to be less good-humoured. They cry (as David Damrosch puts it):

> Should the study of world literature seek to discover unities across the world's traditions [canons], or are such cosmopolitan unities little more than projections of great-power values upon politically and economically subordinated cultures?[8]

---

6   Srinivas Aravamudan, 'In the Wake of the Novel: The Oriental Tale as National Allegory', *NOVEL: A Forum on Fiction* 33 (1999), 5–31, 5.
7   For another suggestive recent examination of this argument, which of course is highly relevant to any study of early modern fiction, see Gu Ming Dong, 'Theory of Fiction: A Non-Western Narrative Tradition', *Narrative*, 14 (2006), 311–38. I discuss it in relation to early Spanish works in a paper given at the seminar: 'Ficciones «orientales»: notas sobra una perogrullada', *Fictiologies médiévales* (Séminaire d'études hispaniques du CIHAM, École Normale Supérieure de Lyon, mars 2018) (in press), from which the above remarks are taken.
8   David Damrosch, 'Introduction', in David Damrosch, ed., *World Literature in Theory* (Chichester: Wiley, 2014), 1–11, 5; to 'cultures' we could easily, of course, add 'genders', etc. See also his 'Comparative World Literature', in Liviu Papadima, David Damrosch and Theo D'Haen, eds, *Canonical Debate Today: Crossing Disciplinary and Cultural Boundaries* (Amsterdam: Rodopi, 2011), 167–78.

In the light of such attacks, it is clear that my opening asseveration concerning the intrinsic value of Golden Age literature is open to rebuff, starting with the question of how we might begin to define such a mythical beast as 'intrinsic literary value'. As it happens, this is a very worthwhile question. Among other things, it has provoked a fruitful reaction to the impasse in literary studies brought about by the demise of the canon. Jonathan Culler, for example, argues that the rapidly burgeoning field of 'world literature' carries the threat of a 'loss of identity' – *not* national, but *creative*.[9] If the specific province of critique, the 'close reading of literary texts in the original languages', is displaced, our discipline risks dwindling into a diluted form of cultural studies in which, shelving the awkward quandary of quality, literature is taken merely as a symptom. We should hold fast, he concludes, to the essence: poetics itself, the aesthetics of 'reading literarily', great literature's immense 'repertoire of possibilities', formal, thematic, and discursive. As Emily Apter argues in her essay 'Against World Literature', invoking Derrida, we must avoid the facile assumption of discursive transparency and be alert to the 'surprising cognitive landscapes hailing from inaccessible linguistic folds' – 'the poetics of translational difference'.[10] It seems we have travelled full circle back to Otherness.

These, then, are some of the theoretical ideas and questions that lay behind my initial remarks about the need to base the defence of our subject on the intrinsic qualities of the texts. Why Golden Age? Straightforwardly, and side-lining for the moment the canonic debate, because it was one of the most significant ages in world history, and because the texts are among the most celebrated not just in Spanish, but in any literature. That celebrity is itself a sufficient source of interest to justify teaching them. We are free to conclude, having read them, that the texts are not in fact great, or that they are ideologically or otherwise objectionable, but if so, it behoves us to argue the case and support our rejection of their celebrity with rational arguments.

---

9   Jonathan Culler, 'Whither Comparative Literature?', *Comparative Critical Studies* 3 (2006), 85–97.
10 Emily Apter, *Against World Literature: On the Politics of Untranslatability* (New York: Verso, 2013), which argues against 'the de-aestheticizing jaws of globalization'; a version of her introduction is reprinted in Damrosch, *World Literature in Theory*, 345–62, from which I take my citations, 346–7.

Of course we shall not uphold the old nationalist concepts of the canon as defended by late nineteenth-century and early twentieth-century scholars such as Menéndez Pelayo and the Francoists, who accorded their accolades on religious and racial criteria, sometimes necessitating notable misrepresentation of the authors concerned.[11] Nevertheless, I believe a renewed vision of canonicity is vital. We must boldly defend, with reasoned demonstrations, the proposition that to study Spanish literature and culture without including Cervantes, Góngora, Garcilaso, Luis de León, Quevedo, Calderón & Co. is a senseless exercise.

So what does all this mean in terms of 'new approaches'? That is the vital matter, and the variety of essays here assembled will explore it. I have already given an indication of where my thoughts will tend by the foregoing remarks on the Benjaminian notion of *Fortleben*. I want to explore an approach to the latter by looking at a film adaptation of Baroque drama that I use in teaching. But first let me to return to another point that arose earlier. In his distinction between material content, the province of commentary,

---

11 See for example the study of Menéndez Pelayo's construction of his image of Calderón as a 'símbolo de la raza' in Bruce W. Wardropper, 'Menéndez Pelayo on Calderón', *Criticism: A Quarterly for Literature and the Arts* 7/4 (1965), 363–72. Significantly, it had the effect of making Spaniards 'hate Calderón' for a century (and not just them: see Edward M. Wilson, 'Gerald Brenan's Calderón', *Bulletin of the Comediantes* 4/1 (1952), 6–7 – though one should note that Gerald Brenan, 'Calderón and the Late Drama', in his *The Literature of the Spanish People* [1951], 2nd edn (Cambridge: Cambridge University Press, 1953), 275–314, remains one of our most interesting essays on the playwright. As for the twentieth century, we need only ponder the incoherent preamble signed 'Año de la Victoria, Francisco Franco' to the law creating the CSIC: 'En las coyunturas más decisivas de su historia concentró la hispanidad sus energías espirituales para crear una cultura universal. Esta ha de ser, también, la ambición más noble de la España del actual momento [...]. Tal empeño ha de cimentarse, ante todo, en la restauración de la clásica y cristiana unidad de las ciencias destruida en el siglo XVIII. [...] Hay que imponer, en suma, al orden de la cultura, las ideas esenciales que han inspirado nuestro Glorioso Movimiento, en la que se conjugan las lecciones más puras de la tradición universal y católica con las exigencias de modernidad' (Francisco Franco, 'Jefatura del Estado: Ley de 24 de noviembre de 1939 creando el Consejo Superior de Investigaciones Científicas', *Boletín Oficial del Estado*, 332, 28 November 1939, 6668–71, 6668). We may laugh at the notion that Fascism was more 'universal' than the Enlightenment, but need one point out that it is precisely ideologies like these that have led to the downfall of the canon?

and truth content, the concern of critique, Benjamin notes the following in 'Goethe's Elective affinities':

> If the works that prove enduring are precisely those whose truth is most deeply sunken in their material content, then in the course of this duration, the more the concrete *realia* die out in the world, the more distinctly they rise up before the eyes of the beholder. [...] Material content and truth content, united at the beginning of the work's history, draw apart [...]. More and more, therefore, the interpretation of what is striking and curious – that is, the material content – becomes a prerequisite for any later critic. (295/125)

The necessity for ever more commentary means that the 'faded text' of our Golden Age masterpieces ends up as a kind of palimpsest 'covered with the strokes of a bolder writing that refers to it'; for just as 'the paleographer must begin with the surface script of the palimpsest, *so the critic must begin with commentary*' (298/125, my emphasis). This touches on a practical problem with which we are all familiar. In teaching Golden Age texts there exists a barrier absent from teaching modern ones, at least on the surface (though perhaps only on the surface – modern works can, for different reasons, be just as difficult): the need to explain their unfamiliar content, language and cultural references. Take, for instance, the following sonnet by Góngora:

> La dulce boca que a gustar convida
> un humor entre perlas destilado,
> y a no envidiar aquel licor sagrado
> que a Júpiter ministra el garzón de Ida,
>
> amantes, no toquéis si queréis vida,   5
> porque entre un labio y otro colorado
> Amor está, de su veneno armado
> cual entre flor y flor sierpe escondida.
>
> No os engañen las rosas que a la Aurora
> diréis que, aljofaradas y olorosas,   10
> se le cayeron del purpúreo seno:
>
> manzanas son de Tántalo, y no rosas,
> que después huyen del que incitan ahora,
> y sólo del Amor queda el veneno.[12]

---

12   *Sonetos amorosos* lxxxii (1584), in Luis de Góngora, *Antología poética*, ed. Antonio Carreira, Clásicos y Modernos, 30 (Barcelona: Crítica, 2009), §24, 116–17.

The subject is one to which modern readers find little difficulty in responding. It is an *enargia* or descriptive visual evocation of what Keats would have called an 'infinitely kissable' pair of lips. Yet it is immediately borne in on us that the description is not simply visual. Instead it is adorned with all manner of Baroque gargoyles and presents the immediate tactile data wrapped up in a dense texture of allusive erudition and metaphysical *agudeza*, or what Dr Johnson called the 'discovery of occult resemblances in things apparently unlike'. Góngora conceives the lovely mouth as a trap, a goblet of delicious nectar at the bottom of which lies curled a serpent – the tongue that titillates, the teeth that bite. This conceit encapsulates the sonnet's truth-content; uncovering what it reveals about human nature constitutes, in Benjamin's terms, the task of critique.

Yet, as critics, we must first perform the rites of commentary. The poem's material content and accidents of form have to be explained: its erudite references (*licor sagrado* = nectar, *Júpiter* = king of the Olympian gods; *garzón de Ida* = Ganymede, Jupiter's handsome cup-bearer and catamite, formerly a shepherd on Mount Ida; *Aurora* = the goddess of Dawn, alluding to the sunrise *púrpura* of the lips; *Tántalo* = the demigod condemned to infinite torture in Hades by being chained between a pool of water and a tree of apples, both out of reach). Then, too, the intertextual *imitatio* of Virgil's myth of Orpheus and Eurydice as recreated in Garcilaso, *Égloga* iii.131–2 'la pequeña sierpe ponzoñosa / entre la hierba y flores escondida', with its allusions to emblem-books; and so on and so forth.

How, then, do we reconcile the two tasks, fuse the details of material content with the truth content? To do so involves, as I have several times hinted, exploring the contours of a mysterious Newfoundland. We must, in short, explicate the strange and complex *motives* that drew the poet to describe something so simple as a pair of lips in this intricate, arcane way. They did not spring from any material cause. It is not the fact (so far as I have been able to determine) that seventeenth-century women had rosier, dewier, more scented lips than now, still less that they had a penchant for hiding nectar and snakes in their mouths. The explanation must go deeper. As Jonathan Culler states in another essay:

> The relationship between literature and society is not one of identity of content but of homology of form: it is the formal organization of literary works, *the operations for the production of meaning* [...], which relate directly to society: the operations

which produce social and cultural objects, *the devices which create a world charged with meaning*.[13]

So what *are* the operations for 'creating a world charged with meaning' in this poem about the idea, the feelings aroused by beautiful lips? As Culler says, they are not embodied in the content, for Baroque society did not believe any more than we do in the classical pantheon or in love as a mythological god (l. 7). What the poem reveals in the first place, then, is the perhaps surprising fact that the meaning of a kiss is profoundly cultural; the semiotics of lips are defined by history and society. To put it another way, Góngora did not conceive of the actual presence in a girl's mouth of a winged god armed with poisoned arrows as the material fact that explains the danger of kissing it. Cupid functions as that peculiar kind of 'operation for the production of meaning' called allegory – one specially 'homologous' with Baroque culture.

In what does this homology consist? Every one of the allusions I listed is calculated to symbolize *tantal*izing desire and it would be easy, no doubt, to proceed to expatiate upon Góngora's situation as a celibate priest, the Ancien Régime's repressed and repressive attitude to sex, the Baroque's terrified fixation with and rejection of the forbidden carnality of the body, especially the female body ... The poem's religious background is not irrelevant, certainly (the mention of a serpent, implying a Fall ...), but I call attention to another unusual and alien detail of its form: the fact that it has a plural addressee, *amantes* (l. 5). The sonnet is a lyric poem, which for post-Romantic readers is supposed to denote intimate introspection. Yet this public illocution gives it a markedly sententious, almost didactic voice – 'no toquéis, si queréis vida'. And from this perspective, what strikes us even more than the metaphors of tantalizing desire is the constant play of appearance and reality. The mouth *looks* inviting, warns the poet, but is really a trap: 'no os engañen las rosas' (l. 9). In short, his poem is a lesson about *desengaño*, and that, in the high tradition of Baroque art, is precisely its 'device for creating a world charged with meaning'. For with *desengaño* goes the Baroque obsession with mortality. 'Si queréis vida' – not because kissing scientifically entails spontaneous combustion, but because these roses, like all flowers (it is nature – the nature

---

13   Jonathan Culler, 'Literary History, Allegory, and Semiology', *New Literary History: A Journal of Theory and Interpretation* 7 (1975–6), 259–70 (260, my emphases).

of the world), are transient symbols of decay and death: 'después huyen', leaving only the bitter aftertaste of disillusion (ll. 13–14).

This, then, is the textbook explanation of the 'homology of form' between Góngora's poem and the culture that produced it; commentary culminates in this. And yet ... is not the truly surprising illumination the *cleft* between this pessimistic *desengaño* and the extraordinary, scintillating sensuality of the poem's imagery? The obsession with mortality goes hand in hand with an agonizing yet joyful celebration of the breath-taking beauty, the triumphant *life* of the fleeting here and now. I cannot persuade myself that any reader of this poem is meant to conclude that they had better simply refrain from kissing; the lips are made far too heavenly for that. But to wrap a kiss in shrouds of mortality is to produce a critical idea – a truth content – to which, though complex, we too can respond.

It seems to me, then, that to address the problem of fusing commentary with critique, some approach that focuses on Culler's relation between the texts' devices for creating meaning and their cultural matrix is one possible starting-point. I cannot claim that it is in any way 'new', of course, but I hope to have suggested it can still be fresh.

I shall end by returning to my main argument, namely, the notion of a work's afterlife as 'transformation and renewal', which makes the same point in another way. I should like to illustrate the concept of 're-creation' by looking at Manuel Iborra's film adaptation of *La dama boba* (2006), one of only two Spanish films of Baroque plays known to me that I consider to be of sufficient quality for students to study them.[14]

Anyone familiar with the first five minutes of Franco Zeffirelli's 1968 and Baz Luhrmann's 1996 land-mark adaptations of *Romeo and Juliet* will be

---

14   Manuel Iborra, dir., *La dama boba* (DeAPlaneta and Flamenco Films, released 24 March 2006), starring Silvia Abascal, José Coronado, Macarena Gómez, Roberto San Martín and Verónica Forqué; the DVD is out of print, but the film is currently online at <https://www1.movies123.be/watch/la-dama-boba-2006-full-movie.html>, accessed 5 August 2018. The other is Pilar Miró, dir., *El perro del hortelano* (1996). On this more conventional, Kenneth Branagh-style adaptation see, for example, Duncan Wheeler, 'We Are Living in a Material World and I Am a Material Girl: Diana, Countess of Belflor, Materialised on the Page, Stage and Screen', *Bulletin of Hispanic Studies* 84 (2007), 267–86.

fully aware of the immense variety of options for recreation offered by screen adaptations.[15] The first is an operatic costume-drama version, beginning with a spectacular aerial shot of Verona through mist golden-lit by the rising sun, and a sonorous voice-over by Sir Laurence Olivier; then a cut to a medieval market square that likewise makes an unashamed appeal to the senses with its picturesque liveried Capulets and colourful fruit-stalls, using Renaissance art to compose the visuals. The second, a flamboyantly modernized version, opens with a conscious ironic reference to the former, a sweeping helicopter view of a sprawling, deliberately ugly millenial metropolis (Mexico City) posing as 'Verona Beach', and a voice-over by a female African-American TV newsreader, the 'ancient rivalry' presented in headlines as a clash between corporate mafia clans, a gang-war given a racial turn (redneck vs Latino) in the immediately following scene set not in a picturesque market but at a gas-station, where – in homage to Sergio Leone-style spaghetti westerns (the slow-motion cigarette drop, ornate boot grinding out the butt) – 'Sword' becomes a brand of handgun, billboards turn Shakespearian quotes into commercials ('Out Damn'd Spot' dry cleaners), and Sampson's opening line "Tis known I am a pretty piece of flesh' gives way to One Inch Punch's *Pretty Piece of Flesh* blaring out of the Montague boys' car radio.

They seem like two different works, yet both screen-plays use Shakespeare's original text, and both directors made a point of asserting their fidelity to it: Zeffirelli called his 'a radical return to the original' seeking 'what no one has bothered to see since the author compiled the work', while Luhrmann said he was 'trying to make the movie rambunctious, sexy, violent and entertaining the way Shakespeare might have if he had been a filmmaker.'[16] From a critical point of view, however, the most striking thing is that each adaptation is overtly and powerfully grounded in its own historical moment. Despite the period costumes, Zeffirelli's film mirrors the

---

15   Franco Zeffirelli (dir.), *Romeo and Juliet* (1968; DVD Paramount 2013) and Baz Luhrmann (dir.), *William Shakespeare's Romeo + Juliet* (1996; DVD 20th Century Fox 2002).
16   Franco Zeffirelli, *The Autobiography* (London: Weidenfeld & Nicolson, 1986), 330; Baz Luhrmann, 'A Note from Baz Luhrmann', in Craig Pearce, Baz Luhrmann, and John Bettenbender, eds, *William Shakespeare's Romeo & Juliet: The Contemporary Film, The Classic Play* (New York: Bantam Doubleday, 1996), i.

youth culture of 1968: the world of hippies, flower-power, anti-Vietnam-war protests and Paris student risings. Romeo's first entrance from the 'sycamore grove' where he hides his narcissistic self ('to himself so secret and so close', *Romeo and Juliet*, i. 1. 149) is in soft focus; he is long-haired and carrying a flower. 'The teenagers should be a lot like kids today,' declared the director, 'they don't want to get involved in their parents' hates and wars. Romeo was a sensitive, naive pacifist'. Thus, the film idealizes the hero and heroine; theirs is a tragedy of innocence. Luhrmann's, by contrast, presents a millennial vision of a crass, blood-sucking, decadent capitalist society in which teenagers are part of the problem (gangs, Romeo tripping on acid). Its Baroque chaos of visual and auditory overkill is designed to lend a *fin-de-siècle* jadedness to its evocation of the forces of wealth and poverty, power and pride. The film is crammed with blasphemous religious icons (the 'Bazmark' cross – *Romeo + Juliet* – shaved on the Capulet boy's heads, tattooed on the Friar's back, engraved on the butts of guns) that mock the positivism of the earlier film; Romeo's Sycamore Grove becomes a delapidated beach haunted by drug-dealers and call-girls. In short, both recreations provide critics with rich scope for delving into Culler's 'devices for creating meaning' and their cultural matrices.

We can apply the same criteria to Iborra's *La dama boba*. Our conclusions will be different, but parallel in kind. The original play's premise is no less simple and universal than Shakespeare's: do you fall in love with someone for their riches, their looks, or their mind? Iborra elects, like Zeffirelli, for a period-costume scenario and he too bases his screen-play on Lope's verse. However, his recreation is no less a product of its own historical juncture and mentality. The Golden Age play is a cynical send-up of its society's iron constraints of class and gender: its themes are money and deception, marriage as a market.[17] Iborra tells the same story, but deliberately feminizes it: the play's father Otavio becomes single mother Otavia (with all the ironic displacements that entails) and the two sisters Finea and Nise are made deeper, more independent, while Liseo is transformed, to begin with, into an effeminate clown, Laurencio into an infantile waster. At the same time

---

17   Lope de Vega, *La dama boba*, ed. Diego Marín, Letras Hispánicas, 50 (Madrid: Cátedra, 1976); my citations below are from this edition, by line number.

Iborra deliberately heightens the element of farce, introducing into the action constant knockabout slapstick – Laurencio's and his servant Pedro's rumbling stomachs, followed by the latter feasting on a cockroach; the risible excess of Liseo's aforementioned foppishness on his first entrance, heavily made-up and obsessed with silk frills, cane, and gloves; the exaggerated pantomime of Finea's antics with farmyard animals; the clumsy slap-and-tickle of the courtship scenes, prat-falls, people falling into puddles or knocking over monks, etc. All this combines to transform the film's subject into an outright mockery of masculinity: there is plenty of rumbustious swash-buckling, but the sword-fights are played for laughs and the ending is entirely despatched by the female characters, while the male suitors gape on humbly, kneeling or from the sidelines.

In doing all this, Iborra knowingly replaces Lope's unrelenting satire with the playful lightheartedness of romantic comedy. The *alegre ligereza* of his treatment ensures that the threat of 'dishonour' that underlay the play's denouement is rendered perfunctory, all but invisible. Instead, Iborra's ending (six minutes, 1.24.44–1.30.52) is a hymn to the power of love. The Neoplatonic philosophy of the ennobling ability of harmony to refine spirits and unite souls is indeed introduced in the first act of Lope's play, when Laurencio answers Finea's innocent question, '¿Qué es amor?' (ll. 769–854), but the scene is entirely playful: Finea insists on getting the wrong end of the stick ('finea– ¿Has visto, Clara,/ lo que es amor? ¡Quién pensara / tal cosa! clara – No hay pepitoria / que tenga más menudencias / de manos, tripas y pies', ll. 850–54), and the *gracioso* Pedro is made to contribute, by mistake, the statement most relevant to her case ('Ciencia es amor, / que el más rudo labrador / a pocos cursos la adquiere', ll. 818–20).[18] We know that Lope subscribed to the theory, and its possible deeper relevance to the meaning of *La dama boba* is by no means precluded by the light-heartedness of its treatment here. Indeed, Finea delivers a notable speech at the start of Act III that describes love as the sunbeam, the 'divine genius' that has released her soul (ll. 2033–80). Nevertheless, the playwright held fast to his plan right up to the end, making clear in the middle of the last act that nitwittery is in fact a deceptive ploy that women can learn and unlearn for their own ends:

---

18   For further remarks on this topic see, for example, James E. Holloway, 'Lope's Neoplatonism: *La dama boba*', *Bulletin of Hispanic Studies* 49 (1972), 236–55.

Why Golden Age?

> LAURENCIO   Pues, ¿sabrás fingirte boba?
> FINEA   Sí; que lo fui mucho tiempo. [...]
> Demás desto, las mujeres
> naturaleza tenemos
> tan pronta para fingir,
> o con amor o con miedo,
> que antes de nacer fingimos. (ll. 2487–95)

Likewise, there is nothing in the least erotic, let alone 'Platonic' or philosophical, about Laurencio's interest in Finea's handsome dowry. His last words are:

> LAURENCIO   Bien merezco esta vitoria,
> pues le he dado entendimiento,
> si ella me da la memoria
> de cuarenta mil ducados. (ll. 3166–9)

In consonance with this uncompromisingly unsentimental ethos, the play's ending is swift and brutally abrupt: Octavio learns that he has been tricked, thunders impotently, is told in a single word ('Desatar') to cut the knot, dismisses the other suitors, and allows the four couples, masters and servants, to conclude their business-like espousals all in twenty brief speeches totalling forty lines – a minute and half (ll. 3141–80). No wonder scholars have pointed out that Lope's apparent love-story comes with a health warning. As Jonathan Thacker puts it, 'the fact that Finea "learns" from a lover whose motivation is greed muddies the waters, leaving the playwright characteristically uncommitted'.[19] A drama critic wrote of John Farndon's production at London's Riverside Studios in 1997:

> The play disturbs because you're never quite sure whether it's an anti-feminist morality tale or a sixteenth-century paean to girl power. For Finea, it turns out, is not as dumb as she seems. 'Girls learn to pretend early out of love and fear', she tells Laurencio; in other words, she is smart enough to know when it pays to be stupid. [...] On the surface,

---

19   Jonathan Thacker, 'Lope de Vega', in Jonathan Thacker, ed., *A Companion to Golden Age Theatre* (Woodbridge: Tamesis, 2007), 23–55, 48; see also Jonathan Thacker, 'Lope, the Comedian', in Alexander Samson and Jonathan Thacker, eds, *A Companion to Lope de Vega* (Woodbridge: Tamesis, 2008), 159–70 on the increasing 'seriousness' of his mature comedies; and, for an exploration based on experience of translating and producing the play, Edward H. Friedman, 'Lope de Vega's *La dama boba* and the Construction of Comedy', *Bulletin of Spanish Studies* 90/4–5 (2013), 599–617.

everything is resolved: four couples are to marry. Yet Finea has only hooked Laurencio by betraying her sister, and she couldn't have done it without a huge dowry. By contrast, Nise's marriage to the fickle Liseo seems a sorry compromise. Having played the game and done her schoolwork, she's now seen as over-educated.[20]

Iborra, by contrast, makes his ending the uplifting centre-piece (if the paradox may be forgiven) of his recreation and, in so doing, creates a skilfully edited montage that is not only absent but would have been totally unthinkable in Lope's play. He preserves every word of Lope's ending, but adds a shot in which the two girls tearfully embrace their mother, and then … the six leading characters are shown in their nuptial beds and, to Luis Ivars' affecting Baroque sound-track, the scene from Act I about the power of love is transposed here, together with quotations on the same topic from other works by Lope, shared between Laurencio/Finea, Nise/Liseo, and Pedro/Clara, delivered with festive smiles but to entirely serious effect, creating a palpably upbeat sense of reconciliation, harmony, and order. In short, Iborra dispenses with the dark side of the play – the side that depended on the antique aspects of early modern patriarchy – to focus on the feminist theme and on love. The cuts he makes for this purpose (e.g. Otavio's pathetic whinge declaring that women's role is not to think but to confine themselves to domestic matters, ll. 225–32, and his mention of the long roster of Finea's suitors 'del oro más

---

20 Adrian Turpin, 'Labours of Love', *Independent*, 30 April 1997 <http://www.independent.co.uk/arts-entertainment/labours-of-love-1270175.html>, accessed 7 August 2018. The players used John Farndon's own fine translation, *Mad for Love*, for a copy of which I thank him (London: John Farndon, 1997, 2008). Michael Billington came to similar conclusions at a recent performance of David Johnston's version directed by Laurence Boswell: it 'leaves a faintly acrid aftertaste; […] there is no mutual maturation process, so the new-flowering Finea winds up with a partner who still believes that "a woman, like a little lamb, is a golden fleece to her husband" [*La dama boba*, ll. 2427–61, at 2439–42 'Laurencio – Inocente te quería, / porque una mujer cordero / es tusón de su marido, / que puede traerla al pecho']. […] Lope pays tribute to female agency and the quickening power of love. But […] you wish he had also found a man worthy of her', 'A Lady of Little Sense', *Guardian*, 15 October 2013 <https://www.theguardian.com/stage/2013/oct/15/lady-of-little-sense-review>, accessed 8 August 2018. *The Lady Boba: A Woman of Little Sense*, trans. David Johnston (London: Oberon Books, 2013). See further Susan L. Fischer, 'Lope and Tirso Translated to the Boards of Bath's Ustinov Studio', *Bulletin of the Comediantes* 66/2 (2014), 229–46, 237–43.

que del ingenio amantes', ll. 249–52; the suggestion that the maidservant Clara plays dumb in order to extract cash from Finea, ll. 493–9; various satiric allusions to literary quarrels about Gongorism, etc.) tend to be what commentators focus upon in their analyses of the play. Perhaps as a result, the film met with some incomprehension.[21] Yet is it not clear that Iborra's is a true 're-creation', every bit as much a 'radical return to the original' as Zeffirelli's or Luhrmann's; and on the other hand, that what he finds and 'unfolds' in *La dama boba* is indeed already coiled in Lope's text?

Misreadings, travesties? No; I contend that each such 'translation' is the 'latest, most complete unfolding' of what is there in the 'living quality of language'. The plot of *La dama boba* presents one fantastic anomaly, an unexplained mystery: how could two sisters in the same household have ended up with such diametrically opposed levels of education, one pedantically erudite, the other entirely illiterate? The answer is, of course, that they embody Lope's own split personality: a child prodigy who wrote sonnets by the age of 9, yet was raucously mocked for his humble origins and lack of any detectible formal education. His play suggests that learning, or the lack of it, is not the issue: schooling the emotions, not the intellect, is the true key to human happiness. Yet it was precisely in this latter, emotional department that his own character was most chaotic, undisciplined, and unfulfilled. 'The more a work's historical *realia* die away, the more its truth content stands apart; [...] historical distance enables critique': as the archaic mindset portrayed in *La dama boba*'s comedy of manners fades into the

---

21   Typical is the review by Rafael Nieto Jiménez, 'Lope de Vega y el cine español, 5: *La dama boba* (Manuel Iborra, 2006)', *Centro Virtual Cervantes: Rinconete. Cine y televisión*, 30 October 2015 <https://cvc.cervantes.es/el_rinconete/anteriores/octubre_15/30102015_01.htm>, accessed 8 August 2018, who finds the film's 'extraño tono cómico' problematic and complains of its 'inconcreción espacial': 'Se ha pretendido romper la unidad escénica de la obra, que trascurría casi toda en la casa, pero nunca sabemos bien dónde están los personajes [...]. La iluminación y los decorados no hacen más que reforzar esta impresión de artificio, solo aceptable si consideramos que es una idealización de la vida muy propia de Lope'. Precisely the aspects of the film that are most creative – it seems – are what prevent him from enjoying it. See Duncan Wheeler, 'A Modern Day *Fénix*: Lope de Vega's Cinematic Revivals', in Samson and Thacker, *A Companion to Lope de Vega*, 285–99, 298–9; he too reckons it 'arguably the most successful film version of a *comedia* ever made' – but not at the box office.

past, we are able to perceive a deeper sense – Lope's anguished *cri de cœur* for grown-up relationships based on true love, a cry more comprehensive, more wide-ranging and profound than simple feminism. He and his contemporaries would doubtless have been shocked by any such way of summing up his meaning; but with our great privilege of hindsight, Iborra's substitution of his distinctive ending can be seen as going to the heart of the matter.

By way of closing remarks, in my experience students respond with enthusiasm to the process of approaching Golden Age masterpieces by thinking about forms of 'after-ripening' such as these. I conclude with a final return to Benjamin in 'Goethe's Elective Affinities': 'So the critic inquires after the truth, whose living flame burns on over the heavy logs and light ashes of the funeral pyre of past experience' (298/126).

Why Golden Age? So we and our students can enquire after the living flame. I conceive our prime task in teaching to be that of communicating the twin pleasures of studying (commentary) and recreating (critique) our texts to new generations of readers.

STUART DAVIS

2 The Golden Age in the Hispanic Studies classroom: The changing shape of what we teach our undergraduates in the UK

ABSTRACT

This chapter examines the history behind the use of the term 'Golden Age', as a framework for investigating the changing shape of its constituent texts, as determined through datasets gathered in a continuing longitudinal study of the syllabuses taught on UK university Hispanic Studies courses. The collected data reveals the range of peninsular literature taught on our courses across eighteen years, with data from the academic years 1998/9, 2006/7 and 2015/16. In order to understand the place of Golden Age culture in the curriculum, the chapter discusses the presence of Golden Age literature in the wider curriculum before examining who are the key authors and texts and how their fortunes have fared over the three sets of data.

It is a truth universally acknowledged that the literature of the Spanish Golden Age is central to the Hispanic literary canon as it is perceived both within and outside Spain. Particularly visible in world literature is Miguel de Cervantes and *Don Quijote* in its many translations and adaptations, permeating the cultural landscape in ways that go beyond direct engagement with the original text, immediate examples including visual imagery, statuary, as well as the concept of the 'quixotic' as idealistic and impractical. Cervantes's presence in the cultural consciousness and sense of literary heritage is strong, reinforced most recently by the commemoration of the 400th anniversary of Cervantes's death, which coincided almost exactly to the day with that of another canonically core writer, William Shakespeare. Indeed, Harold Bloom's infamous *The Western Canon* frequently compares the two favourably, with Bloom paying homage to Cervantes as a writer of 'wisdom' and the creator of 'simply the largest literary characters in the whole Western Canon, except for their triple handful (at most) of Shakespearean peers'.[1] However, we know that Cervantes was not, to paraphrase Shakespeare, born great, but achieved greatness and, over the course of time, has been re-evaluated in ways that caused greatness to be thrust upon him and the epoch in which he lived and wrote.

Although Cervantes is dominant in the literary history of the narrative form, a Golden Age cannot rest on the reputation of one writer only, and a broad range of dramatists, poets and writers coalesce around the canonical core that is Cervantes. The consciousness of who is or is not perceived as canonical is created through a complex interaction of an individual's experiences in education with his or her exposure to references to authors and periods in broader cultural contexts – in short, his or her heritage and cultural capital – which will vary according to the individual's language and geopolitical identity. It would not be surprising if, when requested to name Golden Age writers, a Spaniard were to list Cervantes, Calderón de la Barca, Fray Luis de León, Quevedo, Lope de Vega and many more besides, yet even a reasonably educated Anglophone might struggle to recall any names beyond Cervantes, or even identify how the Spanish Golden Age might be temporally defined. Indeed, as we shall discuss, the 'Golden Age' is a rather nebulous term that incorporates a number of beginning and end date markers and is even unclear in its geographical boundaries. My study interrogates one particular, but revealing, aspect of the changing nature of the Golden Age, through examination of what is presented to non-native students of Hispanism by Hispanists themselves. Following a brief discussion of the terminology that shapes, and is in turn shaped by, the discipline's approach to the literature and culture of this historical period, I reflect on three sets of data, from different academic years over an eighteen-year period, that identify the material taught on undergraduate degrees of Spanish/Hispanic Studies in the United Kingdom. The data reveals how the universities prioritize certain materials and historical periods for the students they teach, who are, by and large, non-native speakers and who are therefore lacking the canonical consciousness and cultural capital acquired through social and cultural immersion. The datasets are a small part of a larger complex picture, yet can nonetheless be read as symptomatic of the regard with which the period is held.

1   Harold Bloom, *The Western Canon. The Books and Schools of the Ages* (London: MacMillan, 1996), 145.

Golden Age: What, when and why?

To understand the importance of the Golden Age for international Hispanism, which as an academic discipline is derived from Spanish culture but also informs and perpetuates it, it will be instructive to consider briefly the origins of the term which reveal much of the conceptualization of the period. As a phrase 'the Golden Age' is not purely literary, but synonymous with Imperial Spain's economic and political power, as much as its cultural output. Indeed, the first acknowledged use of the Spanish term 'Siglo de oro' came after the period, in 1754, when Luis José Velázquez used the temporal markers of politics, through the various Spanish monarchs, to sketch out what he perceived as the four ages of Spanish poetry.[2] Early in his essay Velázquez claims the third age, from Charles V to Philip IV, in effect 1516 to 1665, as the most virile.[3] However, listing the poets in more detail later in his essay, Velázquez singles out the sixteenth century as the focus of this 'third age', in effect a Golden century: 'Esta tercera edad fue el siglo de oro de la Poesía Castellana; siglo, en que no podia dexar de florecer la buena Poesía.'[4] Velázquez's essay concludes by rousing the poets of the fourth age, supposedly in decline, into a return to the glorious past, so that 'la Poesia castellana bolverà à ponerse, sobre el buen pie, en que estuvo en su siglo de oro'.[5] The translation into German and annotation of Velázquez's early literary history by Johann Andreas Dieze, published in Göttingen in 1769, helped bring Velázquez's work to a broader international audience, including the German Romantics and English literary historian George Ticknor,

---

2   Luis José Velázquez, *Origenes de la poesía castellana* (Málaga: Martínez de Aguilar, 1754). While Velázquez is understood to have introduced the nomenclature of a 'siglo de oro', an earlier example of praise for the literary period can be found in the work of Gregorio Mayans y Siscar, who in 1727 rejected the recent Baroque style in favour of the preservation and imitation of what we now consider to be Spanish Golden Age writers. ('Oración en que se exhorta a seguir la verdadera idea de la elocuencia española' in *Ensayos Oratorios de don Gregorio Mayans y Siscar* (Madrid: Juan de Zuñiga, 1739)).
3   Velázquez, *Origenes*, 34.
4   Velázquez, *Origenes*, 66.
5   Velázquez, *Origenes*, 174.

a noted admirer of the translation.[6] More broadly, Juan Manuel Rozas notes that 'entre 1754 y 1779, al menos entre los estudiosos, el término Siglo de Oro literario estaba acuñado'.[7]

With the growth of productions of literary histories in the late eighteenth and nineteenth centuries, the Golden Age began to be defined not only through poetry but also narrative, theatre, politics and, with the growth of the Romantic mindset as an important contributor to the sense of nationalism, national character.[8] Although Ticknor never utilizes a term such as Golden Age to describe the period, for him 1492 acts as a pivotal point in Spanish history and culture, bringing forth a torrent of Empire building.[9] He goes on to note the following: 'Of course, the body of Spanish poetry and eloquent prose produced during this interval – the earlier part of which was the period of the greatest glory Spain ever enjoyed – was injuriously affected by so diseased a condition of the national character'.[10] Indeed, Spain's *leyenda negra* seems to confound early literary historians, predominantly from Northern Europe, who seem surprised at

---

[6] Ticknor states that: 'J. A. Dieze, who was a Professor at Göttingen, and died in 1785, published a German translation of [Velázquez's essay] in 1769, with copious and excellent notes, which more than double, not only the size of the original work, but its value'. *History of Spanish Literature*, iii (New York: Harper and Brothers, 1854), 252. On the cultural transmission of Velázquez's essay see also H. C. Heaton, 'The Case of Parte XXIV de Lope de Vega, Madrid', *Modern Philology* 22/3 (1925), 283–303 and Diego Saglia, 'The true essence of romanticism': Romantic theories of Spain and the question of Spanish romanticism', *Journal of Iberian and Latin American Studies* 3/2 (1997), 127–45.

[7] Juan Manuel Rozas, 'Siglo de oro: historia de un concepto, la acuñación del término', in Manuel Álvar et al., *Estudios sobre el Siglo de Oro. Homenaje a Francisco Ynduráin* (Madrid: Editora Nacional, 1984), 411–28, 420.

[8] On the first literary histories of Spain, see Santiago Pérez-Isasi, 'Building Nations through Words: Iberian Identities in Nineteenth-Century Literary Historiography', in Javier Muñoz Basols, Manuel Delgado Morales, Laura Lonsdale, eds, *The Routledge Companion to Iberian Studies* (London: Routledge, 2017), 333–43; 'The Limits of "Spanishness" in 19th-century Literary History', *Bulletin of Hispanic Studies* 90/2 (2013), 167–88 and Stuart Davis, *Writing and Heritage in Contemporary Spain. The Imaginary Museum of Literature* (Woodbridge: Tamesis, 2012).

[9] Ticknor, *History*, i, 458.

[10] Ticknor, *History*, i, 468–9.

the cultural growth achieved under the zeal of the Inquisition. Friedrich Bouterwek notes that 'The dramatic literature of Spain flourished with most brilliancy during the reigns of the three Philips, from 1556 to 1665, and that is precisely the period when the Spanish inquisition exercised its power with the greatest rigour and the most sanguinary cruelty'.[11] Instead, in tandem with the German Romantic spirit of the time and the writing of Herder, Bouterwek goes on to tell us that 'Spanish literature owes nothing to kings, and has only to thank popular spirit for all its brightest flowers'.[12] It is worth noting that Thomasina Ross's nineteenth-century translation aligns the original's term *Nationalgeiste* [National spirit] with 'popular', making explicit the connection of national identity and the people's identity.[13] Perhaps following the lead of Velázquez, via Dieze, Bouterwek does use the phrase 'in ihrem goldenen Zeitalter' [in their Golden Age] to refer to Spanish poetry of the sixteenth century.[14] Indeed, we find the German equivalent to 'Golden Age' in earlier use by Friedrich Schlegel in 1798, another strong influence on German culture and Bouterwek's approach as a literary historian'.[15]

My study here cannot tackle fully the complexities of the influences and interactions of Romanticism, nationalist approaches and literary history, but the importance of the early to mid-nineteenth century in promoting Spanish literature on an international stage and, perhaps more importantly, within Spain itself, cannot be underestimated. As Barbara Becker-Cantarino notes, 'With the numerous subsequent translations of Schlegel's *Geschichte der alten und neuen Literatur* into most European languages, Spanish literature and Spain regained their place in European cultural history. Even the romantic movement of Spain itself rediscovered and reevaluated its own past largely on the basis of the preceding German

---

11   Friedrich Bouterwek, *History of Spanish Literature* (London: David Bogue, 1847), 106.
12   Bouterwek, *History*, 108.
13   Friedrich Bouterwek, *Geschichte der Poesie und Beredsamkeit seit dem Ende des dreizehnten Jahrhunderts*, iii (Göttingen: Johann Friedrich Röwer, 1804), 155.
14   Bouterwek, *Geschichte*, 157.
15   Barbara Becker-Cantarino, 'The Rediscovery of Spain in Enlightened and Romantic Germany', *Monatshefte* 72/2 (1980), 121–34.

rediscovery'.[16] Spain's own reappreciation of its literary heritage was considered important against its seemingly more culturally, economically and politically advanced neighbours and rivals, whereby an 'asociación de las glorias nacionales con el apogeo literario y artístico fue moneda común en toda la historiografía a partir del siglo XVIII'.[17] Recourse to a myth of times gone past is, in effect, the mode of interaction with any engagement with the canon. Spanish nineteenth-century thinkers felt, according to Rozas, 'una necesidad de entender nuestra historia, en una perspectiva temporal y hacia una renovación desde el presente'.[18] For Becker-Cantarino claims that for those inside and outside the country, 'Spain and her cultural heritage appeared to be one last island of innocence, originality, and ever-lasting beauty – an unreal and, except in a few instances, unattainable counterpart to the real world of political unrest and social impotence. [...] a major force behind this rediscovery of Spain was the search for a viable alternative to the French cultural and political hegemony, to Enlightenment and Classicist literary and intellectual values'.[19]

The Golden Age is thus seen as a source of inspiration by a variety of observers for a variety of reasons. For many it forms a literary highpoint for emulation (a core function claimed for canonicity), produced by a culture whose intellectual and political trajectory stands in marked contrast to the rest of Western Europe. Particular writers within it become symbolic of attitudes or beliefs.[20] Such readings of their own culture from outside seem

---

16 Becker-Cantarino 'Rediscovery', 130.
17 Begoña López Bueno, 'La poesía del Sigo de Oro: historiografía y canon', in María Luisa Lobato and Francisco Domínguez Matito, eds, *Memoria de la palabra. Actas del VI Congreso de la Asociación Internacional Siglo de Oro* (Madrid/Frankfurt am Main: Vervuert, 2004), 55–87, 60.
18 Rozas, 'Siglo de oro', 414–15.
19 Becker-Cantarino 'Rediscovery', 122. Becker-Cantarino's article concludes with the observation that foreign commentators who did venture to Spain were somewhat disillusioned by the lived reality that they encountered!
20 See, for example, August Wilhelm Schlegel's statement that 'If a feeling of religion, a loyal heroism, honour, and love, be the foundation of romantic poetry, it could not fail to attain to its highest development in Spain, where its birth and growth were cherished by the most friendly auspices'. *Lectures on Dramatic Art and Literature* (New York: AMS Press, 1965), 500.

to have both influenced and shaped Spanish culture going forward, whilst also reinforcing their own understanding of their literary heritage.[21]

As a focal point for a constructed canon, writers of the sixteenth and seventeenth centuries become prominent in conceptions of Spanish cultural heritage. Francisco Javier Díez de Revenga's useful survey of academic writing in the early twentieth century suggests that at that time Spanish-language Hispanists were more specific in grouping writers according to the century in which each was active, retaining a more literal concept of 'siglo', whilst Germanic critics such as Pfandl and Vossler used the less temporally circumscribed term *Blütezeit* [blooming/flowering time], employing a discourse of organic growth.[22] These habits persist, whilst in English-language Hispanism, Golden Age continues to be the most frequently used term.

As we have noted earlier, what is included within the term Golden Age may be strongly influenced by the focus laid out by the earliest literary historians, but its precise limits remain indeterminate. Writing recently, Jeremy Robbins notes that its initial referentiality to the sixteenth century has extended to include the seventeenth too; Robbins also quite rightly points out that alternative nomenclature such as 'early modern' is open to debate, and that each term chosen reveals something of the stance and attitude of the person choosing to use it.[23] Equally, the choice of date parameters of the Golden Age/Siglo de Oro have ramifications. We have seen that political dates may be pressed into service as markers – if the seismic year of 1492 may be the start of empire building, then is the 1659 Treaty of the Pyrenees between France and Spain its political end, thus ignoring the final years of Philip IV's reign and the entire reign of his heir Charles II in the seventeenth century? From a literary perspective, such dates would include Nebrija's *Gramática castellana* (1492), the first published grammar of a modern European language in use, but also Juan Ruiz's 1499 publication

---

21 For further discussion see, for example, Derek Flitter, *Spanish Romantic Literary Theory and Criticism* (Cambridge: Cambridge University Press, 1992).

22 Francisco Javier Díez de Revenga, 'El concepto de Siglo de Oro en la encrucijada de dos épocas (1920–36)', *Mélanges de la Casa de Velázquez* 31/2 (1995), 193–206.

23 Jeremy Robbins, 'Renaissance and Baroque: continuity and transformation in early modern Spain', in David T. Gies, ed., *The Cambridge History of Spanish Literature* (Cambridge: Cambridge University Press, 2009), 137–48, 137.

La Celestina, commonly understood to be the last major medieval text in Spanish literary history, although Jo Labanyi describes it as 'strikingly modern nihilism' in *Spanish Literature. A Very Short Introduction*.[24] At the other end, a cut-off of 1659 excludes Calderón de la Barca's later works before his death in 1681 and, from the other side of the Atlantic, Sor Juana Inés de la Cruz's infamous *Respuesta a Sor Filotea de la Cruz* (1691). Indeed, another legacy of the Romantic approach to conflating national history with cultural history has been the marginalization of the trans-Atlantic dimension of sixteenth- and seventeenth-century Spain, whereby Golden Age has come to signify almost exclusively the peninsular. As we will see, this is a false division currently under question.

Ultimately, while a data-led survey of Golden Age syllabuses requires clear beginning and end dates, for our students the Golden Age (or Edad de Oro/Siglo de Oro) presents a challenge linguistically – with unfamiliar structures, idioms and vocabulary – and culturally, as surmised by Terence O'Reilly, writing in *The Companion to Hispanic Studies*, a short volume intended as a guide for new undergraduates of Spanish: 'the literature of the Golden Age is informed by a mentality very different from our own. To read it with understanding, therefore, we must be sensitive to its otherness, otherwise we shall find in it no more than a reflection of our own concerns'.[25]

Presenting the Golden Age to undergraduates

Although the remainder of this essay will take a more empirical view of what constitutes studying the Golden Age, through datasets gathered through a continuing longitudinal study of the syllabuses taught on UK university

---

24 Jo Labanyi, *Spanish Literature. A Very Short Introduction* (Oxford: Oxford University Press, 2010), 47.
25 Terence O'Reilly, 'Golden Age Studies: Spain and Spanish America in the sixteenth and seventeenth centuries', in Catherine Davies, ed., *The Companion to Hispanic Studies* (London: Arnold, 2002), 50–67, 50. Interestingly, O'Reilly's introductory discussion of the politics of the Golden Age takes the reader back to the early years of the reigns of the Reyes Católicos, before even 1492.

Hispanic Studies courses, it is worth spending a moment to consider how the period is presented to students as an option for study, in a sector that is becoming increasingly marketized. At my own institution, the University of Cambridge, my colleagues describe their broad ranging final year options in the following terms, before listing examples of the textual and visual culture material students will encounter: 'This paper covers the period known as Hispanic Golden Age (sixteenth and seventeenth centuries), a moment of cultural change and imperial expansion, of political contrasts and paradoxes. The "discovery" and invasion of America, the Reformation, the rise of philosophical scepticism and the spread of Copernicus' heliocentric theses changed dramatically the way in which the world was understood. This is clearly reflected and interrogated in literature and the arts'.[26] For students at Oxford, where units of study offered are also broad explorations of periods, the period is presented as one of the: 'richest, most varied, and most innovative periods of Spanish literature. A paper offering a wide range of topics and authors that include Cervantes, Lope de Vega, Calderón, Garcilaso, Luis de León, Santa Teresa, San Juan de la Cruz, Góngora, Quevedo, and the Picaresque Novel (among others) gives you the opportunity to engage with a number of the finest literary achievements in the language. It also allows you to study these works in their cultural context, which includes such elements as Golden Age Spain's relations with Renaissance Italy, or the Classical tradition, or the legacy of medieval Spain, or the Spanish intellectual and religious crisis of the sixteenth century'.[27] These units offer students a broad approach that contextualizes textual and visual culture in the history and politics of the two centuries.

At most UK universities, material for study is packaged in smaller module units with a tighter focus. At UCL, a final-year module entitled 'Cervantes and his World' is, like the broader papers, presented as connecting literature with techniques and context: 'Understanding these complex, endlessly fascinating fictions will take in theories of comedy, narrative technique, notions of fiction and fictionality, the history of Golden Age

---

26   <https://www.mml.cam.ac.uk/sp7>, accessed 13 July 2018.
27   <https://weblearn.ox.ac.uk/access/content/group/modlang/general/handbooks/2018-19/Spanish%20FHS%20Handbook%20_2018-19.pdf>, accessed 13 July 2018.

Spain and its global empire'.[28] The University of Exeter's module on Lope de Vega offers students the chance to engage with an unpublished poem in manuscript form, paradigmatic of the research-led teaching expected at that level of study.[29] At the University of St Andrews, a final-year module takes a thematic approach to the period, offering the students an introduction to 'Prose, poetry, theatre and songs that were written mostly for entertainment in the sixteenth and seventeenth centuries in Spain', in which 'works studied for this module feature superhero-like knights, real stories from soldiers of fortune, but also violent men and women on the wrong side of the law'.[30] The thematic approach here appeals to cross-cultural, supposedly timeless archetypes. These descriptions provide just a snapshot of the frameworks through which material is presented to students; there are, of course, many instances in which Golden Age era texts are part of introductory survey courses, or thematic courses that span periods.

The collected data from syllabuses reveals the range of peninsular literature taught on our courses across eighteen years, with data from the academic years 1998–9, 2006–7 and 2015–16. The first data collection took reading lists of peninsular literature material from UK university departments offering degrees in Spanish/Hispanic Studies, to ascertain whether or not any consensus existed as to which were the most important peninsular authors and texts. In the academic year 2006–7 the exercise was repeated but expanded to include non-peninsular literary material and filmic material from across the Spanish speaking world, which was repeated again during the academic year 2015–16. What began as an exercise in canonicity has become over time an exercise in tracing the discipline's change.

In each case the data is compiled from lists of primary reading/texts for study on modules taught; where a text is taught twice within a department on two different courses it is only included once. No distinction is made in the dataset regarding the context of the text's presentation (for

---

28 <https://www.ucl.ac.uk/selcs/study/undergraduate/modules/finalyear-2018-19/finalyear-2018-19/span0039-cervantes-and-his-world>, accessed 13 July 2018.
29 <https://humanities.exeter.ac.uk/modernlanguages/modules/MLS3067/>, accessed 13 July 2018.
30 <https://portal.st-andrews.ac.uk/catalogue/View?code=SP4015&academic_year=2018/9>, accessed 13 July 2018.

example, whether it is part of a compulsory or optional course), the level of study it is taught or whether it is taught alongside other Golden Age texts. Sections of texts are taken to mean the whole, a frequent example being Cervantes's *Novelas ejemplares*, which in practice is virtually never studied in its entirety, but is encountered through one or two of its constituent stories. Anthologies were listed as just the anthology title, as it was not possible to ascertain which texts were studied within the anthology (in practice few published anthologies are used). Frequently, lecturers would take a range of works from one poet's body of work, rather than any one collection; on such occasions, it was necessary to list the text for a poet as simply *Obra selecta*. The data collated includes only taught material whose primary language is Spanish, although texts translated from other languages of the Iberian peninsula and its overseas territories are included when read in Castilian. All forms of writing are incorporated into the data collection, including, for example, essay work or travel writing as well as fiction; as long as the text is treated as an object of study, as primary reading rather than secondary reading, then it is included. There were three main forms of locating the information: lists of primary reading as provided on openly accessible departmental internet pages; lists of a module's key texts provided by an institution's library catalogue for its users; information and handbooks supplied directly by colleagues.[31]

Although it is impossible to capture the primary reading lists of every module on every course, the intention is to arrive at as clear a snapshot of what is taught as is possible. Inevitably there will be some differences if a text is substituted at the last moment or if a list has not been updated. In very few instances I was unable to secure any information on the texts chosen for study on a particular module. Most importantly, as suggested earlier, my construction of a list cannot convey the context of the presentation of each author and text in the pedagogical moment: how is it presented? What is it compared to? Which other authors are mentioned but not studied, particularly in non-cultural focused classroom settings, for example language classes? Equally, the data collection cannot understand how Golden Age

---

31 I wish to express here my gratitude to all colleagues who assisted me in the task of collecting this information.

material is referenced and used in other contexts, an experience I know myself as a Modernist teaching Zorrilla's *Don Juan Tenorio*, with necessary reference to Tirso de Molina's *El burlador de Sevilla*, or Lorca's *Romancero gitano* with reference to Luis de Góngora's poetic techniques. Such reference points are the hallmarks of the affiliation to a cultural consciousness of canonicity that cannot be captured by a syllabus database.[32]

Nonetheless my data works to reveal two things. First, the nature of disciplinary change in UK Hispanism through the lens of what we teach, which is informed both by what we research and also what we believe to be important for the student to encounter within a languages undergraduate degree. Second, it reveals the nature of what we present from Spanish-language literary heritage as of value to the non-native speaker through access to and study of the original text.[33] As I have written elsewhere, we as educators have a responsibility to translate that culture to them through pedagogy, since our choice of text sends an authoritative signal of what is of value in the other culture.[34] Yet, in addition to these value-laden reasons for text choice, pragmatic motives also play their part: primarily the text's length, its availability and its level of linguistic difficulty. Our choice of text is also informed by what we studied ourselves and what we engage in our research. As Colin Evans suggested back in 1988, in relation to the presentation of the studied text as a gift, 'the staff give, the students receive. So all the onus is on the staff to get it right. Occasionally we try to guess what the students want; very rarely we ask; but the usual method is to give what we ourselves love or used or think we ought to love'.[35] The changes I will present suggest

---

[32] It is worth noting that UK students studying Spanish below degree level are exposed to some literature and film alongside what is almost predominantly a language course. A survey of Spanish university entry qualifications reveals that only one of the five UK exam boards offers Golden Age texts (*Fuenteovejuna* and *Lazarillo de Tormes*) on its syllabus.

[33] The possibility of accessing other cultures through translation is also always present, but in the Anglophone context is often limited.

[34] Stuart Davis, 'Close encounters of the cultural kind: The peninsular Spanish canon in a pedagogical context', *Journal of Iberian and Latin American Studies* 16/2–3 (2010), 107–26.

[35] Colin Evans *Language People. The Experience of Teaching and Learning Modern Languages in British Universities* (Milton Keynes: Open University Press, 1988), 131.

that perhaps now we are better at asking and responding to what students want, as well as adapting our objects of love.

Bearing in mind the earlier discussion of nomenclature and periodization as an act from the present moment, for this data analysis 'Golden Age' is taken at its broadest temporal limits, from the momentous political events in 1492 to the death of Sor Juana Inés de la Cruz in 1695, a span of 200 years that lives up to the discourse of an 'age' and not a 'siglo'. The term is also understood to include material produced outside the Iberian peninsula. The dataset will be discussed first in relation to the place of Golden Age literature in the wider curriculum before examining in more detail who the key authors and texts are, and how their fortunes have fared over the three sets of data.

In the most recent data collection, from the academic year 2015–16, I was able to obtain complete or almost complete data from thirty-nine departments. As a dataset, 74 per cent of the material offered for study was textual and 26 per cent film. A total of 617 different authors and film directors were present (not including anonymous texts and editors of anthologies), split equally as 50 per cent peninsular and 50 per cent non-peninsular.[36] There were 1,228 different books or films, divided as 51 per cent peninsular and 49 per cent non-peninsular. The average size of a list was thirty-nine books and indeed, as we will see when comparing this data with earlier collections, in 2015–16 there was little consensus as to the most important. If we take as a benchmark 50 per cent of departments teaching one specific author as a mark of consensus then there are only two canonical authors and one filmmaker for our students: Pedro Almodóvar (taught by 74 per cent of departments), Gabriel García Márquez (64 per cent) and Federico García Lorca (54 per cent). Extending our criterion for inclusion to an arguably generous 25 per cent rate of consensus creates a longer list of twenty-one authors and directors (see Table 2.1).

This list of twenty-one comprises eight film directors and thirteen authors and eighteen of the list are men and three are women. There are thirteen from Spain and eight Latin American (half of which are Mexican); three are Golden Age writers and the remainder from the twentieth and

---

36   I use the phrase 'non-peninsular' to reflect the presence of African and Asian Spanish-language material from Equatorial Guinea and the Philippines, as well as Latin America.

Table 2.1. Authors and directors taught in at least 25 per cent of surveyed departments in 2015–16 data collection.

Author/director	Percentage of departments teaching at least one text/film
Pedro Almodóvar	74
Gabriel García Márquez	64
Federico García Lorca	54
Luis Buñuel	46
Carlos Saura	44
Icíar Bollaín	38
Víctor Erice	36
Jorge Luis Borges	33
Lope de Vega	
Miguel de Cervantes	
Mario Vargas Llosa	
Juan Rulfo	31
Guillermo del Toro	
Alejandro González Iñárritu	28
Carlos Fuentes	
Isabel Allende	
Carmen Martín Gaite	26
Javier Cercas	
Luis García Berlanga	
Miguel de Unamuno	
Pedro Calderón de la Barca	

twenty-first centuries. Within the material represented by these figures, there is a dominance of film and narrative (novel/short story), with some drama, poetry and essaywork figuring in several profiles.

In order to examine the consensus around texts and films, it is instructive to lower the threshold slightly more to 20 per cent consensus, which also produces a list of twenty-one (see Table 2.2).

Table 2.2. Texts taught in at least 20 per cent of surveyed departments in 2015–16 data collection.

Author/Director	Title	Percentage of departments teaching the text/film
Erice	*El espíritu de la colmena*	33
Cervantes	*Novelas ejemplares*	31
García Márquez	*Crónica de una muerte anunciada*	28
Almodóvar	*Mujeres al borde de un ataque de nervios*	
García Lorca	*Bodas de sangre*	26
García Lorca	*La casa de Bernarda Alba*	
González Iñárritu	*Amores perros*	
Cercas	*Soldados de Salamina*	
Bollaín	*Te doy mis ojos*	23
Rulfo	*El llano en llamas*	
Puenzo	*La historia official*	
Saura	*Cría cuervos*	
Anon	*Lazarillo de Tormes*	21
García Márquez	*El coronel no tiene quien le escriba*	
Borges	*Ficciones*	
Arguedas	*Los ríos profundos*	
Puig	*El beso de la mujer araña*	
Cervantes	*Don Quijote*	
Calderón de la Barca	*La vida es sueño*	
Buñuel	*Viridiana*	
Buñuel	*Un chien andalou/Un perro andaluz*	

Of these twenty-one, eight are films, with the remainder confirming our expectations arisen from the list of authors previously presented. There are four Golden Age texts included, one from the sixteenth century and three from the seventeenth. The remaining texts focus on the so-called Silver Age of early twentieth-century Spain and twentieth-century Latin American narrative. Missing from these lists of authors and texts are the pre-1492 period, and the eighteenth and nineteenth centuries. This identified core represents just a handful of texts and authors amongst a great many more.

What the data shows us so far is, arguably, in line with our expectations for a higher education level course aimed at non-native speakers; it focuses on material that is perceived to be most accessible from a linguistic and historical perspective, with the presence of what is considered to be a key moment in the cultural and political history of Spain: the Golden Age. That there are three authors and four texts from this period represented in these core lists is an achievement, given the fact that of the thirty-nine departments in the dataset, sixteen (41 per cent) did not offer any Golden Age material for study. As noted earlier, this does not prevent engagement with the period through the study of later texts and periods, and it may be that these departments offer history or visual culture focused modules instead, or indeed offered Golden Age texts for study in other years.

The body of Golden Age material taught in 2015–16 comprises sixty-eight authors, plus five anonymous texts. Of those sixty-eight authors, fifty-seven were men and eleven (16 per cent) women. Fifteen were born in the fifteenth century, forty-four in the sixteenth century and nine in the seventeenth century. When the five anonymous texts are included, fifty-three of the total seventy-three authors/texts were peninsular, with twenty living and writing entirely or predominantly in Colonial Latin America. It is of interest to note that of the seventy-three authors/anonymous texts, forty-six (62 per cent) appear on just one university reading list, suggesting that a diverse body of material is being employed by lecturers. However, there is a relatively strong sense of a core within the Golden Age material (see Table 2.3).

Table 2.3. Golden Age authors or anonymous texts taught in at least 13 per cent of surveyed departments in 2015–16 data collection.

Author/anonymous text	Percentage of departments teaching the author/text	Number of different titles by that author taught
Lope de Vega	33	29
Miguel de Cervantes	33	5
Pedro Calderón de la Barca	26	22
Francisco de Quevedo	23	4
Sor Juana Inés de la Cruz	23	2

The Golden Age in the Hispanic Studies classroom

Author/anonymous text	Percentage of departments teaching the author/text	Number of different titles by that author taught
Lazarillo de Tormes	21	1
Tirso de Molina		9
Bartolomé de las Casas	18	1
Garcilaso de la Vega		2
Cristóbal Colón	15	3
Fernando de Rojas		1
Luis de Góngora		4
Hernán Cortés	13	1
María de Zayas		2

All of the thirteen authors plus one anonymous text listed were taught that year by five or more UK universities, representing some of the best known peninsular fiction writers and playwrights we would expect to see, plus Cortés and Bartolomé de las Casas who represent study of the textual culture of conquest and colonization in Latin America.[37]

The most commonly taught texts are illustrated in Table 2.4.

Table 2.4. Golden Age texts taught in at least 35 per cent of surveyed departments in 2015–16 data collection.

Author	Title	Genre	Percentage of departments teaching the text
Miguel de Cervantes	*Novelas ejemplares*	narrative	31
Anon	*Lazarillo de Tormes*	narrative	21
Miguel de Cervantes	*Don Quijote*	narrative	
Pedro Calderón de la Barca	*La vida es sueño*	theatre	
Bartolomé de las Casas	*Brevísima relación de la destrucción de las Indias*	non-fiction	18
Tirso de Molina	*El burlador de Sevilla*	theatre	

(*Continued*)

---

37 Just outside this group are three more recognizably canonical writers, across a range of genres: Fray Luis de León, Álvar Núñez Cabeza de Vaca and Santa Teresa de Ávila.

Table 2.4. (*Continued*)

Author	Title	Genre	Percentage of departments teaching the text
Fernando de Rojas	*La Celestina*	narrative	15
Francisco de Quevedo	Selected poetry	poetry	
Cristóbal Colón	*Diario de Colón*	non-fiction	13
Francisco de Quevedo	*El Buscón*	narrative	
Garcilaso de la Vega	Selected poetry	poetry	
Hernán Cortés	*Cartas de relación*	non-fiction	
Lope de Vega	*El perro del hortelano*	theatre	
Sor Juana Inés de la Cruz	Selected poetry	poetry	

Amongst these fourteen texts, two authors appear twice, Cervantes and Quevedo. It is also interesting to note the range of genres represented here: five fiction narrative texts; three plays; three poetry collections; three 'essays' (non-fiction texts).

The 2015–2016 data in comparison to earlier years

In order to understand fully the changes in the presence of Golden Age material across all three datasets, it will be instructive to briefly examine the fuller picture within which Golden Age studies is to be found. The fullest comparison is to be found by comparing the 2015–16 data with that of 2006–7, since both encompassed the full range of taught material: film and text, peninsular and non-peninsular.[38] From the academic years 2006–7 to 2015–16 there was a 42 per cent increase in the number of authors and directors taught. However,

---

38 The 2006–7 collection included forty university departments, one more than the 2015–16 collection, so although they are not all the same degree courses surveyed,

there was only a 22 per cent increase in the number of different titles taught and a much smaller 2 per cent increase in the body of material taught, suggesting very strongly that students are not encountering more material in their courses than nine years previously, but a greater diversity within that body of material. This is in part due to a growth in film within our degree courses, since the percentage share of directors and film titles has grown from roughly a fifth to a quarter, indeed almost a third of the authors/directors list in total. The differences between the two data collections confirm an observation often made anecdotally; that the canonical core is dissipating, with an increasing shift towards visual culture and Latin American studies.

As the 1998–9 data collection had included peninsular textual material only, it is not possible to look back further at the divisions between filmic and textual, peninsular and non-peninsular (including non-peninsular Golden Age material). However, we can examine the changing fortunes of those peninsular texts that we have identified as core in the 2015–16 data collection. Table 2.5 lists all the Golden Age authors and anonymous texts that have been taught by at least 10 per cent of departments in any one of the three data collections:

Table 2.5. Authors taught in at least 10 per cent of surveyed departments in at least one of the three data collections.

	Percentage of depts teaching at least one text – 1998–9	Percentage of depts teaching at least one text – 2006–7	Percentage of depts teaching at least one text – 2015–16
Miguel de Cervantes	68	45	33
Lope de Vega	58	33	33
Pedro Calderón de la Barca	55	38	26
Francisco de Quevedo	42	28	23
Sor Juana Inés de la Cruz	unknown	18	23
Lazarillo de Tormes	58	33	21
Tirso de Molina	48	33	21

(*Continued*)

they represent the Spanish/Hispanic Studies degrees available in those years and, as such, represent the discipline in the UK Higher Education sector as a whole.

Table 2.5. (*Continued*)

	Percentage of depts teaching at least one text – 1998–9	Percentage of depts teaching at least one text – 2006–7	Percentage of depts teaching at least one text – 2015–16
Garcilaso de la Vega	26	15	18
Bartolomé de las Casas	unknown	1	18
Fernando de Rojas	45	25	15
Luis de Góngora	39	13	15
María de Zayas	6	1	13
Cristóbal Colón	unknown	1	13
Hernán Cortés	unknown	1	13

Reflective of the large increase in the overall number of authors between the two later data collections, there were forty new Golden Age authors on the 2015–16 list who were not taught in 2006–7, but as sixteen were 'lost', there was a net gain of twenty-four new authors. None of these authors would have appeared on the list of 'the most commonly taught'. There are two key observations to be made regarding the table of Golden Age authors across the three datasets: the first is the sharp decline in the visibility of canonical authors, many of whom are taught by significantly fewer departments by 2015–16 than was previously the case. Secondly, although the presence of Latin American focused texts was unknown in 1998–99, there has been a striking growth in their presence between 2006–7 and 2015–16. These observations are, unsurprisingly, reflected also in the presence of Golden Age texts on the degree courses (see Table 2.6).

Table 2.6. Texts taught in at least 10 per cent of surveyed departments in at least one of the three data collections.

Title	Percentage of depts teaching at least one text – 1998–9	Percentage of depts teaching at least one text – 2006–7	Percentage of depts teaching at least one text – 2015–16
Novelas ejemplares	52	35	31
Lazarillo de Tormes	58	33	21
Don Quijote	52	38	21

(*Continued*)

The Golden Age in the Hispanic Studies classroom

Title	Percentage of depts teaching at least one text – 1998–9	Percentage of depts teaching at least one text – 2006–7	Percentage of depts teaching at least one text – 2015–16
La vida es sueño	39	18	21
Brevísima relación de la destruición de las Indias	unknown	5	18
El burlador de Sevilla	45	33	18
La Celestina	45	25	15
Quevedo: Selected poetry	13	13	15
Diario de Colón	unknown	5	13
El Buscón	32	18	13
Garcilaso de la Vega: Selected poetry	26	15	13
Cartas de relación	unknown	5	13
El perro del hortelano	13	18	13
Sor Juana Inés de la Cruz: Selected poetry	unknown	18	13
Góngora: Selected poetry	39	13	15
El alcalde de Zalamea	35	13	5

Again, we see a decline in the visibility of most of the core canonical texts and some growth in the Latin American textual material.

It is also instructive to see the place of Golden Age material within each data collection. The comparison in Table 2.7 does not include non-peninsular material, to ensure the three datasets are comparable.

Table 2.7. The presence of Golden Age material in each data collection.

	Number of peninsular Golden Age authors/ anonymous texts (percentage of all peninsular authors)	Number of corresponding titles (percentage of all peninsular titles)	Number of corresponding objects of study (percentage of all peninsular objects of study)
Data collection 1998/9	19 (11%)	93 (19%)	311 (24%)

(*Continued*)

	Number of peninsular Golden Age authors/ anonymous texts (percentage of all peninsular authors)	Number of corresponding titles (percentage of all peninsular titles)	Number of corresponding objects of study (percentage of all peninsular objects of study)
Data collection 2006/7	28 (14%)	103 (20%)	245 (23%)
Data collection 2015/16	53 (17%)	136 (22%)	245 (22%)

It is clear that there is now a greater number and broader range of Golden Age material; although there has been an increase in the range of material overall on undergraduate degrees nonetheless Golden Age material has increased as a percentage of overall peninsular material taught, suggesting strength in the field. However, the greater dispersal of the material across authors and texts means that there is a less clear core of authors and texts to which the majority of undergraduate students are exposed. Additional to this, the growth in teaching in colonial Latin American textual (and visual) culture can only be empirically evidenced through future data collections, but does seem to be symptomatic of a shift in the discipline away from the peninsular canonical core (a shift that includes, as suggested before, a growth in the presence of visual culture and history focused modules and material available to students). The movement to see Hispanic Studies as an intrinsically trans-Atlantic discipline has not only been recognized in research publications, but also texts that are designed to introduce undergraduates to the field, as evidenced by Luis Fernando Restrepo's exploration of colonial cultures and Amerindian writing in *The Companion to Latin American Studies*, where he recognizes the shift: 'For a long time Hispanic literary studies neglected this plurilingual and multiform cultural repertoire, focusing more on European-style literature'.[39]

---

39   Luis Fernando Restrepo, 'The Cultures of Colonialism', in Philip Swanson, ed., *The Companion to Latin American Studies* (London: Arnold, 2003), 47–68, 59. Terence O'Reilly's essay on the Golden Age for *The Companion of Hispanic Studies*, referenced

The importance of the Golden Age for a sense of canonicity and literary heritage remains demonstrably important, as evidenced through these data collections as a snapshot of a much larger picture. The period remains visible, despite there being a dispersal of the canon. The most famous Golden Age texts remain central to the core, alongside more contemporary material from the twentieth century to the present day; amongst the most frequently taught texts in all the data collections have been *Lazarillo de Tormes*, *La vida es sueño*, *Don Quijote* and Cervantes's *Novelas ejemplares*. Their place in the pantheon of stars is assured, it would seem, and they outshine authors we might well have expected to see instead such as Pérez Galdós, Pardo Bazán, Unamuno or Cela. The increase in the quantity of authors and texts is also to be celebrated, revealing to our students the diversity of voices within a period that we call the 'Golden Age', not as static as the temporal distance may lead us to assume. As Hispanic Studies continues to diversify, so does its most celebrated moment of cultural heritage. As López Bueno notes: 'Es como mirar el cielo: en una simple mirada observamos las estrellas que más brillan; pero, cuanto más limitamos el punto de mira, más estrellas logramos ver, aunque su intensidad es diferente'.[40]

---

earlier, also spends some time drawing on the relationship of Spain to the so-called New World and the writings that detailed conquest and life there.
40 López Bueno 'La poesía del Sigo de Oro', 80.

PART II

Teaching the old through the new

ALMUDENA GARCÍA GONZÁLEZ

3   El estudio del mundo literario de la España del siglo diecisiete desde la ficción televisiva del siglo ventiuno: autores, obras y contexto presentes en *El Ministerio del Tiempo*

[Studying the literary world of seventeenth-century Spain using a twenty-first-century TV fiction series: Authors, works and contexts in *El Ministerio del Tiempo*]

ABSTRACT

The Spanish TV series *El Ministerio del Tiempo* portrays a secret Ministry entrusted with the job of ensuring that no significant changes occur to the history of Spain. In addition to twenty-first-century officials, the Ministry employs a range of agents, recruited from different periods, who use secret doors to travel back in time. The choice of Golden Age Spain as the scenario for a number of secret missions, coupled with the presence of characters such as Lazarillo and authors such as Lope de Vega and Cervantes, makes the TV series an excellent tool for introducing students to the period and to some of its most renowned literary figures. It subsequently enables them to approach their reading of the texts with an appropriate knowledge base and a curiosity triggered as a result of viewing the popular series.

El 24 de marzo de 2015, Televisión Española estrenó una nueva serie: *El Ministerio del Tiempo*. Se trataba de una propuesta arriesgada por lo rocambolesco y atrevido de su argumento: la existencia de un Ministerio secreto, cuyos trabajadores pueden viajar a través de unas puertas del tiempo a cualquier época pasada y desde el pasado, hasta la actualidad. Su principal función es la de velar por que no se produzcan cambios en la Historia, ni viajen por las puertas del tiempo intrusos ajenos al Ministerio. En dicha institución, además de funcionarios del siglo veintiuno, trabajan una serie de agentes reclutados de diferentes épocas, asegurándose de que todo se mantiene tal y como las crónicas, libros de historia y literatura, cuadros, fotografías y películas nos han ido relatando del pasado.

En la primera parte de este trabajo haré una relación y un breve análisis de la presencia de la literatura áurea en la serie, que servirán de base para un segundo apartado, en el que se señalan algunas líneas concretas de trabajo. Este primer acercamiento considero que resulta fundamental para poder aprehender lo que la serie nos ofrece y llegar, a partir de esto, a explorar las posibilidades pedagógicas que encontramos en ella. El simple visionado de unos capítulos concretos puede crear curiosidad en nuestros alumnos por conocer más sobre determinadas épocas, autores y obras. Y este es un primer paso muy importante, pero solo si nosotros hacemos una labor previa de análisis y trazamos unas líneas de trabajo claras y rigurosas a partir de las que nuestros alumnos puedan profundizar, lograremos realmente explotar todo el potencial de una herramienta como esta. El objetivo: que nuestros estudiantes desarrollen un espíritu crítico sobre este tipo de producciones y lleguen al aprendizaje sobre la literatura áurea en el grado de profundidad que nosotros deseemos.

Son tres las temporadas que se han emitido del *El Ministerio del Tiempo* y, en todas ellas, la literatura áurea se ha visto representada y ensalzada en algún capítulo. En la temporada uno, ya en el episodio dos, la patrulla protagonista habrá de salvar a un joven Lope de Vega que va a embarcar en la Grande y Felicísima Armada, más conocida con el irónico apelativo de la Armada Invencible. El papel del dramaturgo tuvo tanto éxito de audiencia, que en las siguientes temporadas estuvo de nuevo presente. También en la primera temporada tuvo su papel, en el episodio seis, Lázaro de Tormes. Aunque *La vida del Lazarillo de Tormes* sea una obra temprana, de mediados del dieciséis, todos sabemos la relevancia de esta pieza para la evolución de la literatura barroca. En el tercer episodio de la segunda temporada, los agentes del Ministerio habrán de viajar a 1604. Esta vez el protagonista será Miguel de Cervantes y la misión, asegurarse de que se publica la obra insignia no solo de este autor, sino de las letras españolas: *El ingenioso hidalgo Don Quijote de la Mancha*. Junto a Cervantes, veremos de nuevo a Lope de Vega. Finalmente, en el episodio veintiséis de la serie, noveno de la temporada, 'Tiempo de esplendor', los agentes del Ministerio velarán por la firma

El estudio del mundo literario de la España del siglo diecisiete 59

del tratado de paz entre Inglaterra y España, que había sido previamente firmado en Londres en 1604 e iba a ser ratificado en Valladolid, en 1605, con las firmas de Felipe III y Lord Howard, como representante de Jacobo I. Lope y Cervantes serán testigos privilegiados y tendrán un papel importante en este suceso.

Junto a los episodios relacionados, encontramos otros en los que la literatura no será la protagonista, pero las situaciones históricas relatadas sí nos llevan a momentos claves y a personajes que pueden ayudar a conocer mejor la sociedad española de los siglos dieciséis y diecisiete, como Felipe II, el pintor Diego Velázquez, el General Spínola o Bernal Díaz del Castillo. Finalmente, considero también relevante el hecho de que uno de los miembros de la patrulla, Alonso de Entrerríos, sea un soldado de los tercios procedente del siglo dieciséis, con lo que ello conlleva respecto a su forma de expresarse, comportarse y pensar. Es reclutado por el Ministerio en 1569, tras ser condenado a muerte por rebelarse ante la incompetencia de su superior. Los otros dos agentes que conforman la patrulla protagonista son Julián Ramos, enfermero del Servicio de Emergencias de Madrid reclutado en el 2015, y Amelia Folch, joven barcelonesa y, según la serie, primera mujer en España en acceder a la Universidad, donde estudia Filología Hispánica. A partir de la segunda temporada entra en escena, por la marcha de Julián, Jesús Méndez, conocido como Pacino, policía en los años 80 del siglo veinte. En definitiva, la suma de la elección de la España áurea como destino de varias de las misiones y la presencia de todos los personajes, reales y ficticios, anteriormente señalados, creo que convierte a esta serie en una excelente herramienta para introducir a los estudiantes en la época y presentarles a dos de los autores más representativos para, después, poder llegar a la lectura de los textos con una base de conocimientos adquiridos y, sobre todo, una curiosidad ya creada. Además, el juego constante entre los referentes culturales de las épocas visitadas, los propios de las épocas de cada agente y los de la actualidad, suponen un aliciente más para que los alumnos extranjeros que estudian la lengua española y su literatura disfruten y aprendan con esta serie.

Señalaba que el primer episodio en el que la literatura del Siglo de Oro se ve directamente representada es el segundo de la primera temporada, 'Tiempo de gloria'. El capítulo comienza en la Lisboa de 1588. Gil Pérez, un funcionario del Ministerio del Tiempo de la época descubre que Lope de

Vega no aparece en el listado de hombres que componen la tripulación del San Juan, el barco en el que supuestamente debía ir para regresar vivo de la empresa. Rápidamente avisa a los responsables actuales de la institución para que le envíen refuerzos que le ayuden a investigar y paliar lo sucedido. La patrulla formada por Amelia, Julián y Alonso será la encargada de ayudar a Gil Pérez con la misión. Localizan a Lope en las listas del navío San Esteban y, tras comprobar que este barco se hundió con toda su tripulación, habrán de lograr que Lope no viaje en este, sino en el San Juan, y así asegurar que el dramaturgo volverá vivo de la expedición.

En el último número publicado de la revista *Anuario de Lope de Vega*, encontramos diversos trabajos que analizan, en mayor o menor medida, la figura de Lope en *El Ministerio del Tiempo*. Tanto Esther Fernández, como Simon Breden, como Héctor Urzáiz, coinciden en la caracterización canalla que se da a Lope. A lo largo de su artículo, Breden desgrana cómo los creadores y guionistas de la serie juegan con la faceta donjuanesca de Lope y cómo esta atrae al gran público (una muestra de esto es el hecho de que el personaje de Lope, tras su primera aparición, fuera *trending topic* durante 24 horas en Twitter).[1] Por la entrevista que incluye al final de su artículo a Javier Olivares, uno de los creadores del *Ministerio*, vemos que la elección de este marco histórico y del personaje de Lope de Vega no se debe a una especial admiración de estos por el madrileño. Fue en su supuesta participación y supervivencia en la Armada Invencible donde vieron un ejemplo perfecto para destacar una de las claves que pretenden con la serie: 'hablar de los perdedores y los olvidados en contraposición con los grandes nombres de la Historia'.[2] Los protagonistas habrán de salvar a un personaje relevante para la historia de la literatura española, pero tendrán que dejar morir a todos los soldados que fueron en los navíos que no lograron volver. Alonso, como soldado, no

---

1   Esther Fernández, 'Lope de Vega en televisión', *Anuario Lope de Vega* 24 (2018), 10–37, <http://revistes.uab.cat/anuariolopedevega/article/view/v24-fernandez-1/246-pdf-e>, consultado 29 junio 2018; Simon Breden, 'La presencia de Lope de Vega en *El Ministerio del Tiempo*', *Anuario Lope de Vega* 24 (2018), 75–93, <http://revistes.uab.cat/anuariolopedevega/article/view/v24-breden>, consultado 29 junio 2018; Héctor Urzáiz, '"¡Maldito Lope de Vega!": la polémica Cervantes-Lope en las pantallas de hogaño', *Anuario Lope de Vega* 24 (2018), 38–74, <http://revistes.uab.cat/anuariolopedevega/article/view/v24-urzaiz>, consultado 29 junio 2018.

2   Breden, 'La presencia de Lope', 88.

puede dejar de exclamar al conocer la misión: 'Espero que los méritos de ese tal ... Lope ... sean muchos, para salvarle y dejar que mueran los demás'.[3]

Y esto se acentúa si, además, la caracterización que se da de ese gran nombre es la de un mujeriegoególatra y vanidoso.[4] La primera vez que los agentes ven a Lope, el encuentro se produce en una taberna y el madrileño acaba de arrebatarle una conquista a otro soldado embriagado. Alonso exclama: '¿A este botarate es al que hemos de salvar?'[5] Por su parte, Julián, al regresar de la misión, expresa abiertamente ante sus jefes su opinión en caso de que debieran intervenir una vez más para salvar al dramaturgo: 'Si eso ocurre, mejor que manden a otros. Es un tipo insoportable, engreído, mujeriego ...'[6] No será esa, sin embargo, la impresión de Amelia, que conoce a fondo la obra de Lope y le admira. No considero una casualidad que en el primer episodio se presenta a Amelia en clase, mientras el profesor explica a Lope de Vega y la influencia del *Orlando furioso* en su obra *La hermosura de Angélica*. En el segundo episodio, justamente, son unos versos del *Orlando* los que delatan la identidad de Lope a los agentes en la pelea con el soldado, anteriormente referida. La joven los identifica y señala rápidamente a sus compañeros la identidad del escritor: 'dudo que haya muchos soldados capaces de citarlo de memoria ... aparte de él'.[7]

Los defectos personales de Lope son de nuevo resaltados en los capítulos que comparte con Cervantes, 'Tiempo de hidalgos' y 'Tiempo de esplendor'. En el capítulo 'Tiempo de hidalgos', vuelven a resaltarse la vanidad del autor y su desmedido gusto por las mujeres. Pacino es enviado a averiguar si han contactado también con Lope los ingleses que han comprado el manuscrito de *Don Quijote* con la intención de evitar que Cervantes lo lleve a la imprenta y así la obra nunca llegue a publicarse. El nuevo agente recibe el siguiente consejo por parte de uno de los jefes: 'Lope es un hombre sensible

---

3   Javier Olivares y Pablo Olivares, 'Tiempo de gloria', guión del capítulo dos, temporada uno, 19, <http://www.rtve.es/contenidos/el-ministerio-del-tiempo/ministerio_del_tiempo_guion_capitulo_2.pdf>, consultado 29 junio 2018.
4   Motivo por el que no va en el San Juan. Carta real al Duque de Sessa.
5   Olivares y Olivares, 'Tiempo de gloria', 22.
6   Olivares y Olivares, 'Tiempo de gloria', 59.
7   Olivares y Olivares, 'Tiempo de gloria', 22.

a los halagos. Regálele el oído y le tendrá ganado'.[8] A los vicios ya conocidos, se le suman otros dos: se nos muestra a un Lope competitivo y envidioso, además de autor de un teatro de masas que lo único que busca es la fama. Para evitar que Cervantes estrene *Los baños de Argel*, pues la pieza nunca llegó a verse en las tablas, Gil Perez y Pacino hacen creer a los actores de la compañía de Cervantes que Lope los reclama para una obra suya, ante lo que el protagonista exclama: '¡Ese monstruo de la naturaleza no se detendrá hasta acabar conmigo! ¿No tiene bastante con su fama y su fortuna que tiene que hundir a los demás?'[9] La crítica mayor viene cuando Alonso lo anima para que convenza a los actores de que se queden con él. En su discurso acusa de baja calidad a las obras de Lope y defiende su concepción del teatro:

> Lope es autor de fama y nombre, lo sé. Pero ¿de verdad queréis trabajar para alguien que la consigue como él lo hace? ¡Lope desprecia a su público! Cientos de veces ha dicho que en el *Arte nuevo al vulgo es justo hablarle en necio para darle gusto*.[10] Yo soy de otro parecer. El pueblo merece ser mejor, y se le hace mejor dándole buen alimento y buena letra.[11]

Ante este alegato, Gil Pérez comenta con Amelia 'Cómo se nota que no ha trabajado en televisión'.[12] El reclamo de Cervantes de un teatro mejor, seguido del chiste de Gil Pérez, supone un paralelismo entre el teatro de los Siglos de Oro como espectáculo de masas y ciertos programas y retrasmisiones de la televisión, que ejercerían ese papel en la actualidad.

La pugna entre ambos autores por la fama presentada en este capítulo es de nuevo desarrollada en 'Tiempo de esplendor', constituyéndose en el hilo principal de las intervenciones de ambos personajes. Asimismo, en este

---

8 Carlos de Pando y Anaïs Schaaff, 'Tiempo de hidalgos', guion del capítulo once, temporada dos, 34, <http://www.rtve.es/contenidos/ministeriotiempo/guion-ministerio-del-tiempo-capitulo-11-T2XE03.pdf>, consultado 29 de junio 2018.

9 Pando y Schaaff, 'Tiempo de hidalgos', 43.

10 Con esta referencia al *Arte nuevo*, los guionistas juegan con una de las citas más famosas del tratado de Lope sobre su visión del género dramático. La acción del episodio se desarrolla a finales de 1604 y el texto de Lope no se publicó hasta 1609. Aunque circulara manuscrito con anterioridad, Pedraza defiende que 'tuvo que redactarse a finales de 1608 o en los primeros días de 1609'. Felipe Pedraza, *Lope de Vega vida y literatura* (Valladolid: Universidad de Valladolid, 2008), 65.

11 Pando y Schaaff, 'Tiempo de hidalgos', 44.

12 Pando y Schaaff, 'Tiempo de hidalgos', 44.

episodio aparecerá el último de los defectos achacado al Fénix de los Ingenios que, además, hará que Amelia pierda toda la admiración que sentía por él hasta entonces: el servilismo a los poderosos. A través de la correspondencia conservada entre Lope y el Duque de Sessa, a menudo se ha resaltado esa faceta del madrileño.[13] En la serie, será al Duque de Lerma al que rinda pleitesía, traicionando, incluso, el trato al que había llegado previamente con la reina. Sin embargo, esta vez Lope no es el objeto principal de crítica para los guionistas, la amenaza del privado de retirarle la licencia para poder actuar lo convierte en esta ocasión en víctima. Es la figura de Lerma la que se intenta denunciar como la de uno de los primeros políticos corruptos de nuestro país.

El tratamiento dado a la personalidad de Lope dista bastante del empleado respecto a la figura de Cervantes, quien recibe un trato bastante más amable. De hecho, el personaje de Alonso, quien desde un principio había mostrado sus reticencias por salvar a Lope y en ningún momento muestra interés por su obra, antes de marchar a la misión de recuperar *Don Quijote*, se entrega a su lectura y, entre risas, exclama divertido: '¡A fe mía que es bueno este libro ... ¡muy bueno!'[14] Asimismo, muestra una empatía y admiración por la obra teatral de Cervantes y sus deseos de ser un dramaturgo de éxito muy lejos de la consideración de 'botarate' que tiene de Lope. En la ya citada entrevista de Breden a Olivares podemos ver las claves de esta diferencia. La primera es su consideración sobre la relevancia y calidad de *Don Quijote*, frente a las composiciones lopescas. La segunda estaría en la respuesta a la cuestión de si cree que Lope de Vega ha sido 'maltratado por la educación y la escena':[15]

> Como todos, convirtiendo esas materias como algo aburrido que habla del pasado como si estuviera muerto. Y está bien vivo. Y sin él, no se puede entender el presente. Pero considero más víctima a Cervantes que a Lope. En su época y aún hoy en día.[16]

---

13 Para Pedraza, este 'servilismo desmedido' de Lope lo que nos demuestra es que el dramaturgo 'utilizó siempre su única arma, la palabra, para obtener provecho de sus protectores [...] Escribe sus cartas pensando en quien ha de leerlas'. Pedraza, *Lope de Vega vida y literatura*, 40–1.
14 Pando y Schaaff, 'Tiempo de hidalgos', 11.
15 Breden, 'La presencia de Lope', 89.
16 Breden, 'La presencia de Lope', 89.

Así, comprendemos como mientras a Lope se le afea su gusto por la fama, en Cervantes se justifica como una cuestión de justicia por los méritos literarios del autor. Si bien, en algún momento, sí se muestra como su enfrentamiento con Lope le lleva a comportarse de forma ansiosa e infantil. En 'Tiempo de esplendor', Cervantes está dolido porque ante la visita de la comitiva inglesa para la firma del tratado, a él se le ha encargado escribir la crónica, mientras la representación que se llevará a cabo para homenajearlos correrá a cargo de Lope de Vega. Además, le obsesiona que Lope pueda conocer a Shakespeare, que ha viajado con la delegación y él no. Cervantes y Lope protagonizan ante esta situación una cómica escena que les vale una reprimenda de Amelia. Al final, Cervantes se verá recompensado, pues solo él conocerá a Shakespeare y, además, le puede entregar un ejemplar de su recién publicado *Don Quijote*. Por su parte, Lope no solo no logra entrevistarse con el genio inglés, sino que perderá el favor de la reina y de Amelia por haber claudicado ante las exigencias del de Lerma.

> A pesar de que la relación de Cervantes y Lope se centra en su enfrentamiento por el éxito teatral y de Lope se destaca esencialmente su labor como dramaturgo, la mayor parte de las obras de Lope que se citan en la serie no son comedias. En ella se habla de *La hermosura de Angélica*, el *Isidro* y *La Dragontea*. Como obras teatrales solo se nombra a *Los embustes de Fabia* y *La dama boba*, título que, además, aún Lope no había escrito.[17]

Por último, en el caso de Lázaro de Tormes, los creadores juegan con que este personaje habría existido en la realidad. En el sexto episodio de la primera temporada, mientras la patrulla debe buscar a un empresario condenado en el siglo ventiuno por malversación, que se ha escondido en el siglo dieciséis, se topan casualmente en el camino con un joven al que están asaltando unos ladrones. Alonso no puede evitar actuar en su defensa y el joven, agradecido, los acompaña hasta su destino y les invita a verlo actuar esa noche. Al decirles su nombre y relatarles una parte de su vida, tanto Amelia, como Julián, reconocen al joven y quedan impactados al descubrir que estaban

---

17   Se hace también referencia, pero sin llegar a nombrarla, a la comedia *Las ferias de Madrid* por la escena en la que Lope intenta conquistar a Amelia salvándola del ataque de dos hombres que él mismo ha preparado para impresionar a la joven. Sin embargo, el dramaturgo no contaba con la cultura e inteligencia de Amelia, que reconoce la escena y no duda en dejárselo claro al galán.

ante el que creían hasta entonces un personaje de ficción. La presentación de Lázaro muestra la tendencia de los hermanos Olivares a ponerse de parte de quienes consideran más desfavorecidos o que han sufrido el abuso de otros hombres más poderosos. El joven es retratado como un personaje inteligente, ingenioso, agradecido y honrado, que no duda en exponer su propia integridad para ayudar a los agentes que previamente lo habían salvado a él. Al final de este capítulo, los guionistas nos ofrecen su propia teoría sobre quién escribió *La vida del Lazarillo de Tormes*: un fraile amigo de Lázaro que los ha ayudado en la misión. Amelia anima a Lázaro a escribir su vida al despedirse y el religioso se ofrece a ayudarlo con la condición de que no aparezca su nombre. Tras todo lo sucedido, Julián se pregunta si no habrán sido ellos los que han promovido la existencia de la famosa novela por las palabras de su compañera.

A la hora de analizar todos los elementos literarios que aparecen en la serie, no debemos olvidar que nos encontramos ante un producto de ficción, no un documental histórico-literario objetivo. Los guionistas se toman diversas licencias dependiendo de sus intereses, así como de sus impresiones y gustos personales. En este sentido, es una lástima que la caracterización de Lope y, en especial, la de su obra, se vean perjudicadas por resaltar tan solo una faceta y olvidar la profundidad y valor de una parte importante de sus creaciones. Pero como bien ha señalado Wheeler a propósito de la visión que ha habido en España después del régimen franquista sobre nuestro teatro clásico, por el tratamiento que se le dio en los años previos 'hubo más rechazo que reevaluación de las obras de Lope, una oportunidad perdida dadas las posibilidades de sacar lecciones sobre la dignidad del ser humano presentes en obras como *Fuente Ovejuna* o *Peribáñez*'.[18]

A pesar de todo esto, considero que la serie tiene un gran potencial como herramienta didáctica, especialmente como medio para acercar a los estudiantes los autores y obras en ella presentes y despertar su curiosidad.[19]

---

18   Duncan Wheeler, 'Las adaptaciones cinematográficas como (posible) herramienta pedagógica', *Anuario Lope de Vega*, 24 (2018), 260–88, 266, <http://revistes.uab.cat/anuariolopedevega/article/view/v24-wheeler>, consultado 29 junio 2018.

19   Coincido con Wheeler cuando en el artículo anteriormente citado afirma: 'Las adaptaciones cinematográficas y televisivas no son ni una panacea ni una traición en sí, y en cuanto a la enseñanza del Siglo de Oro hemos intentado dar ejemplos concretos

No podemos quedarnos tan solo con la anécdota o la imagen creada de los personajes, pero sí puede ser un motivador punto de partida. Solo el hecho de poner cara a los autores, aunque sea realmente la de unos actores – magníficamente caracterizados, por cierto –, de verlos actuar y comportarse 'en vivo' con sus virtudes y defectos, considero que hace que la actitud ante el aprendizaje y la lectura de sus composiciones sea más receptiva. Además, la serie tiene un punto de comicidad importante, entre otras cosas por los constantes guiños que nacen de la mezcla de elementos y lenguajes de muy diversas épocas: siglos dieciséis y diecisiete por los destinos de las misiones y el personaje de Alonso; siglo diecinueve, por Amelia; y finales del veinte, principios del veintiuno por los agentes Julián y Pacino y por la época desde la que parten todas las acciones del Ministerio. Todo ello acerca, incluso sin que ellos mismos sean conscientes, la literatura del Siglo de Oro a la realidad actual de nuestros estudiantes. La tecnología está presente de forma constante en la serie: en todas las épocas en las que viajan, los agentes del Ministerio utilizan móviles y tienen conexión a internet. En la Universidad de Alicante, un grupo de docentes de la Facultad de Educación ha dedicado diversos trabajos a las posibilidades didácticas de la serie desde el universo transmedia: los capítulos del Ministerio no solo han podido verse en televisión.[20] A ellos se puede acceder desde su página web oficial

---

para demostrar cómo y por qué deberíamos buscar parámetros evaluativos que van más allá de la fidelidad para considerar cómo y en qué contextos se puede sacar mejor provecho de su existencia con la esperanza de que funcione como un acercamiento de los estudiantes al teatro áureo a la vez que fomente el pensamiento crítico y brinde la oportunidad de desarrollar habilidades transferibles de comunicación'. Wheeler, 'Las adaptaciones cinematográficas', 277.

20 José Rovira Collado, Ramón R. Llorens García y Sara Fernández Tarí, 'Una propuesta transmedia para la Educación Literaria: *El Ministerio del Tiempo*', en María Teresa Tortosa Ybáñez, Salvador Grau Company, José Daniel Álvarez Teruel, coord., *XIV Jornadas de Redes de Investigación en Docencia Universitaria: Investigación, innovación y enseñanza universitaria: enfoques pluridisciplinares* (Alicante, Universidad de Alicante, 2015), 569–84; Isabel María Gómez-Trigueros, José Rovira-Collado y Mónica Ruiz-Bañuls, 'Literatura e Historia a través de un universo transmedia: posibilidades didácticas de *El Ministerio del Tiempo*', *Revista Mediterránea de comunicación*, 9/1 (2018), 217–25; Mónica Ruiz Bañuls e Isabel María Gómez Trigueros, 'Herramientas innovadoras para futuros docentes de enseñanza Secundaria: *El Ministerio del Tiempo* como herramienta metodológica interdiciplinar', en Rosabel Roig-Vila, coord., *Redes*

(<http://www.rtve.es/television/ministerio-del-tiempo/>), pero, además, en torno a ellos hay una intensa actividad en las redes sociales, una webserie, un canal de gifs, un videojuego, programas alternativos en los que los actores participan (*Las puertas del tiempo* y *Los archivos del Ministerio*), una aplicación para el móvil e, incluso, algunos capítulos han sido diseñados para poder ser vistos con dispositivos de realidad virtual.

Son varias las perspectivas de estudio desde las que podemos acercarnos a la serie con una finalidad pedagógica como, por ejemplo, el estudio de la biografía de los autores, el conocimiento y análisis de sus obras o teorías sobre el teatro, o un acercamiento a su contexto. A continuación, propongo varias posibles líneas de trabajo en torno a estos puntos. No se trata de ejercicios concretos, pues considero que, de esta forma, a partir de las propuestas presentadas, cada docente puede elegir la fórmula que mejor se ajuste a las características y al nivel de cada uno de sus grupos.

En cuanto a los autores, una posible vía de trabajo sería la de proponer un trabajo de investigación a nuestros alumnos sobre cuáles de los aspectos de la serie son reales y cuáles licencias televisivas. Asimismo, podemos buscar ejemplos y debatir sobre los tópicos que la historia transmite en torno a las grandes figuras y las leyendas que se crean en torno a ellos. Por ejemplo, en el capítulo 'Tiempo de hidalgos', hay una anécdota con el personaje de Pacino que podemos utilizar para introducir esta cuestión. Cervantes tradicionalmente ha sido referido como 'El manco de Lepanto', alegando que perdió su mano izquierda en dicha batalla. Sin embargo, parece que lo que Cervantes sufrió realmente fue una lesión en los tendones que hizo que perdiera gran parte de la movilidad. En el caso de Lope, su fama de conquistador puede ser un punto de partida interesante para conocer mejor la biografía del autor. Un posible proyecto que podemos plantear a nuestros alumnos sería el de averiguar cuáles fueron realmente sus esposas y amantes conocidas y, especialmente, la presencia y relevancia de estas en su obra.

Por otra parte, ya que en la serie solo aparecen Lope de Vega y Cervantes, sin que haya apenas mención a otros de los grandes autores áureos de su misma generación, como fueron Quevedo y Góngora, el enfrentamiento

---

colaborativas en torno a la docencia universitaria (Alicante: Universidad de Alicante/ Instituto de Ciencias de la Educación, 2017), 554–62.

entre los dos literatos representados puede ayudarnos a introducirlos por la aún más profunda enemistad que existió entre ellos. Para esta propuesta, es el personaje de Julián el que puede darnos el pie: en 'Tiempo de gloria', cuando la patrulla localiza a Lope en la taberna, el escritor trata abiertamente de seducir a Amelia ante la presencia de Julián, a pesar de que este se está haciendo pasar por su marido. Como Lope utiliza el verso para ganarse el favor de la joven, Julián, poco conocedor de obras literarias, recurre a una de las canciones más conocidas de Leño, un grupo de rock famoso de los años 80, para demostrarle que él también puede utilizar el verso para enviar mensajes sobre sus intenciones: 'No sé si estoy en lo cierto/ lo cierto es que estoy aquí/ otros por menos han muerto/ maneras de vivir'. Lope queda desconcertado por las palabras de Julián y pensativo se pregunta retóricamente '¿Góngora?'[21]

Respecto a las obras, son varios los títulos que se mencionan de ambos autores, aunque no excesivos. De Cervantes, tan solo tres: *La Galatea, Don Quijote* y *Los baños de Argel*. De Lope, ya las hemos mencionado anteriormente. Las obras reseñadas no parecen las más apropiadas para proponer como lectura a estudiantes que el español es su segunda lengua – y ni tan siquiera para aquellos que la tienen como lengua materna –, exceptuando *La dama boba*, pieza que probablemente es destacada, además de por su calidad, por conservar de ella un manuscrito autógrafo en la Biblioteca Nacional de España y a cuya digitalización todos podemos tener acceso desde el catálogo de la 'Biblioteca Digital Hispánica' de esta institución. Sin embargo, creo que lo referenciado puede ser suficiente como para despertar el interés de los alumnos por acercarse a algunas de las obras que aparecen en la serie y, sobre todo, para querer conocer más, jugando precisamente con la baza de que son pocos los títulos que se nos dan a conocer.

En cuanto a las teorías dramáticas de ambos autores, de nuevo *El Ministerio del Tiempo* puede servirnos como punto de partida para trabajar con los testimonios escritos que Lope y Cervantes nos dejaron en sus obras, especialmente en *Don Quijote* (capítulos 47 y 48) y en el prólogo de sus *Ocho comedias y ocho entremeses nuevos, nunca representados*, en el caso de Cervantes y en su *Arte nuevo de hacer comedias* en el de Lope. Por ejemplo,

---

21 Olivares y Olivares, 'Tiempo de gloria', 26.

El estudio del mundo literario de la España del siglo diecisiete

Simon Breden, en su trabajo para el *Anuario de Lope de Vega*, nos muestra como la definición que da el personaje de Lope sobre el teatro cuando conoce a Amelia y a Julián, coincide con lo escrito por el autor, tanto en el *Arte nuevo*, como en unos versos de *El castigo sin venganza*.[22]

Finalmente, la calidad de esta serie en la ambientación de los diversos escenarios y en la caracterización de los personajes en los viajes temporales de nuestros protagonistas, es una excelente aliada para situar a los estudiantes en la época y los usos propios del período estudiado. Destacamos tres ejemplos:

- El primero son las imágenes que podemos ver del corral de comedias de Almagro, lugar de los ensayos de la compañía que monta Cervantes en 'Tiempo de Hidalgos'. Conocer el tipo de escenario en el que se representaba el teatro áureo es parte fundamental de la comprensión de lo que supuso este género y de cómo se desarrollaban las representaciones entonces: el horario diurno, cómo se configuraba el espectáculo, los diferentes espacios que ocupaba el público según el género y la clase social, etc.
- El segundo es, en el mismo capítulo, la caracterización de Pacino como miembro de la Santa Hermandad. Se trata del disfraz idóneo para que pueda interrogar a Cervantes sobre los hombres a los que ha vendido su manuscrito de *Don Quijote* sin levantar sus sospechas. Este 'cuerpo policial', creado en el siglo quince y activo hasta la primera mitad del diecinueve, formaba parte de la vida cotidiana de la España de los siglos dieciséis y diecisiete y, como tal, está presente en muchas de las piezas literarias de la época como, por ejemplo, en *Don Quijote*. Si a través del visionado de este capítulo, nuestros alumnos ya conocen de la existencia de esta corporación y cuál era su función, entenderán mejor aquellos fragmentos de la genial obra de Cervantes en los que esta está presente. Asimismo, la presencia de esta figura también nos puede servir para que los estudiantes conozcan el origen de una expresión coloquial bastante habitual en la lengua española: 'A buenas horas, mangas verdes', que nacería por el color del uniforme de los representantes de la Santa Hermandad y su fama de llegar tarde a los lugares donde se requerían sus servicios.
- Por último, fijamos nuestra atención en la presencia de Shakespeare en 'Tiempo de esplendor', el capítulo de la tercera temporada en el que una delegación inglesa llega a Valladolid para la firma del tratado de paz con España. A pesar de que la aparición de este autor es muy breve, su nombre está presente en todo el capítulo por la pelea entre Lope y Cervantes por lograr el privilegio de conocerle y hacerle llegar su obra. Como ya sabemos, es Cervantes el que consigue el encuentro y el

---

22 Breden, 'La presencia de Lope', 80.

que le regala una copia de su recién publicado *Don Quijote*. De esta forma, los creadores de la serie toman partido por los defensores de la teoría de que el genial dramaturgo formó parte de la comitiva británica y que así conoció la obra de Cervantes, como explicación a su *Cardenio* perdido.

Las propuestas aquí presentadas suponen tan solo una parte de todas las posibilidades que creemos que ofrece la serie de *El Ministerio del Tiempo* como herramienta pedagógica. Se han destacado aquellos aspectos que consideramos más significativos y que podían ser desarrollados en el espacio de este trabajo. Trabajar con seriedad y rigor con este tipo de recursos puede suponer contar con un apoyo que, lejos de desvirtuar la enseñanza de los clásicos, nos permita hacer de la necesidad virtud, convirtiendo el obstáculo en estímulo.

TED BERGMAN

4   What 50 Cent can teach us about Quevedo: The case for using analogy and video clips

ABSTRACT
This paper explores the use of modern video clips taken from entertainment media to provide students with content analogous to works of Golden Age literature. The examples of content provided in the paper will all be drawn from an honours-level university module titled 'Action Heroes and Anti-Heroes in Early Modern Spain'. To provide material for a broader discussion of anti-heroes in which to take a closer look at Golden Age texts, the instructor plays modern video clips that contain analogous characters, such as criminal alter egos of hip-hop artists (such as 50 Cent) or iconic figures played by actors such as Clint Eastwood in the role of 'Dirty Harry'. While not guaranteed to eliminate all barriers to understanding the material, modern video clips are useful in stimulating students' analytical imagination. These supplementary media make it easier for seminar participants to name relevant abstract themes to be applied to specific difficult texts, including *jácaras* containing obscure slang and unfamiliar contexts.

As Stephen M. Buhler has written in a recent article, 'Some educators have understandably urged caution when adopting pop cultural approaches to earlier literatures'. Among particular concerns, he invokes a 'recent variation on old "High Culture" attitudes (art is complex; pop culture is simplistic) that persists.' At the same time, he cites specific 'cautionary examples [that] remind us that the use of popular music materials to explore Early Modern works requires awareness of difference/s as well as resonances.'[1] Buhler is mainly referring to teaching Shakespeare, but the concerns he addresses echo reservations one may have regarding the use of pop culture to teach Spanish Golden Age literature. These reservations seem implicit in a 2005 special volume of *Calíope* titled *Teaching Golden Age Poetry*. It is filled with pedagogically useful articles that still manage to omit nearly any mention of

---

1   Stephen M. Buhler, 'Palpable Hits: Popular Music Forms and Teaching Early Modern Poetry', *The CEA Critic* 78 (2016), 229–41, 229–30.

popular culture that is not early modern. The exceptions are Luis F. Avilés and Bradley J. Nelson, who both touch on the matter in a general sense. Avilés mentions that 'en muchos sentidos la música popular contemporánea, con su combinación heterogénea de tradiciones y géneros diversos, no se comporta de forma tan diferente a la poesía'.[2] Without citing specific examples either, Nelson muses further that 'although the social and cultural differences are staggering, a curiously framed allusion to contemporary rap or hip-hop music brings home some of the more pertinent characteristics of Renaissance poetry, not least its musical and theatrical qualities'.[3] Over the last decade, since the inception and inevitable ubiquity of YouTube videos, teachers of undergraduates in other subjects have published reflections such as 'Promoting Student Understanding of Petrarch's *Canzionere* through Popular Music' or an entire book titled *Shakespeare and YouTube* that ends with a chapter reflecting on 'The Teaching and Learning Tube: Challenges and Affordances'.[4] Meanwhile, while YouTube has been successfully integrated in the teaching of Spanish Golden Age literature, the methods involved mainly focus on primary works and their interpretation. In other words, we continue to eschew the wealth of relatable popular culture and entertainment that the platform makes available to students and can connect them with texts from far away and long ago.[5] Edward H. Friedman writes of 'Góngora, Quevedo, and other Baroque poets [who] recoil from the popular, and from the *vulgo*', who also belong 'to a system of erratic, ironic,

---

[2] Luis F. Avilés, 'Poesía y diferencia cultural: prácticas para el estudio de textos poéticos de los Siglos de Oro', *Calíope* 2 (2005), 7–19, 10.

[3] Bradley J. Nelson, 'Capes and Swords: Teaching the Theatricality of Golden Age Poetry', *Calíope* (2005), 111–24, 114.

[4] Silvia Ross, 'Promoting Student Understanding of Petrarch's *Canzionere* through Popular Music', in Christopher Kleinhenz and Andrea Dini, eds, *Approaches to Teaching Petrarch's* Canzoniere *and the Petrarchan Tradition* (New York: The Modern Language Association of America, 2014), 136–48. Stephen O'Neill, *Shakespeare and YouTube: New Media Forms of the Bard* (London: Bloomsbury Methuen Drama, 2015).

[5] Compare the following articles with a similar focus, written 'pre' and 'post' YouTube, so to speak. Ignacio Navarrete, 'Teaching Golden Age Poetry: Modeling Intertextuality through Hypertext', *Calíope* 2 (2005), 91–109; Charles Patterson, 'Lope on YouTube: Film Analysis and Amateur Video Production in a "Comedia" Course', *Hispania* 98 (2015), 522–32.

and subtly or not so subtly subversive centers'. While Friedman treats this as an area of study in which students can be aided through 'a metacritical or metatheoretical reading of studies', perhaps we are siding too much with Góngora and Quevedo in our own teaching.[6] Perhaps we unwittingly 'recoil from the popular' for fear of dumbing down or simplifying our subject of study, especially at the level of encouraging student engagement in difficult texts. On the other hand, perhaps the 'centers' that poets and playwrights occupy, be they many or few, can alternately be explained with less erudition instead of more. It is my intention here to prompt those teaching within our discipline to rethink their own classroom practice, specifically how to use popular culture through YouTube video clips to explain theme, tone, and even poetic technique through analogy. We explain things to ourselves in this way as researchers, so why not share these types of explanations with our students, even expand upon them, however whimsical or *vulgo* they may seem at first? Inspired by a director's comments that 'many of our female icons from pop culture behave in manner similar to Fenisa [from María de Zayas's *Friendship Betrayed*]', Barbara Mujica goes on to conspiratorially admit that 'Zaya's readers loved trash, and so do we. As scholars, we are reluctant to admit watching *Desperate Housewives* – although some of us not only watch it, but read the secrets of Eva Longoria in the supermarket check-out line'.[7]

There exists a recognition within our discipline that pop-culture references can connect a modern audience with an early modern Spanish work of literature, but it is not commonly apparent that the audience can also consist of students in the classroom with the text alone, without the need for performance. Often as fans of pop-culture productions ourselves, we can be quick to recognize their potential and how they inform our own understanding of the texts; but this recognition stops short at 'bringing home some of the more pertinent characteristics of Renaissance poetry' as stated by Bradley J. Nelson above. Twelve years after he wrote his 2005 article in the special

---

6   Edward H. Friedman, 'Teaching Golden Age Poetry: The Old and the New', *Calíope* 2 (2005), 59–68, 64.

7   Barbara Mujica, 'Maria de Zayas's *Friendship Betrayed* à la Hollywood: Translation, Transculturation, and Production', in Susan Paun de García and Donald R. Larson, eds, *The Comedia in English: Translation and Performance* (Woodbridge: Tamesis, 2008), 240–54, 247.

teaching issue of *Calíope*, Nelson – along with his co-editor Julio Baena – urged readers of their 'polemical companion to *Medialogies*' to read a chapter from that volume or the original study 'while listening to Kendrick Lamar's militant hip-hop'. They go on to lament that they 'put together this volume without an essay articulating the resistance powers of poetry – non-fictional writing – as seen from the pastoral (one of us has actually written an in-your-face pastoral novel) to the hip-hop modes'.[8] In Nelson and Baena's choice of Kendrick Lamar, a politically engaged rapper and Pulitzer Prize winner, one can detect a lingering implication that popularity and widespread consumption are not enough. Entering a sort of defensive stance still preserves the impulse to fall back on links through erudition represented by 'the greatest rapper alive'.[9] Choosing other rappers or other examples may risk endorsing Mujica's admission that, when it comes to pop culture, many of us simply 'love trash'. It is time to rethink and even abandon any wariness that we may have to using pop-culture analogies, the sort that are wholeheartedly adopted by directors who are obligated to have their audience understand and enjoy 400-year-old Spanish texts. Along with teaching the finer points, we also have that same obligation as a director of our students' learning, for them to enjoy and understand what they are reading. YouTube allows us as both researchers and fans of Golden Age literature to share our enthusiasm through a nearly limitless supply of pop-culture examples. If my colleagues are anything like me, these examples often inspire analogies that are simply too good to keep to ourselves.

The module in which I have used examples in the form of video clips is called 'Action Heroes and Anti-heroes in Early-Modern Spain'. The title itself reflects the challenging prospect of attenuating wariness among students who may balk at the thought of reading an early modern text and wrestle with its language to the point of frustration. Thus, the term 'Action Heroes and Anti-heroes' is meant to counterbalance that wariness as it promises

---

[8] Bradley J. Nelson and Juio Baena, 'Introduction: A Polemical Companion to Medialogies: Reading Reality in the Age of Inflationary Media', *Hispanic Issues On Line Debates* 8 (2017), 1–21, 7–8.

[9] Dorian Lynskey, 'From street kid to Pulitzer: why Kendrick Lamar deserves the prize', *The Guardian* online, 22 April 2018, <https://www.theguardian.com/music/2018/apr/22/kendrick-lamar-wins-pulitzer-prize-damn-album>, accessed 12 May 2019.

cross-medium comparisons that will provide a modern perspective on works that might otherwise appear inaccessible. In a very general thematic sense, the module assumes that everybody at some point has been entertained by 'action' in movies and television, and that most people are intrigued by the idea of an 'anti-hero'. There is always a risk in employing modern analogies to gain access to the thematic essence of a work of literature, not only in a pedagogical context, but also in the very act of adaptation. This is exemplified in H. R. Coursen's opinion of the 1995 film adaptation of Shakespeare's *Richard III*:

> The film's explicitness robbed the play's metaphor of its suggestive bridge between unlike things. Pulled in the direction of its 1930-ish motif, the film loses contact with all but the words of the originating script. They are not enough. The film detaches from its archetype – whatever it is.[10]

These comments remind us that analogous video clips may not always turn a student's modern mind towards identifying transhistoric 'archetypes'. This term, employed somewhat surreptitiously by Coursen, is appropriate since the first class meeting of my module is dedicated to asking questions about the appeal of archetypal heroes and anti-heroes. To avoid overwhelming the students, I employ only two secondary texts as a point of departure for conversation. The first is Chapter 3 of Part II of Joseph Campbell's *Hero With a Thousand Faces*, titled 'Transformations of the Hero'. The myths that the author cites may seem unfamiliar to the students, but the main point as stated by Campbell in his preface is clear:

> It is the purpose of the present book to uncover some of the truths disguised for us under the figures of religion and mythology by bringing together a multitude of not-too-difficult examples and letting the ancient meaning become apparent of itself. The old teachers knew what they were saying. Once we have learned to read again their symbolic language, it requires no more than the talent of an anthologist to let their teaching be heard.[11]

---

10   H. R. Coursen, 'Filming Shakespeare's history: three films of Richard III', in Russell Jackson, ed., *The Cambridge Companion to Shakespeare on Film* (Cambridge: Cambridge University Press, 2010), 102–19, 102.
11   Joseph Campbell, *The Hero with a Thousand Faces* (Princeton, NJ: Princeton University Press, 1968), vii.

In a sense, as the instructor I am the 'anthologist', curating students' learning. To better ensure that the 'teachings be heard', I include a video clip in the class before we enter into a discussion of what makes a hero. In the clip, the interviewer Bill Moyers speaks directly to Campbell about the author's ideas in relation to *Star Wars*, as snippets of the film occasionally overlay the recording of the men in conversation. Students are likely to be familiar with the Star Wars characters and mythos, especially with the continuation of the original timeline in films like *The Force Awakens* (J. J. Abrams, 2015) and *The Last Jedi* (Rian Johnson, 2017). For this reason, a simple short burst of imagery from the original movie is all that is required, without requiring students to see the entire film or many minutes of it. During the clip, Moyers asks Campbell: 'Do you, when you look at something like *Star Wars*, recognize some of the themes of the hero throughout mythology?' As images of the Millennium Falcon, Luke Skywalker with his lightsabre and Obi Wan Kenobi flash on the screen, Campbell answers: 'Well, I think that George Lucas was using standard mythological figures. The old man as the adviser, well, specifically what he made me think of is the Japanese swordmaster'.[12] The purpose of the clip is to reinforce and clarify the idea that there are ways to define archetypal heroes and their journeys, and that we in class can adopt these definitions or craft our own definitions of types to apply the Golden Age texts.

On the subject of anti-heroes, the secondary source used to stimulate conversation is a brief column from a series called 'The Hero in You', written by Brian A. Kinnaird. The specific piece is titled 'Anti-Heroes: Is There a Goodness of Purpose?' and Kinnaird begins his argument as follows:

> In our literature and films, the term anti-hero has come to mean a fictional character with characteristics that are antithetical to those of the traditional hero. Anti-heroes perform acts that are heroic but only do so through methods or manners not appearing heroic at all.[13]

---

12 This interview is available at Bill Moyers's website. Bill Moyer, 'Moyers & Campbell on *Star Wars*' Mythological Influences', 21 June 1988, <https://billmoyers.com/content/moyers-campbell-on-star-wars-mythological-influences/>, accessed 28 June 2018.

13 Brian A. Kinnaird, 'Anti-Heroes: Is There a Goodness of Purpose?', *Psychology Today* online, 26 September 2013, <https://www.psychologytoday.com/gb/blog/the-hero-in-you/201309/anti-heroes-is-there-goodness-purpose>, accessed 28 June 2018.

He quickly adds that 'Scholarly definitions of anti-hero are few and far between'. To bring concreteness to his explanations, the author provides examples from popular culture, the main one being the first and eponymous *Dirty Harry* (Don Siegel, 1971) movie. Because it is often better to show than to tell, instead of explaining the character to my students and what makes him 'dirty,' I play them a clip from the first film in the series.[14] In a sequence that lasts about two minutes, the anti-hero protagonist chases down the serial-killer villain until he collapses in an empty football field and is forced to confess as Dirty Harry stomps on his wounded leg and causes him excruciating pain.

The clip makes viscerally clear Kinnaird's observation in his column that 'Criminal investigators typically use the sliding scale of criminal culpability to gain a suspect's confidence in eliciting a confession, however, Dirty Harry went from asking a question at gunpoint to torture'. In the first class meeting of the module, with its specific quotes and video clips, we begin a semester-long discussion of terms and how to apply them with easily relatable points of reference so that students can determine their own definitions 'hero', 'anti-hero' and 'villain'.

The texts that are covered in the module on a week-by-week basis are the following: *Historia del emperador Carlo Magno* by Nicolás de Piamonte; Catalina de Erauso's *La historia de la monja alférez; Rinconete y Cortadillo;* selections from *Guzmán de Alfarache;* a selection of *romances de valientes y bandoleros* from Agustín Durán's nineteenth-century collection; a selection of *jácaras*, taken from John Hill's anthology of *Poesías Germanescas;* Calderón's *La puente de Mantible;* the comedia *El valiente Juan de Heredia* of indeterminate authorship; and, finally, selections from Quiñones de Benavente's *Jácaras entremesadas*. Since space is limited in this article, we will discuss examples from the *romance* genre; however, it is important to note that every text for every week has accompanying video clips to better equip students in making thematic connections between an early modern Spanish context and more familiar, modern, pop-culture examples.

---

14   Movieclips, 'Dirty Harry (7/10) Movie CLIP – Where is the Girl? (1971) HD', *YouTube*, 31 December 2014, <https://www.youtube.com/watch?v=buNwwAximcE>, accessed 28 June 2018.

Because the module in question is for fourth-year students, many of them would have already studied the *romancero* in a previous year, and they would have some familiarity with the metre, rhyme and storytelling elements of the early modern ballad style. We start with less difficult romances (for which basic *romance* literacy skills will suffice) from the section in Agustín Durán's *Romancero General* titled 'Sección de romances vulgares que tratan de valentías, guapezas, y desafueros'.[15] Like many ballads in this collection, the first in the section is anonymous. It tells the tale of Doña Victoria Acevedo who is married against her will. While in her wedding bed, Doña Victoria slashes the throat of her husband so that she can return to the arms of her lover. As the couple in the ballad seek to escape the law, they kill two 'ministros' or 'alguaciles' and injure one 'corregidor' in the process. The lover is captured but Doña Victoria escapes, after which she encounters ten *bandoleros* while she attempts to hide in a forest. 'Por sus valerosos arrestos', she is chosen as the leader of this criminal gang while keeping herself disguised as a man.[16] Further violent adventures ensue after Doña Victoria and her gang break her lover out of jail. As she leaves a trail of bodies throughout the rest of the ballad, it should become quite clear to students reading the *romance* that she is an anti-heroine. She is precisely the type discussed in the first day of class and exemplified by video clips of charismatic and violent anti-hero characters like 'Dirty Harry'. At the same time, despite the students' basic comprehension skills, the action in the ballad may not be sufficiently clear in their mind's eye. The immediate solution is to play some more video clips. Some of these feature sword-fighting scenes from movies, but since the essential thematic element, that of a 'bad-ass' woman 'kicking ass', is of utmost importance, it is not enough to simply recreate the action from the ballad. Instead, it can be just as important to employ an analogy that highlights the themes of gender, violence, female empowerment, revenge and flouting of authority. To ensure extra thematic clarity, I play a short video clip from Taylor Swift's 'Bad Blood' video.[17] As

---

15 Agustín Durán, ed., *Romancero general o colección de romances castellanos anteriores al siglo XVIII: Tomo 2* (Madrid: M. Rivadeneyra, 1882), 359–90.
16 Durán, *Romancero*, 360.
17 The video can be accessed in its embedded form through the *New York Times* online article cited below.

Emily Yahr explains, 'The song is widely known to be about Swift's feud with pop star Katy Perry', but there is a deeper meaning in the song's video:

> If you missed it, the plot is an action movie that starts as Selena Gomez (alter ego 'Arsyn') goes to battle and pushes Swift out of a window. Swift is unscathed as she spends the rest of the video recuperating and training for revenge, with the help of her fellow warriors/pals. The all-female army of supermodels and actresses marches across an abandoned city, a huge fire blazing in the background as they go to fight Swift's enemy once more. [...] And if this video teaches us anything, Taylor Swift is not someone who you want to have as an enemy.[18]

It is also clear that Swift is re-working the trope of the Hollywood anti-hero by incorporating women singers and actors, much like Doña Victoria Acevedo from the seventeenth-century *romance* is a woman adopting the compulsive violence linked to a personal code ordinarily associated with male *guapos* and *valientes* in the ballad tradition. The video clip of 'Bad Blood' is played for students to foster thinking around questions of violence, protagonism, gender, entertainment, morality and how all these themes relate, intersect, or possibly contradict each other. Often there is insufficient time in class to watch an entire movie, sometimes not even an entire video. Happily, short clips can deliver a sort of visual shorthand cut to bring up universal themes that are easily applicable to works that initially might seem too far removed from immediate experiences with pop culture.

It is true that the methods described above are fairly basic. Students come to the module with a solid understanding of what constitutes a Hollywood action-hero and have some notion of what constitutes an anti-hero. Even so, at times a little coaxing of imagination is required. This additional thematic prodding aids them in making connections between the pieces of information that lie before them. Thanks to programs like *Breaking Bad* and *Sons of Anarchy*, criminal anti-heroes with a fan base of millions of viewers are not too distant in the cultural memory. Even questions of morality and entertainment that may seem disconnected from a modern relativistic point of

---

18 Emily Yahr, 'What Taylor Swift's "Bad Blood" music video actually says about power in Hollywood', *New York Times*, 17 May 2015, <https://www.washingtonpost.com/news/arts-and-entertainment/wp/2015/05/17/what-taylor-swifts-bad-blood-music-video-actually-says-about-power-in-hollywood/>, accessed 28 June 2018.

view can be shown to bridge great distances in space and time. Just as early modern moralists decried the excesses and poor moral examples of anti-hero protagonists, the same complaints appear in similar fashion in recent examples. The example I provide to students is from the programme *Sons of Anarchy*. It takes the form of an 'indecency' complaint against the show made to the United States' Federal Communications Commission by a viewer. The document states:

> This program is the most sadistic program on TV. It shows women being hung in handcuffs in a cage and graphic killings. It is all about the hatred and sadism of a bunch of bikers and there is even a dark color to everything. I turned if off but before I did I saw a group of bikers getting ready to do who knows what to an average guy in a suit. It is frightening and destructive to our society. I hate to think that people are watching this and we walk among them.[19]

To stimulate further discussion related to the 'romances de valentías, guapezas, y desafueros', the students must decide if the modern material is indeed morally repugnant or something else. They are shown a promotional video clip for the programme that is full of action, threats and violence.[20] The students are then encouraged to discuss if they see the same 'dark color to everything' in the clip and in the ballads that they have read for the class. One cannot deny the appeal of the modern biker-gang characters, given the series' run for seven years, just as it is clear from Durán's notes to his edition that early modern ballads about criminals enjoyed the same popularity.[21] The students are then left to reconcile or explain the relationship between audience appeal and the violent anti-heroism on visceral display in the video clip, with the relevant themes now in clearer relief.

Analogies of criminal anti-heroes are not difficult to explain in terms of plot and action. Pedagogically speaking, however, analogies become

---

19   Robert Delaware, 'FCC complaints about the television program "Sons of Anarchy"', *MuckRock News*, 28 June 2018, <https://cdn.muckrock.com/foia_documents/7-27-12_mr1417_ACK.pdf>, accessed 28 June 2018.

20   SonsofAnarchyEngland [*sic*], 'Sons Of Anarchy Season 1 Promo/Trailer HD', *YouTube*, 14 February 2012, <https://www.youtube.com/watch?v=Gr9_lvMuYrE>, accessed 28 June 2018.

21   Durán, *Romancero*, 389.

complicated as they approach more obscure areas of research. I am specifically speaking of criminal ballads called *jácaras* that were highly popular in the Golden Age and are one of my areas of specialization. The most famous author of *jácaras* is Quevedo, a man who loved underworld subject matter in both his poetry and prose. The genre stands apart from the *romances* collected by Agustín Durán because *jácaras* are typically filled with criminal jargon known as *germanía*. This linguistic marking adds a layer of difficulty for experts in Golden Age literature, let alone undergraduate students. So, how does one remove barriers to understanding in a limited amount of class time? First, one needs to provide students with a glossary. This is not difficult to do because there exists such a glossary from a 1609 collection edited by Juan Hidalgo called *Romances de germanía*, which is found in a modern anthology compiled by John M. Hill titled *Poesías germanescas*.[22]

The ideal process for achieving basic comprehension among the class is as follows: students sit down with a Spanish-English dictionary, access to the *Diccionario de Autoridades* online, and a glossary of specialized criminal terms, and they slowly make their way through a single *jácara*. They have been reading standard-language *romances* from the *romancero* beforehand and this gives them an idea of what some of the *jácara* narratives are about. The main difference in content is that many more of the *jácara* protagonists are pimps, prostitutes, thieves, or plain murderers, instead of noblemen or noblewomen who simply end up on the wrong side of the law. This difference in characterization is not itself a problem if students are alerted beforehand. As they wrestle with the text, I am forced to recall what a professor of mine once reminded us as undergraduates: 'La literatura se lee para pasarlo bien, no solo para estudiarla y comentarla'. How can one get the students as excited about these ballads as I am about my research? Thanks to the students' exposure to 'romances de valentías, guapezas, y desafueros' beforehand, the main content, including the themes, is not out of reach; however, themes in themselves do not make the experience entertaining. Since the entertainment value of the sub-genre is found in its ironic, detached and humorous treatment of violent criminality, students must be given access to a tone from long ago, and the swiftest way to achieve this is through analogy.

---

22   John M. Hill, *Poesías germanescas* (Bloomington: Indiana University, 1945).

As a researcher, I used to explain to anybody who would listen that my area of interest was 'seventeenth-century Spanish gangsta rap'. I thought perhaps that I was being slightly glib but then, why not embrace this idea in an effort to connect the material with students? Why not use actual 'gangsta rap', even if its popularity has faded in the last decade, to convey the tone and the themes of the *jácara*? Additionally, comparing the modern and early modern genres of song can demonstrate the connection between difficult language, criminal subculture and the appeal of anti-hero subcultures. In his understated way, Ignacio Arellano explains that 'En el caso particular de las jácaras la base material del léxico de germanía sobre la que se edifican los conceptos supone el extremo de la ingeniosa dificultad en la poesía satírica y burlesca de Quevedo'.[23] So that the reader of this article can gain some idea of the level of difficulty, I provide a fragment from one of Quevedo's *jácaras* below:

> Ya está metido en la trena
> Tu querido Escarramán,
> Que unos alfileres vivos
> Me prendieron sin pensar.
> Andaba a caza de gangas,
> Y grillos vine a cazar,
> Que en mí cantan como en haza
> Las noches de por San Juan.
> Entrándome en la bayuca,
> Llegándome a remojar
> Cierta pendencia mosquito,
> Que se ahogó en vino y pan ...[24]

The ballad aims to recreate the language and tone that form the basis of a particular sub-culture's 'street cred'. This in-group has its own expressions for breaking the law communicates a mix of pride and fatalism in doing so. In an effort to bridge the 400-year gap in space and time between two strands of 'street cred' homogenized through popular culture, I use analogous examples of songs with heavily concentrated criminal jargon. The best example that I can find for my students is 50 Cent's song 'Bloodhound', for

---

23 Ignacio Arellano, *Comentarios a La poesía satírico burlesca de Quevedo* (Madrid: Arco Libros, 1998), 65–6.
24 Hill, *Poesías germanescas*, 127

which there is no official video. Instead, I show the class a homemade version from YouTube.²⁵ Although it is not of professional quality and is made from edited chunks of other videos, its images clearly convey the 'gangsta' lifestyle proudly declared in the lyrics of the song.

> Then we go through the strip,
> hangin' up out the whip
> Dumpin' clips off at they whole clique, man (clique, man)
> When witnesses around,
> they know how we get down
> So when the cops come they ain't see shit, man (shit man)
> My soldiers slangin' 'caine,
> sunny, snow, in sleet or rain
> Come through the hood and you can cop that (cop that)
> I'm sittin' on some change,
> G-Unit that's the gang
> Come through here stuntin' you get popped at (popped at)
> [Chorus]
> I love to pump crack,
> love to stay strapped
> Love to squeeze gats
> but you don't hear me though
> I love to hit the block,
> I love my two Glocks
> Love to bust shots
> but you don't hear me though.²⁶

In the video, there are flashes of 1990s gangsters firing guns, standing near luxury or customized cars and restraining pit bull terriers with chain leads. These are all symbols of a world view that is equally violent, exuberant, fatalistic and wryly humorous, much like that of a narrative voice from a seventeenth-century *jácara*. The video even features darkly humorous timing through the use of barking pit bulls that coincide with the sampled barking noise in the song. Both Quevedo's *jácara* and 50 Cent's rap song require a glossary to understand the terms, but the second of the two has

---

25   Creapofluigi, '50 Cent – Blood Hound ft. Young Buck VIDEO', *YouTube*, 25 August 2008, <https://www.youtube.com/watch?v=t-Qmzjo5OyI>, accessed 28 June 2018.
26   50 Cent, 'Blood Hound', *Get Rich or Die Tryin'* (Europe: Interscope records, 2015).

the advantage of an accompanying visual culture to grant easier access to the song's meaning, themes and tone.

Quevedo's turn of phrase, 'unos alfileres vivos me prendieron sin pensar' can be explained in terms of its word play on 'prender' and the 'afileres vivos' representing 'live pins' that are the catchpoles who arrest/pin-down ('prendieron') the gangster *Escarramán*. But understanding something is not the same thing as accessing its tone, its dark humour tied to criminal behaviour. As E. B. White wrote in 1941: 'Humor can be dissected, as a frog can, but the thing dies in the process and the innards are discouraging to any but the pure scientific mind'.[27] The same risk of tone 'death' occurs when one deciphers the lyrics of 50 Cent's song. One can discover the meanings of 'pump crack' (a not-too-obscure reference to dealing crack cocaine), 'stay strapped' (a somewhat general-use term for staying armed) and 'squeeze gats' (a more specialized 'gangsta') term for firing off guns, but this is not enough for a full appreciation and understanding. And yet, there is hope for saving the tone and humour from 'death' under a barrage heavy analysis. For example, the line 'My soldiers slangin' 'caine, / sunny, snow, in sleet or rain' is relatively intelligible – in the Mafia, 'soldato' means a low-level member – while the irony (soldiers bringing crime instead of order) is highlighted in the video clip by a brief flash of 50 Cent and his crew dressed as officers with people standing at attention in fatigues in the background. So far, the barriers against basic comprehension are not too great. But the joke that is worthy of Quevedo's wit, and which remains to be sprung on the listener and viewer, is attached to the punchline 'sunny, snow, in sleet or rain'. It is a parody of the US Postal Service Postman's creed, originally dating from Herodotus's *Histories*.[28] 50 Cent is describing his army of drug dealers as if they were reliable postmen making their rounds and their deliveries without fail. The discovery of this joke by the students, with a little coaxing, may not result in guffaws, but if only wry smile comes forth, I consider it a great accomplishment. The *jácara* by Quevedo is also full of irony, dark humour, bravado, cynicism, and this may be more difficult to access. It is hoped that

---

27 E. B. White, *In the Words of E. B. White: Quotations from America's Most Companionable of Writers*, ed. Martha White (Ithaca, NY: Cornell University Press, 2011), 129.
28 Smithsonian National Postal Museum Website, 'Frequently Asked Questions (FAQs)', <https://postalmuseum.si.edu/about/frequently-asked-questions/index.html#history10>, accessed 28 June 2018.

through the power of analogy, when students make a connection with the rap lyrics and video, they will be able to make a tonal, perhaps even visceral connection with criminal *romances* from the early modern time period.

When students gain an appreciation of the tone and wordplay of the *jácara* through modern analogy, they are better equipped to explore the genre on its own terms. At the same time, there is no point in fully disengaging from an analogy that leads one to a better understanding of 400-year-old texts of an intentionally obscure nature. For example, taking the parodic aspect of the 50 Cent rap cited above as a point of departure can lead students to discover the dark parodies that exist in the seventeenth-century criminal ballads, and how these parodies are constructed. The example from Quevedo cited above is from his best known *jácara*, 'Carta de Escarramán a la Méndez'. Students who are familiar with literary models from previous modules can hopefully detect within the ballad a parody of sentimental romance or of mythic figures whose 'gestas' are enshrined in heroic verses.[29]

Likewise, students already familiar with Quevedo's strain of sarcasm and satire, both literary and social, or his *conceptismo* on a general level, can see the poet's skills on full display, much as the same students can appreciate a virtuoso rapper from the 1990s who uses the backdrop of the criminal underworld to show off his mastery of rhyme, metre and imagery. It is this last item, imagery, that reminds us that audio recordings in themselves are not always sufficient when we live in such a visual age.

As a method driven by the understanding that students live in an increasingly dominant visual culture, using films for the study of early modern Spanish texts is certainly nothing new. At the same time, there is always room for exploring new ways to employ film and related media, such as music videos. Experience and close familiarity with Golden Age texts have taught us as researchers that many early modern authors are 'strikingly modern' and that barriers to comprehension for our students may not be as insurmountable as first thought. Video clips can offer us a shortcut in class for providing concrete examples of how the more things change, the more they stay the same.

---

29   David Becerra Mayor, 'Acercamiento social e ideológico a las jácaras de Quevedo. "Carta del Escarramán a la Méndez"', *La Perinola* 13 (2009), 183–208, 202; María José Tobar Quintanar, 'La originalidad de Cervantes en *El rufián viudo*', *Artifara* 17 (2017), 279–94, 287.

COLLIN McKINNEY

5 The next best thing?: Introducing *Don Quijote* as a graphic novel

'Retráteme el que quisiere,' dijo don Quijote, 'pero no me maltrate.'
— MIGUEL DE CERVANTES, *Don Quijote*

ABSTRACT
This chapter begins with an overview of popular practices in the profession – looking at how most students are introduced to *Don Quijote* – and a brief survey of the existing scholarship on the subject of teaching the novel to undergraduates. Next I address the advantages and shortcomings of using an alternate version of the work, specifically Rob Davis's graphic-novel adaptation of *Don Quijote*. Published in 2014, Davis's book has been warmly received by critics, but little has been written about attempts to introduce the work into the classroom. I will describe my own experience using the book in an undergraduate course at Bucknell University. I will address some of the practical considerations of using a less traditional text as well as deeper questions that arise due to the changing learning style of current students and the role of literary studies in undergraduate education in the US.

Perhaps you have been there too. You want to teach *Don Quijote* to undergraduate students, but worry that they (or you) will not be up to the challenge. Do you omit what is arguably the most important work of Spanish literature from a survey course because it is too long or too difficult? Do you include a single chapter, knowing that such an incomplete encounter with the text will hardly do justice to Cervantes's masterwork? Or, a new possibility, do you give students an adaptation of the tale of Alonso Quijano, one that is faithful to the original, has literary merit, and is ideally suited for the tastes and habits of millennials?

This chapter begins with an overview of popular practices in the profession, looking at how most instructors choose to present *Don Quijote*.

Next I address the advantages and shortcomings of using an alternate version of the work, specifically Rob Davis's graphic-novel adaptation.[1] First published in its complete form in 2013 (the Spanish edition was released in 2014), Davis's book has been warmly received by critics, but little has been written about attempts to introduce the work into the classroom. In this chapter I will describe my own experience using the graphic novel in an undergraduate course at Bucknell University, touching on some of the practical considerations of using a less traditional text like this one, as well as deeper questions that arise due to the changing learning style of current students.

There is universal agreement that *Don Quijote* is one of the most important texts of world literature, but this does not mean that its place in the college curriculum is straightforward. *Don Quijote* appears in many shapes and sizes in the American university classroom. Some instructors dedicate an entire course to the novel, ranging anywhere from one quarter to a full year. Others ask students to read large portions of the book as part of a comparative literature course, comparing it with classics like *Madame Bovary* or more contemporary figures like the Marvel antihero Deadpool. Still others include only a chapter or two as part of a survey course. According to the instructor's survey carried out by James A. Parr and Lisa Vollendorf in preparation for the second edition of *Approaches to Teaching Cervantes's* Don Quixote, the two biggest obstacles facing American undergraduate students charged with reading all or part of *Don Quijote* are its length and complexity.[2] Not only is the sheer volume of the book daunting, but for non-native Spanish speakers a lack of linguistic ability can lead to significant difficulties in deciphering Cervantes's prose 'both in terms of vocabulary and syntax'.[3] Add to these challenges the problem posed by an unfamiliar historical context and you end up with a tall order for both instructors and students. In short, Parr and Vollendorf agree with the respondents, who state that the work is a joy to

---

1   Rob Davis, *The Complete Don Quixote* (London: SelfMadeHero, 2013). [Trans. José C. Vales, *Don Quijote* (Madrid: Kraken, 2014)].
2   James A. Parr and Lisa Vollendorf, eds, *Approaches to Teaching Cervantes's* Don Quixote (New York: Modern Language Association of America, 2015), 3–5.
3   Parr and Vollendorf, *Approaches to Teaching Cervantes's* Don Quixote, 3–4.

read and teach, but at the same time the 'challenges of teaching *Don Quixote* were felt to be significant'.[4]

Teachers have worked hard to overcome these hurdles. From bilingual editions to supplemental readings and film adaptations, instructors use a variety of approaches to make *Don Quijote* more accessible to contemporary students. Parr and Vollendorf's survey offers another key bit of advice: 'respondents all identified the same two key components for successfully teaching *Don Quixote*: literary background and historical context'.[5] In his essay, 'Quixotic Pedagogy; Or, Putting the Teacher to the Test', Edward Friedman explains that he spends two to three weeks (four to six class sessions) on introductory materials in order to give students 'a general idea' of the political climate and literary tradition of the day.[6] To be more specific, some of the contributors to Parr and Vollendorf's volume suggest that 'students should have some exposure to the Habsburg era, including the rise and decline of the empire and the role of the Inquisition in building the early modern nation-state'.[7]

I work at Bucknell University, a private liberal arts college in central Pennsylvania. One of the courses that I teach regularly is titled Spanish Cultural Traditions. It is a mid-level survey course covering key episodes and works from Spain's history, art and literature. The course, which is geared towards second and third-year students and typically taken right before they study abroad, begins with the period of the Punic Wars and goes all the way to the present day, and acts as something of a gateway course for our upper division literature classes. The class is capped at twenty-four students, is taught entirely in Spanish, and meets for three hours per week for approximately fifteen weeks.

Over the years I have tried different textbooks. Currently I am using the sixth edition of *España y su civilización*, which I heavily supplement

---

4   Parr and Vollendorf, *Approaches to Teaching Cervantes's* Don Quixote, 4.
5   Parr and Vollendorf, *Approaches to Teaching Cervantes's* Don Quixote, 5.
6   Edward Friedman, 'Quixotic Pedagogy; Or, Putting the Teacher to the Test', *Hispania* 88/1 (2005), 20–31, 22.
7   Parr and Vollendorf, *Approaches to Teaching Cervantes's* Don Quixote, 11.

with additional materials.⁸ A quick glance at the table of contents shows that Chapter 4 contains historical information on the Habsburg reign, while Chapter 5 offers an introduction to the literature of the Golden Age, especially poetry.⁹ Chapter 6 is devoted to Cervantes and *Don Quijote*, and includes information on the author's life as well as a short summary of the novel and its impact. Students get only a slight taste of *Don Quijote* from this chapter, and I had long toyed with the idea of giving them something more substantial to chew on. For me the tipping point came in the form of a note scribbled in the margin of an exam: 'I don't understand what all the fuss is about,' the student wrote, 'Why are people so crazy about *Don Quijote*?' I realized that if I wanted students to understand the importance of the work I would have to show them and not just tell them.

As I contemplated how to go about doing this I was particularly influenced by Patricia Manning's 'Don Quijote on the Plains: Harnessing Enthusiasm for the *Quijote* at the Undergraduate Level' as well as the many excellent essays in MLA's *Approaches to Teaching Cervantes'* Don Quixote, edited by Richard Bjornson.¹⁰ Likewise, the second edition of that work, edited by Parr and Vollendorf, provided several illuminating insights as I grappled with what place Cervantes and his work would have in my course. In the end I decided that whichever version of the *Don Quijote* I chose it would have to meet four criteria. It would have to be accessible, faithful, funny and self-reflexive.

I needed a text that was accessible to students with limited time, limited linguistic ability, and, sadly, limited attention spans. *Don Quijote* is a fabulous read, yes, but not necessarily an easy one. As noted above, it is a

---

8   Francisco Ugarte, Michael Ugarte and Kathleen McNerney, *España y su civilización* (New York: McGraw-Hill, 2009).

9   To some extent my pairing of the graphic novel and the textbook, with its chapters on the Habsburg reign and the Siglo de Oro, mirrors Friedman's approach described earlier, albeit on a much smaller scale. With less time at my disposal I devote one class to the period of the Habsburg dynasty and a second to the literary landscape of the Siglo de Oro prior to our reading of Davis's adaptation.

10   Patricia Manning, 'Don Quijote on the Plains: Harnessing Enthusiasm for the *Quixote* at the Undergraduate Level', *Hispania* 88/1 (2005), 64–71. Richard Bjornson, ed., *Approaches to Teaching Cervantes'* Don Quixote (New York: Modern Language Association of America, 1984).

notoriously difficult work to teach because of its complexity as well as its length: 'Don Quixote requires us to slow down, attend to detail, and allow our in-boxes to fill as we read all 126 chapters'.[11] In his excellent edition for Spanish-language learners, Tom Lathrop gives running headlines on every page with important details from the text, uses modern spelling, and provides a glossary of over 10,000 terms.[12] That such steps are necessary is a pretty good indication of the difficulty faced by young American students for whom Spanish is not their first language.

Don Quijote poses many problems for undergraduates in part because it requires a slow, careful reading and intellectual perseverance. The very nature of a survey course on culture means that I do not have time to use any of the many excellent complete versions of the original. In situations like this it is not uncommon for instructors to include an excerpt, typically Don Quijote's iconic encounter with the windmills in Chapter 8. However, my own experience with this approach was less than satisfactory. I found that students did not engage with the text in the way I had hoped, perhaps because that particular story is so familiar that it does not strike them as revolutionary, or perhaps because taking the episode out of context inevitably truncates and distorts ideas and themes, leading to false impressions about the book. My failure left me with an all-or-nothing attitude. The responses to Bjornson's survey suggest that I am not unique in this respect:

> There is enormous resistance to the use of anthologies in teaching *Don Quixote*. 'I find anthologies so poor in conveying the feeling of *Don Quixote*,' declares one respondent to the survey, 'that I avoid them at all costs'. Others claim that students need access to the whole book even if only part of it is taught in class, for as one instructor explains, an anthology creates 'a mistaken notion regarding the unity and complexity of a work; it obscures relationships of one part to another and can only give isolated impressions'. Another respondent, himself a writer of fiction, states categorically that 'you cannot read and comment on novels ... by sampling them'.[13]

---

11   Parr and Vollendorf, *Approaches to Teaching Cervantes's* Don Quixote, x.
12   Miguel de Cervantes Saavedra, *Don Quijote de la Mancha*, ed. Tom Lathrop (Newark, DE: Juan de la Cuesta, 2000).
13   Bjornson, *Approaches to Teaching Cervantes'* Don Quixote, 11.

This may explain why some literary collections intended for survey classes opt for alternative Cervantine texts. The anthology *Aproximaciones al estudio de la literatura hispánica*, for instance, includes the play *El juez de los divorcios*.[14] Another popular textbook, *Voces de España: Antología literaria*, numbers *El celoso extremeño* amongst its Golden Age texts, whereas *Texto y vida: Introducción a la literatura española*, contains the entremés *El retablo de las maravillas*.[15] Clearly these are wonderful works, but in a course meant to introduce students to the most iconic literary masterpieces some might consider it unthinkable to exclude *Don Quijote* altogether, a work without equal in the Spanish literary canon.

Because I had used graphic novels in other classes with positive results, I looked into the possibility of teaching a graphic version of Cervantes's masterpiece.[16] Rob Davis's adaptation is part of a long tradition of illustrated and comic-book versions of *Don Quijote*. Some are good, some are bad, and some are very bad. Such a format certainly has its advantages. Barbara Stafford is not alone in her opinion that 'our postmodern times are indeed pre-eminently visual times'.[17] In her aforementioned article on teaching *Don Quijote* to undergraduate students, Patricia Manning argues that visual aids provide a 'contextualization of the text in a manner that resonates with learners of the digital generation'.[18] Furthermore, she suggests that the use of visual imagery makes an unfamiliar time period more 'readily comprehensible to students accustomed to the slick visuals of television and video games'.[19] While some might view Manning's statement as a lamentable accommodation, there is evidence from the field of cognitive science to suggest that we are witnessing a paradigm shift in the way that students learn and interact

14   Carmelo Virgilio, Edward Friedman and Teresa Valdivieso, eds, *Aproximaciones al estudio de la literatura hispánica* (New York: McGraw-Hill Education, 2012).
15   Francisca Paredes Méndez, Mark Harpring and José R. Ballesteros, *Voces: Antología literaria* (Boston, MA: Cengage Learning, 2014). Bárbara Mujica, ed., *Texto y vida: introducción a la literatura española* (New York: John Wiley, 1990).
16   In another course on the novels of Benito Pérez Galdós I had used a graphic adaptation of *Marianela*. Rayco Pulido Rodríguez, *Nela* (Bilbao: Asteberri, 2013).
17   Barbara Stafford, *Good Looking: Essays on the Virtues of Images* (Cambridge, MA: MIT Press, 1998), 22.
18   Manning, 'Don Quijote on the Plains', 64.
19   Manning, 'Don Quijote on the Plains', 65.

with books. Alarmingly for teachers of literature, one study showed that the ubiquitous smartphone has increased distractibility in college students, leading to impaired performance in academic tasks that require sustained concentration such as reading.[20] Worse still, following a large-scale survey conducted by the National Endowment for the Arts, researchers reached an even more sombre conclusion:

> The accelerating declines in literary reading among all demographic groups of American adults indicate an imminent cultural crisis. The trends among younger adults warrant special concern, suggesting that – unless some effective solution is found – literary culture, and literacy in general, will continue to worsen.[21]

Now is not the time to turn our noses up at graphic literature. We must do whatever we can to help our students rediscover the pleasure of reading.

For students more accustomed to the silver screen than the printed page, multi-modal texts like graphic novels feel familiar and prove easier to digest in short bursts. The first page of Chapter 3 (in Davis's book), for instance, begins with three panels of Alonso Quijano as he lays in bed recovering from the sound beating he received at the hands of the Toledan merchants (see Figure 5.1).

Davis employs a classic cinematic technique, a zoom out, that will feel natural to a modern audience. The combination of words and images allows the text to multi-task. The panels signal a subtle change in focalization as the receding view draws us away from the protagonist and turns our attention to the other characters as they discuss how to break the spell that the *libros de caballerías* have cast on their beloved neighbour and uncle. Their dialogue, shown as speech bubbles, lets us follow the thoughts and actions of the other characters even before we see them. The overall effect is a narrative that progresses quickly. Because the text here is only a fraction as long as the original, students can read the entire book in a few days. This chapter, which

---

20 Laura E. Levine, Bradley M. Waite and Laura L. Bowman, 'Electronic Media Use, Reading, and Academic Distractibility in College Youth', *CyberPsychology & Behavior* 10/4 (2007), 560–6.
21 Tom Bradshaw and Bonnie Nichols, 'Reading at Risk: A Survey of Literary Reading in America', National Endowment for the Arts (2004), xiii, <https://www.arts.gov/sites/default/files/ReadingAtRisk.pdf>, accessed 1 July 2018.

Figure 5.1. Don Quijote recovers at home (Davis, *The Complete Don Quixote*, 25).

includes the inquisition of the library as well as Don Quijote's departure with Sancho on his second adventure, runs a total of eight pages (thirty-seven panels), with a total word count of 1,052, whereas the corresponding pages in the original (most of Chapters 6 and 7) have a total word count of just over 4,000.

Not only does the format reduce the text load for readers, but the visual cues help students quickly overcome what Manning describes as their 'linguistic discombobulation' with Cervantes's literary style.[22] According to Stephen Cary's *Going Graphic: Comics at Work in the Multilingual Classroom*, with the aid of visual cues students demonstrate better comprehension and retention when reading multi-modal texts while also showing fewer instances of misinterpretation.[23] Keeping track of multiple characters, frequent dialogue and diverse settings is easier for readers when they can both read the words and see the images. Similarly, unfamiliar words like *bacía* and *yelmo*, which would normally leave second-language learners scratching their heads, pose fewer problems because they are also rendered in visual form, meaning fewer pauses to consult the dictionary and thus a more natural reading experience.

But as I searched for an appropriate edition of *Don Quijote* for my class I did not *just* want a version that was easy to consume; it also had to have literary merit, and it had to be faithful in both content and spirit to the original. It is precisely on this point that most graphic adaptations fail. They are frequently incomplete, omitting tangential storylines and glossing over all but the most iconic chapters. They also often ignore the self-reflexive frame, re-presenting the story as an uninterrupted, linear narrative. A comic-book version adapted by Lloyd S. Wagner for Campfire's graphic novel series, for example, is too earnest in my opinion, lacking the nuance and absurdity of the original.[24] Don Quijote is not the withered, incompetent knight errant found in the novel. Instead, he is an inexplicably muscular middle-aged

---

22   Manning, 'Don Quijote on the Plains', 66.
23   Stephen Cary, *Going Graphic: Comics at Work in the Multilingual Classroom* (Portsmouth, NH: Heinemann, 2004).
24   Lloyd S. Wagner, *Don Quixote* (New Delhi: Campfire, 2010). [Volume I illustrated by Richard Kohlrus].

man who, although prone to flights of fancy, often seems far too heroic. In Davis's adaptation, by contrast, Don Quijote is equal parts pathetic and idealist, self-destructive and noble of spirit, frustrating and endearing. In short, he is a complex character that fascinates us more and more with each misadventure.

Other versions are undoubtedly excellent, such as the recent adaptation by German illustrator Flix.[25] It strikes the right tone, but it diverges too much from the original. In Flix's *Don Quijote*, Alonso Quijano is a nutty old man trying to prevent the creation of a wind-farm in his hometown of Tobosow, Germany, Dulcinea is his lost cat, and his comic-obsessed grandson, who thinks that he is Batman, becomes a Sancho-like side-kick who is arguably more quixotic than the protagonist (see Figure 5.2). The author is fully aware of these differences and argues that his version is a 'reposición' of Cervantes's tale rather than an 'adaptación'.[26]

Rob Davis's adaptation manages to find the sweet spot. It feels fresh and innovative, but it remains faithful to the original both in content and spirit. As much as possible this edition uses Cervantes's own text. Chapter 1 begins with the iconic words: 'En un lugar de la Mancha, de cuyo nombre no quiero acordarme'.[27] It is also remarkably complete, including most of the storylines, the *cuentos intercalados*, and even little details such as the mystery of Sancho's lost donkey.

In addition to having a comprehensive storyline, a key part of being faithful to the spirit of the original means that it should be funny. I agree wholeheartedly with Daniel Eisenberg who, in his essay 'Teaching *Don Quixote* as a Funny Book,' states that 'Cervantes wrote *Don Quixote* to make us laugh'.[28] Eisenberg notes that the comedic element 'is one of the most often missed by modern readers'.[29] It is also often overlooked, I might add, by adapters.

---

25 Flix, *Don Quijote* (Hamburg: Carlen Verlag, 2012). [Trans. María Dolores Pérez Pablos, *Don Quijote* (Madrid: Dibbuks, 2014)].
26 Flix, *Don Quijote*, 12.
27 Rob Davis, *The Complete Don Quixote*, 9.
28 Daniel Eisenberg, 'Teaching *Don Quixote* as a Funny Book', in Richard Bjornson, ed., *Approaches to Teaching Cervantes' Don Quixote* (New York: Modern Language Association of America, 1984), 62–8, 62.
29 Eisenberg, 'Teaching *Don Quixote* as a Funny Book', 65.

The next best thing?

Figure 5.2. Alonso Quijano and his grandson come upon the windmills (Flix, *Don Quijote*, 95).

Let us compare a scene from Wagner's adaptation and the same scene from Davis's book. The episode in question occurs when Don Quijote and Sancho are staying at an inn, and Maritornes, 'la criada malencarada de cuerpo gallardo' sneaks into the room to see her admirer, the muleteer.[30] In Wagner's version, Maritornes is plain, but hardly ugly. And the dialogue, simplified for a younger readership, comes across as clunky and antiquated.[31] Davis's drawing of Maritornes, who has one bulging eye as well as a moustache, borders on caricature (see Figure 5.3). But that is what makes Don Quijote's subsequent actions all the more ridiculous and therefore more humorous! His declaration, '¡Oh dama de sin par fermosura!' is silly because it is so far from the truth.[32] Cervantes's work is rich and multi-dimensional, and humour is obviously not his only tool nor laughter his only goal, but as Eisenberg observes, 'to claim that *Don Quixote* is not primarily a work of humour is to claim that it is a failure'.[33] *Don Quijote*, after all, is a parody, and parody is meant to make us laugh as it critiques. It is a goal of which Davis does not lose sight.

As anyone who has travelled to another country knows, humour is highly contextual and culturally specific. Even more so when it is in a foreign language. Eisenberg makes the following observation: 'Spaniards are correct when they claim that *Don Quixote*, like much verbal humour, is to some extent untranslatable ... [and] can only be explained, never translated'.[34] Yet I would counter that the visual element of graphic novels can reduce this communication gap. After all, visual images, while not free of culture, are perhaps more universal, and, as the old saying goes, an image is worth a thousand words. Davis's visual rendering of the narrative works especially well with instances of physical humour in the novel. 'One of the book's humorous elements involves its many sexual and excretory allusions,' Eisenberg notes, 'a fact of considerable interest to contemporary American students'.[35] In this, Davis's version does not disappoint. A scene which perfectly captures Eisenberg's comment comes in the sixth chapter of Part I (see Figure 5.4).

---

30 Davis, *The Complete Don Quixote*, 63.
31 Wagner, *Don Quixote*, 31–3.
32 Davis, *The Complete Don Quixote*, 65.
33 Eisenberg, 'Teaching *Don Quixote* as a Funny Book', 63.
34 Eisenberg, 'Teaching *Don Quixote* as a Funny Book', 66.
35 Eisenberg, 'Teaching *Don Quixote* as a Funny Book', 65.

The next best thing?

Maritornes
(La criada malencarada de cuerpo gallardo,
que anda enredada con el arriero)

Figure 5.3. Maritornes, 'La criada malencarada de cuerpo gallardo' (Davis, *The Complete Don Quixote*, 63).

Sancho gives Don Quijote the 'bálsamo de Fierabrás' after one of their numerous smack-downs, causing the knight errant to promptly vomit in Sancho's face. Sancho turns in shock and stares out toward the reader as if to say, 'Seriously? Can you believe this just happened?' For me this is the perfect moment because it captures the humour as well as the self-reflexive element that are at the core of the original.

This brings me to my final criterion. I felt that it was crucial to find a version that did not overlook the metafictional qualities of the novel. Carroll Johnson has observed that *Don Quijote* 'is a book made out of other books and it is a book about books'.[36] Similarly, Ulrich Wicks notes that, '*Don*

---

36   Carroll Johnson, *Don Quixote: The Quest for Modern Fiction* (Long Grove, IL: Waveland Press, 2000), 71.

Figure 5.4. Don Quijote drinks the 'bálsamo de Fierabrás' (Davis, *The Complete Don Quixote*, 78).

The next best thing? 101

Quixote is a self-reflexive work: the acts of reading, the responses of readers, and the implications of reading – both within the narrative and outside it – are the real substance of the book'.[37] This quality is undoubtedly one of the main reasons that Carlos Fuentes, among many others, refers to *Don Quijote* as 'the first modern novel [...] born as both an encounter of genres and a refusal of purity'.[38]

Unlike other adaptations, Davis does not shy away from this aspect of the original. In fact, one might argue that, given the visual format of Davis's adaptation, the self-reflexiveness of the work is even more obvious than in other versions. We see this, for instance, in the speech bubbles of the narrator and the unique formatting of the intercalated stories. Figure 5.5 shows the title page of Davis's adaptation, where it reads: 'Donde se cuentan las verdaderas aventuras del valeroso caballero don Quijote de la Mancha, escritas por Miguel de Cervantes y publicadas en 1605. Cervantes ideó la historia de Don Quijote mientras estaba encarcelado en Sevilla'.[39] Right below this we have a speech bubble coming out of a prison cell. It says 'No, mentira. Yo no he inventado nada. ¿Quién ha dicho eso?'[40] On the next page we find the narrator/implied author speaking again: 'No podéis creer todo lo que leáis, apreciado lector. Estas aventuras son ciertas y verdaderas porque son historia, y no un cuento. Y, contrariamente a lo que se asegura en la página anterior, ¡yo soy el traductor, no el autor!'[41] From the moment readers open the book they are confronted with a narrator who delights in breaking the fourth wall, turning self-consciousness into one of the main themes of the story.

The metafictional element is also present in the embedded stories, like the story of Cardenio or that of the 'Curioso impertinente' (see Figure 5.6). Here Davis alters the style of the drawings, often making them more

---

37 Ulrih Wicks, 'Metafiction in *Don Quixote*: What is the Author Up To?', in Richard Bjornson, ed., *Approaches to Teaching Cervantes' Don Quixote* (New York: Modern Language Association of America, 1984), 69–76, 70.
38 Carlos Fuentes, 'Tilt: The errant knight of La Mancha rides again in a new English translation', *The New York Times* (2 November 2003).
39 Davis, *The Complete Don Quixote*, 5.
40 Davis, *The Complete Don Quixote*, 5.
41 Davis, *The Complete Don Quixote*, 6.

Figure 5.5. Title page (Davis, *The Complete Don Quixote*, 5).

cartoonish or using a monochromatic colour scheme. This stylistic change makes them seem a further step removed from reality, more fictional if you will, leading the reader into a mise-en-abyme literary world. And finally, throughout Davis's book we have the same ongoing discussion of books and reading that we find in the original, from the library purge carried out by Alonso Quijano's friends and family, to the conversation between Sansón Carrasco and Don Quijote in which they discuss the possibility of a second

The next best thing?

part of Don Quijote's story. Throughout it all, the narrator steps in and out of the spotlight, whether he is pausing the narrative mid-battle to describe his search for the lost manuscript, or handing a scroll to Sancho with the ending to the very story we are reading.[42] Like the original, this is a book about books, a story about storytelling.

Figure 5.6. Tale of the 'Curioso impertinente' (Davis, *The Complete Don Quixote*, 124).

42   Davis, *The Complete Don Quixote*, 41 and 145.

Davis's text is accessible, faithful, funny, and self-reflexive, and because of this it has the depth needed to withstand the scrutiny of the cleverest and most demanding students. As with any literary text that I use in class, students are guided through a close reading of Davis's adaptation, one that draws on their newfound knowledge of Spanish history and culture. At the end of the unit students are required to write a response to a question from a bank of prompts, some of which are unique to this graphic adaption ('How does the interplay of text and image in this graphic adaptation complement the bending and blending of genres in the story itself?'), while others are not ('How does the self-reflexivity found in the novel complicate the question of narratorial reliability?'). This focus on close reading and analysis means that students are practising the same skills that they will use in other literature courses, which is one of the learning goals for this course.

In conclusion, this edition is not perfect, but then again no adaptation is. Its biggest shortcoming is that it is not the original, whose genius can never be matched. But this version certainly checks enough boxes for a course like mine. (Besides, if we take into account the limitations of our students or the constraints of the courses we teach, not even the original is without problems). Just as Davis's book can never replace the original, my course cannot do for Cervantes and *Don Quijote* what courses like Friedman's or Manning's courses do. But it does not have to. I am offering students an appetizer (to build on Friedman's gastronomic metaphors), enough to give them a taste of the feast that awaits them if they sign up for a semester-long class on *Don Quijote* in their senior year. In this regard I believe my approach succeeds. As one student recently commented, 'I loved this book, which I didn't expect. In fact, I think I'm ready to read the real thing now'. When you cannot have the original, this is the next best thing.

IDOYA PUIG

6 Teaching literature and language using a multiliteracies framework: Exploring intercultural skills with Cervantes's *La española inglesa*

ABSTRACT
There is concern that reading literary classics is becoming harder, especially for young people. For some years, literature has been excluded from the study of the foreign language and has lost ground in university studies. However, studies in pedagogical theory show the benefits of a multiliteracies approach, which combines different channels of communication and multimodal forms of linguistic expression. When used creatively, this approach can be applied to the study of literary texts to foster traditional reading skills. This chapter looks specifically at *La española inglesa*, one of Cervantes's *Novelas ejemplares*, and presents examples showing how language and cultural context can be studied successfully through this short story by using a multiliteracies framework. In particular, the text can be harnessed to highlight intercultural elements relevant to present-day discussions.

Introduction: Accessing literary classics in the twenty-first century

There is a growing concern that the advent of new media has reduced reading habits, particularly among young people. Reading seems less appealing and more challenging. However, studies confirm that rather than decreasing, reading habits are changing and moving from print to digital media:

> La lectura digital se va consolidando con un carácter hegemónico en la población más joven. Por niveles de estudios son los estudiantes universitarios los que presentan mayores porcentajes de incremento.[1]

1 Julio Alonso-Arévalo, José-Antonio Cordón-García and Raquel Gómez-Díaz, 'Comparación de los hábitos y perfil del lector digital entre Estados Unidos y

In the UK, a new GCSE and A-Level syllabus is being introduced in the study of languages to address the excessive focus on isolated and repetitive tasks and the abdication of more challenging skills such as deep reading. In the new A-Level exams, students will be required to read texts, including one book. In the words of Stephen Parker, chair of the panel for modern and ancient languages on the A-Level Content Advisory Board:

> While changes to the A-level modern languages curriculum over the past 10 years aimed to make it more relevant, recycling topics about family life could be uninspiring. Students were no longer required to read a book in a foreign language [...] and the emphasis was often on rote learning rather than on engaging with a different society and culture.[2]

In higher education, language teaching has lost considerable ground in recent years.[3] A fall of 22.8 per cent in UK applications to European languages courses at university was observed in 2017 compared to the same point in 2012.[4]

This situation necessarily impacts on the reading of foreign literature, which is becoming more and more inaccessible. The introduction of high university fees and the widespread practice of measuring student satisfaction regularly through formal surveys put pressure on universities to only offer popular subjects and discontinue units that attract a smaller intake of students due to their perceived difficulty or less immediate appeal.

España', *Anales de Documentación* 17/1 (2014), <http://dx.doi.org/10.6018/analesdoc.17.1.193111>, accessed 7 June 2018.

2   *Living Languages Report*, British Academy and *The Guardian* (2015), 4, <http://static.guim.co.uk/ni/1428923743291/BritAcFINAL_living_language.pdf>, accessed 5 June 2018.

3   *Living Languages Report*, 8–10.

4   Kershaw, Alison, 'Fall in number of students taking up foreign languages prompts Brexit concerns', *The Guardian* (5 August 2017), <https://www.independent.co.uk/news/education/education-news/fall-in-number-of-students-taking-modern-foreign-languages-brexit-british-council-prompts-concerns-a7877491.html>, accessed 9 September 2018.

In the field of Hispanic Studies, particularly in the English-speaking world, the literary offer is being replaced by films, with older or longer works of literature being pushed to one side for fear of failing to attracting sufficient numbers and/or jeopardizing student satisfaction. Comments below from a number of scholars consulted on whether Spanish literary classics such as Cervantes's *Don Quijote* were being taught at university level confirm the challenge posed by books of this nature. In some cases, undergraduates are asked to read *Don Quijote* but, very often, other shorter works by Cervantes are used, including one or two of the short stories from the *Novelas ejemplares*. In other cases, *Don Quijote* is accessed in translation only or is read partially at best (a few chapters or selected extracts), as the following responses illustrate:

> I have found out that a great work, such as *Rinconete y Cortadillo* cannot be taught to American students at an undergraduate level in the USA. Even if their Spanish is good, they lack the expertise to flavor the word-play and linguistic nuances of this novel. (xx, email dated 26 April 2015)

> I do not teach Cervantes because the grad students do not take any course in Golden Age. They receive the Ph.D. without ever having read/studied Don Quijote. This is like grad students in English graduating without taking Shakespeare. (xx, email dated 21 February 2015)[5]

Recent years have seen the publication of two comprehensive studies on the state of the 'literary canon' taught in universities in the US and UK.[6] Both studies confirm the shift away from older classic works of literature, which are being replaced increasingly by films or by more recent texts by contemporary authors.

---

5   I have deleted individual names and university affiliation for data protection.
6   Winston R. Groman, 'The Hispanic Literary Canon in U.S. Universities', *Instituto Cervantes at FAS Harvard* (2016), <http://cervantesobservatorio.fas.harvard.edu/sites/default/files/026_en.pdf>, accessed 4 June 2018 and Stuart Davis, 'The state of the discipline. Hispanic literature and film in UK Spanish degrees', *Journal of Romance Studies* 18/1 (2018), 25–44. This study is further developed in Davis's article included in this collection.

New approaches to teaching: Multiliteracies and traditional skills

In the light of this growing trend, it is relevant to take into account studies which explore alternative means of learning through new media. Literacy in the twenty-first century is 'the set of abilities and skills where aural, visual, and digital literacy overlap. These include the ability to understand the power of images and sounds, to recognize and use that power, to manipulate and transform digital media, to distribute them pervasively, and to easily adapt them to new forms'.[7] It is important to integrate these new skills with what one might consider the traditional skill of reading, which remains an essential skill for all:

> Textual literacy remains a central skill in the twenty-first century. Before students can engage with the new participatory culture, they must be able to read and write. Youth must expand their required competencies, not push aside old skills to make room for the new. [...] New media literacies include the traditional literacy evolved with print culture as well as the newer forms of literacy within mass and digital media.[8]

It is not a question of displacing skills but rather developing them through new media. Instead of reading less, we read in a different way. However, such reading runs the risk of being much more superficial, in some cases consisting of little more than jumping from link to link. It becomes harder for the brain to analyse data and perform deep reading. It is important therefore to harness new media to foster and consolidate deep reading skills and understand how internet-mediated communication works.[9]

In addition, new technologies offer a strong social element, which brings other advantages. New media facilitate interaction with a much wider

---

7   'A Global Imperative: The report of the 21st Century Literacy Summit', *New Media Consortium* (2005), 8, <http://www.nmc.org/pdf/Global_Imperative.pdf>, accessed 7 June 2018.

8   Henry Jenkins, ed., *Confronting the challenges of Participatory Culture: Media Education for the 21st century*, MacArthur Foundation (2006), 19, <http://www.newmedialiteracies.org/wp-content/uploads/pdfs/NMLWhitePaper.pdf>, accessed 7 June 2018.

9   Francisco Yus, *Ciberpragmática. El uso del lenguaje en Internet* (Barcelona: Ariel, 2001).

audience and make it possible to create texts which can be shared in a global setting, thus aiding the development of intercultural skills:

> The new media literacies should be seen as social skills, as ways of interacting within a larger community, and not simply as individualized skill to be used for personal expression. [...] Disparate collaboration may be the most radical element of new literacies: they enable collaboration and knowledge-sharing with large-scale communities that may never personally interact.[10]

Accordingly, the social and collaborative aspect of new technologies has great potential for development and, as a result, should be incorporated into new teaching practices. Students who are comfortable writing their own posts on a social network can utilize and integrate this skill in the more formal context of education. Henry Jenkins and his team define a number of new skills to be developed in educational settings, including play, multitasking, networking, and negotiation, among others. All these skills can be put into practice using different channels of communication, old and new, in a multiliteracies approach that fully integrates multiple forms of media into learning processes. The term multiliteracies was defined in 1994 by the New London Group. This approach highlights two key aspects of literacy: linguistic diversity and multimodal forms of linguistic expression:

> The 'multi-' of enormous and significant differences in contexts and patterns of communication, and the 'multi-' of multimodality. In the case of the first of these 'multi-'s, the Multiliteracies notion sets out to address the variability of meaning making in different cultural, social or domain-specific contexts. [...] The other 'multi-' response to the question of the 'what' of Multiliteracies arises in part from the characteristics of the new information and communications media. Meaning is made in ways that are increasingly multimodal – in which written-linguistic modes of meaning interface with oral, visual, audio, gestural, tactile, and spatial patterns of meaning.[11]

Applied to the study of literary classics, the multiliteracies approach bridges the gap between traditional reading skills and new approaches to learning

---

10 Jenkins, *Confronting the challenges of Participatory Culture*, 20-1.
11 Bill Cope and Mary Kalantzis, 2015. 'The Things You Do to Know: An Introduction to the Pedagogy of Multiliteracies', in B. Cope and M. Kalantzis, eds, *A Pedagogy of Multiliteracies: Learning By Design* (London: Palgrave), 1–36, 3.

rather than viewing them as mutually exclusive. It highlights ideas and values that can be found in both cultures or historical periods and, at the same time, allows differences to be defined and explained, leading ultimately to a better appreciation of both historical moments (the Spanish Golden Age and the present day, for example). The multiliteracies approach brings classic texts to life in the classroom rather than relegating them to the past as something outdated or inaccessible: 'The new media literacies could supplement and expand traditional print literacies in ways that enriched our culture and deepened our appreciation of classical stories'.[12] To achieve this, the new remix or interpretation needs to engage in a meaningful manner with the old. At the same time, embracing elements of participatory culture and multimodality can help foster traditional reading and writing skills in learners.

Viewed from this perspective, new trends appear less threatening and more easily adoptable: 'Changes in educational practices are more often evolutionary than revolutionary'.[13] We do not have to sacrifice the study of literary classics or avoid teaching texts that we value and recognize as classics in a particular language or country. A balance is required: 'It would be tragic if we allowed new media literacy practices to totally displace traditional print literacy practices, but refusing to engage with new media out of a misplaced fear of change would be equally tragic'.[14]

There is an inherent value in literature which can be applied to language learning. The benefits of literature include the recognition of the value of authentic texts to reinforce language competency, foster student engagement and develop intercultural communication.[15]

Janet Swaffar and Katherine Arens apply this multiliteracies perspective to language learning in particular, focusing on the actual text and adopting

---

12 Clinton, Jenkins and McWilliams, 'New Literacies in an Age of Participatory Culture', 5.
13 Clinton, Jenkins and McWilliams, 'New Literacies in an Age of Participatory Culture', 9.
14 Clinton, Jenkins and McWilliams, 'New Literacies in an Age of Participatory Culture', 11.
15 Amos Paran, 'The role of literature in instructed foreign language learning and teaching: an evidence-based survey', *Language Teaching* 41/4 (2008), 465–96, <https://doi.org/10.1017/S026144480800520X>, accessed 7 June 2018.

a critical approach to explore 'the social and linguistics frameworks of texts and genres for spoken and written communication across time periods, across cultures, and in multicultural frameworks'.[16] Following this line also, Paesani, Willis and Dupuy have produced a specific framework to implement a multiliteracies approach to teaching the foreign language.[17]

The multiliteracies framework identifies four pedagogical acts: situated practice, overt instruction, critical framing and transformed practice. Situated practice is the immersion in the language, including the knowledge and experience already possessed by students. It invariably entails some presentation of resources and provision of background information to facilitate understanding and engagement with the text, and these elements together are termed overt instruction. The students are encouraged to reflect and analyse in a critical manner the texts presented to them (critical framing). Finally, there is an act of transformed practice given that students apply their learning to other contexts, creating and developing new texts. These categories combine the simultaneous development of different skills and can incorporate diverse media and technologies. In this way, the four pedagogical acts serve as a bridge connecting (old) traditional literacy skills and (new) twenty-first-century multiliteracies.[18]

Ana López Sánchez is among those to have adopted the multiliteracies framework for the study of Spanish poems.[19] The present paper further develops the application of the framework, presenting as a case study a classic short story from Spanish literature: Cervantes's *La española inglesa*. The aim is to show how it is possible to offer texts from earlier centuries to a twenty-first-century audience. As will be demonstrated below, classic literary texts initially deemed too difficult or too remote for young people to relate to can be made more accessible and be explored using the multiliteracies framework described above.

16   *Remapping the Foreign Literature Curriculum: An Approach through Multiple Literacies* (New York: The Modern Language Association of America, 2005), 5.
17   Kate Paesani, Heather Willis Allen, and Beatrice Dupuy, *A Multiliteracies Framework for Collegiate Foreign Language Teaching* (Boston, MA: Pearson, 2014).
18   Paesani, Willis and Dupuy, *A Multiliteracies Framework*, 27–8.
19   Ana López Sánchez, 'Hacia una pedagogía para la *multialfabetización*: El diseño de una unidad didáctica inspirada en las propuestas del New London group', *Hispania* 97/2 (2014), 281–97.

La española inglesa and intercultural awareness

Having outlined the multiliteracies approach and the four pedagogical acts of the framework, we can now turn to the study of a Spanish literary classic from the sixteenth century: *La española inglesa* by Miguel de Cervantes. It goes without saying that Cervantes is an obligatory point of reference in any discussion of Spanish literature. His literary masterpiece, *Don Quijote*, continues to be recognized as an essential element of Spanish culture, while Cervantes himself is widely considered the greatest writer in Spanish literature and deserving of study. As with other Golden Age authors, it is vital to seek out new ways of bringing his texts to twenty-first-century readers and younger generations through new methods and approaches.

Don Quijote has been recreated in a variety of media, with numerous films, comics strips, plays, ballets, paintings, and now iPad resources featuring Don Quijote as a protagonist. However, as a book it is difficult to access due to its length and complexity. Although much quoted, it is widely acknowledged that not many people have actually read it. The celebration of the 400th anniversary of the deaths of Shakespeare and Cervantes led to the organization of a large number of events that clearly demonstrated the creative use of new formats to make this literary classic known. An excellent effort was undertaken to gather information on events during 2016 in a systematic manner, facilitated by new technologies. By way of example, a specific website was created to provide details of events held, to link up different institutions and provide a good search engine to locate events with ease. The Spanish government's official commemoration programme classified the activities under headings such as exhibitions, performing arts, music, cinema, literature, education and promotion, digital contents, research and academic activities, cultural tourism and legacy.[20] This is a useful example of the adoption of a multiliteracies approach in educational and cultural settings.

---

20   *IV Centenario de la muerte de Cervantes* (2017), <http://400cervantes.es>, accessed 7 June 2018.

Teaching literature and language using a multiliteracies framework 113

The aforementioned initiatives parallel the resources developed by the British Council specifically for the study of English through Shakespeare's plays: on-line courses which harness technologies for literacy purposes using different texts and media, including videos, exercises, quizzes, opportunities to take part in on-line chats and create texts, etc. In addition, an extensive programme of events has been put in place to link up with schools throughout the country. These and other examples demonstrate how the use of a multiliteracies approach can enhance the study and enjoyment of literary classics.[21]

While a range of new pedagogical approaches have been suggested for the study of *Don Quijote*,[22] other texts by Cervantes or by other Golden Age authors have not been explored to the same degree and require greater attention if they are to remain accessible to the modern reader. One such case is *La española inglesa*, one of the short stories of Cervantes's collection *Novelas ejemplares* (1612), which can also be exploited using the multiliteracies framework.[23] For those unaccustomed to reading older literary texts, it can prove more realistic and satisfying to commence with a shorter and easier work. Equally, a shorter story can still be effective in introducing the reader to the main style and literary characteristics associated with the author.

The *Novelas ejemplares* comprise twelve stories with very different themes and styles. Cervantes claims in the prologue to the collection that he was the first to write *novellas* in the Spanish language. He is credited in particular with originality of style:

> The essence of Cervantes's claim to originality, however, lies in the way in which he took the form and gave it a life of its own, liberating it from dependence on a larger structure. In this, his antecedents are Italian rather than Spanish: the 'Decameron'

---

21 *Shakespeare*, British Council (2017), <https://learnenglish.britishcouncil.org/en/listen-and-watch>, accessed 7 June 2018.

22 Edward H. Friedman, 'Quixotic Pedagogy; Or, Putting the Teacher to the Test', *Hispania*, 88/1 (2005), 20–31; Lisa Vollendorf and James A. Parr, eds, *Approaches to Teaching Cervantes's Don Quixote* (New York: Modern Language Association of America, 2015); Margaret Boyle, 'Teaching *Don Quixote* in the Digital Age: Page and Screen, Visual and Tactile', *Hispania*, 99/4 (2016), 600–14.

23 Miguel de Cervantes, *Novelas ejemplares*, ed. Juan Bautista Avalle-Arce (Madrid: Castalia, 1987).

(c. 1348) of Giovanni Boccaccio [...]. Such collections were popular throughout Europe and provided playwrights in several countries, Shakespeare among them, with handy ideas for plots.[24]

Even though written in the late sixteenth and early seventeenth centuries, the *Novelas ejemplares* address timeless and universal themes such as love, friendship and freedom. It is, therefore, possible to use the work to establish links with present day issues and identify elements common to different cultures and contexts. Intercultural competence is the capacity to communicate effectively in intercultural situations and to establish appropriate relationships within diverse cultural contexts:

> Developing intercultural competence does not mean doing away with the information gap or related activities, but developing them so that (1) culture becomes a regular focus of the information exchanged, and (2) learners have the opportunity to reflect upon how the information is exchanged, and the cultural factors impinging upon the exchange.[25]

The use of literary texts in the language class allows students to experience different cultures in context, thus encouraging familiarity with traditions and values and, in turn, fostering intercultural awareness: 'Language learning helps learners to avoid stereotyping individuals, to develop curiosity and openness to otherness and to discover other cultures'.[26]

A number of intercultural elements are explored in *La española inglesa* and it is an appropriate text to study in this regard. Themes such as abduction, religious tolerance, the value of the dignity of the individual regardless of their beauty or external traits, the freedom to choose one's marriage partner and the scope of parental authority in such matters, all make an appearance in the story and offer suitable pretexts for critical analysis.

La española inglesa presents the story of a girl, Isabela, who is abducted from her parents by an English nobleman during a battle in Cadiz and is taken to England. She is adopted and looked after by her new family and, although she is a captive, the son of the family, Ricardo, falls in love with her

---

24 Barry W. Ife, ed., *Exemplary Novels* (Warminster: Aris & Phillips, 1992), ix.
25 John Corbett, *An Intercultural Approach to English Language Teaching* (Multilingual Matters, 2003), 32.
26 Council of Europe, *Council of Europe white paper on intercultural dialogue* (2008), 29, <http://www.coe.int/t/dg4/intercultural/source/white%20paper_final_revised_en.pdf>, accessed 7 June 2018.

and her incredible beauty and his parents agree to their marriage. The Queen of England learns of her existence and refuses to sanction the marriage until Ricardo proves he is worthy of her and embarks on a mission to defend the interests of the crown. He has to fight Turkish pirates and decides to show clemency to the pirate leader. The same Turk will, in turn, save Ricardo later from execution. The story is full of action and unexpected twists: Ricardo finds Isabela's parents who are then reunited with their daughter; Isabela is poisoned by the mother of a rival suitor and loses all her beauty; Ricardo's parents want him to marry somebody else as a result, etc. Eventually the efforts and perseverance of the two lovers are rewarded and the marriage takes place. *La española inglesa* offers an abundance of adventure and some degree of suspense, features which make it appealing and entertaining. The blend of settings and cultures also make it an appropriate story to explore intercultural themes.

La española inglesa: Multiliteracies framework applied to a literary classic

Having considered the value and appropriateness of *La española inglesa* as a text for study in the present context, we can now present some examples illustrating the application of the multiliteracies approach to the study of this short story. Given the extensive range of new media, it is necessary to focus on one specific manifestation. Film is a familiar medium and is particularly appropriate because of its popularity, accessibility and appeal to the younger generation:

> Film in the target language is an efficient and effective link to the target culture(s) in that it is highly visual; it is authentic in that it is made for the target culture audience: it is readily available; it is attractive to students accustomed to a multimedia environment.[27]

The discussion concerning the relationship between film and literature lies beyond the scope of the paper. However, it is clear that critics increasingly

---

27 Jessica Sturm, 'Using film in the L2 Classroom: A Graduate Course in Film Pedagogy', *Foreign Language Annals* 45/2 (2012), 246–59, 246.

perceive the advantages of the dialogue between literature and film adaptations of classic or older literary texts: 'studying adaptations of literature offers students a better, more effective way to study literature'.[28] Duncan Wheeler is among those who recognize the usefulness of films and visual materials and states that there is a responsibility to make good use of them so they can be effective instruments to make works of literature known and promote classic texts.[29]

In this case, a film version of *La española inglesa* (2015) produced by Spanish Television (RTVE) is a further tool that may be harnessed for the study of the short story. This film recreates the sixteenth-century setting in a visual way and brings the action to the screen, taking the story closer to the twenty-first-century reader.

If we apply the multiliteracies framework described above to *La española inglesa*, the four pedagogical acts of situated practice, overt instruction, critical framing and transformed practice will help address sections of the text alongside the film. Certain chapters will be read in different stages with the aim of ultimately reading the whole work of literature, while also engaging with multimodal elements and different literacies.

A pilot project to apply the multiliteracies approach to *La española inglesa* is outlined briefly in the following section. Sessions were delivered for first-year undergraduate students and Erasmus students at Manchester Metropolitan University at the beginning of the academic year 2017–18. The students had an advanced level of language. The aim of the sessions was to trial the level of engagement with and response to the literary work through initial contact with the film. None of the students was familiar with the work and they had very little or no knowledge of sixteenth-century Spain.

The sessions included some element of overt instruction as the teacher provided information on the historical and literary context, as well as clarifying certain language issues. Situated practice occurred given that students

---

28 Dennis Cutchins, Laurence Raw, and James M. Welsh, *The Pedagogy of Adaptation* (Plymouth: Scarecrow Press, 2010), viii.
29 Duncan Wheeler, 'Las adaptaciones cinematográficas como (posible) herramienta pedagógica', *Anuario Lope de Vega* 24 (2018), 260–88, DOI: <https://doi.org/10.5565/rev/anuariolopedevega.257>

watched the film clip, listened to Spanish and completed a series of comprehension exercises. Critical framing and transformed practice were present in the form of detailed discussion of intercultural issues, subsequently leading to the production of written and oral work.

The very title of the text proved a good starting point to engage critically with cultural references. Students identified aspects which defined Spanish and English cultures and initiated discussion on language, character traits and traditions. As the title suggests, in *La española inglesa* there are a number of cultural opposites which can be explored both from the perspective of the historical moment of the time of writing and the present day. Other opposing terms in the story include Catholic and Protestant, Christian and Muslim, captive and free, rich and poor, lower and upper class: 'It is a story of dissimulation and unpacks the condition and practice of hybrid identity in the early modern period'.[30] For all these reasons, it can be considered an appropriate text to explore in for the language classroom.

A series of exercises served to introduce students to the historical context and help them identify ethical issues appearing in the story, including rivalry between countries in the sixteenth century, issues of religion, relationships between parents and children in terms of choice of partner and the understanding of marriage, and even concepts of friendship in past times. The participation of Erasmus students in the classes broadened the range of cultural points of view offered. From the outset, students were able to make connections between Cervantes's times and aspects of the present.

Following introductory considerations, students watched a clip from the film and explored the scene using multimodal designs (linguistic, visual, audio, spatial and gestural). The clip provided an opportunity for situated practice as they had to understand the original Spanish track supported by the Spanish sub-titles. The palace scene, when the Queen meets Isabela and her family, was particularly useful: each of the designs was identified in the scene and helped to define the characters and the relationships between them. The verb tenses and forms of address used helped to recognize attitudes of

---

30 Emily Colbert Cairns, 'Crypto-Catholicism in a Protestant Land: *La española inglesa*', *Cervantes* 36/2 (2016), 127–44, 127.

power and submission. The Queen, for example, speaks using imperatives and determines what is to happen to the two main characters in the immediate future.

The colours of the costumes worn by the characters reinforced their position and challenged these relationships: Isabela was portrayed as being submissive, yet appeared in red, suggesting her inner strength and value as she stood before the rich and powerful Queen, dressed in contrasting white. The action was supported by gestures such us pointing, looks and bowing, which determined the position of each character in the social hierarchy. The grandiose setting of the palace and the solemn music contributed to provide a quasi-religious character to the Queen and the ceremony watched by the students.

The scene is engaging and full of emotion and it prompted student discussion of the specific issues arising, including the clash of cultures and, in particular, the free choice of marriage partner and the interests of other parties such as the Queen, parents and society in general. The transition to present-day situations was smooth as students were able to relate the content to analogous situations which still arise today.

This initial stage of film analysis helped capture the interest of students and familiarize them with the story. At this point it was appropriate to introduce into the session the original Cervantes text, which would otherwise have held little initial appeal for students. The text of the same scene seen in the film clip was presented in class. Evidently, the visual elements of the film were lacking in the text but students were nonetheless able to appreciate the power of the highly expressive and effective written metaphors and images describing the beauty of Isabela and the solemnity of the setting. Participating students realized that the lack of visual elements was compensated by vivid images and metaphors, which were equally or more effective than what they had viewed in the film clip: 'The descriptions in the novel are very interesting and create great images' (student comment). In this way, the link between the text and the film was made and the use of different media was clear.

Additional exercises allowed the four key language skills of reading, writing, listening and speaking to be practised using digital tools, namely, a Quizlet (to build up vocabulary and understand the text) and a Webquest (with links enabling students to obtain further information on the context of the scene viewed in the film or in the text read). Most of the students were already familiar with the Quizlet and Webquest tools.

Situated practice and critical framing actions were implemented throughout the sessions. Intercultural issues were examined and students gave examples of integration and respect for different cultures in society. The theme of friendship was also discussed, as Ricardo's close friendship with his servant overcame class barriers of the day. In addition, a Turkish pirate saves Ricardo and his servant, just as the former had saved him at the beginning of the story, thus revealing a sense of loyalty that transcended the religious barriers and prevailing divisions between countries in the sixteenth century. Students read sections of the original work and analysed in depth these intercultural issues and their representation in the text, identifying multimodal elements and discovering how they changed over time.

In order to demonstrate that students could apply their learning to other contexts, they were encouraged, as an act of transformed practice, to identify in news items and magazines further representations of the story and references to the themes discussed. Finally, they were asked to write their own conclusions using multiliteracies or other modes of communication, such as a book trailer, film review, a film clip to be uploaded to YouTube, etc.

Combining the four different pedagogical acts from the multiliteracies approach, additional exercises were created to facilitate the reading of the short story in full. Students worked with the plot, structure, characterization, themes and language (including imagery and register) of the story. Quotes were selected to check understanding and generate discussion. Meanwhile, other exercises developed vocabulary and grammar structures and all contributed to helping the students engage with the story and familiarize themselves further with the Golden Age text.

Conclusion

As this paper has highlighted, numerous studies explore the potential of new technologies and define new ways of learning. A multiliteracies approach can be used to develop language and literary skills and incorporate new practices for learners, particularly young people. Instead of being fearful of new multiliteracies skills, it is important to understand them and embrace them as instruments which can help develop and promote more traditional skills of reading and writing which, it is worth emphasizing, are here to stay. It is important also to identify and harness existing resources to discover literary texts.

As illustrated in the preceding pages, there are multiple benefits to the application of this specific multiliteracies framework to activities deemed challenging in the current context, among them the study of literary classics:

> It facilitates development of grammatical and lexical knowledge as resources for meaning making put into practice through contextualized language use within the context of FL texts. Because this pedagogy places texts at the center of the curriculum from the very start of language study, even introductory learners can engage in the kinds of critical framing and transformed practice activities to which they are exposed at this level.[31]

In the words of Donnell, through innovative pedagogies 'early modern literary works have a crucial role to play in the teaching of language, of culture, and of genres as acts of communication'.[32]

Further examples can be devised by teachers and academics and shared to enable us to undertake the study of many classic works of literature with renewed creativity and flexibility. It is hoped that the case presented here has demonstrated how a literary classic written centuries ago remains relevant to present-day issues, generates constructive ethical and intercultural debate, and fosters the creation of transmedia texts.

The exercises described represent an attempt to marry theory and practice in order to show that canonical works can be made more engaging for students by applying skills belonging to the new participatory culture of the twenty-first century and the multiliteracies framework. The combination of the four pedagogical acts described in the framework proves an effective

---

31   Paesani, Willis and Dupuy, *A Multiliteracies Framework*, 43
32   Sidney Donnell, '*Don Quixote* in the Balance: Early Modern Studies and the Undergraduate Curriculum', in Lisa Vollendorf and James A. Parr, eds, *Approaches to Teaching Cervantes's Don Quixote* (New York: Modern Language Association of America, 2015), 197–205, 204.

tool to approach not just this particular classic text but many others also. As shown here, in the case of *La española inglesa*, the application of new angles and different media helps make this short story from the sixteenth century more accessible to our times and context, while at the same time aiding the development of intercultural skills.

JULES WHICKER

7 Technologically assisted translational activity: An approach to teaching Spanish Golden Age literature

ABSTRACT
To engage with a literary text, readers require some means of obtaining a mental purchase on it. As teachers of Spanish Golden Age literature, we try to provide such a foothold by linking the texts to ongoing societal narratives. We harness digital resources to ground the students in the material culture of the period, helping them visualize, situate and relate its referents graphically and geographically. This leaves us with the 'problem' of the text itself and of how to persuade students to swap haste for traction, skimming for immersion. One way to do this is through translation. Instead of teaching through or alongside a modern English translation, students translate sections of the Spanish source text for themselves, initially within peer groups and then independently. The translator's duty to understand before expressing requires thorough scrutiny of the text and motivates imaginative visualization, empathy in characterization, and confirmatory research, all of which renders them more appreciative or critical of English translations.

Introduction

This paper is based on a final-year module developed for the undergraduate Translation Pathway at the University of Birmingham, but the approach described here combines elements used previously in other modules, both in Hispanic Culture and Translation Studies. It presents in outline some ways in which the challenge of teaching literary texts from the Spanish Golden Age – texts that are linguistically, aesthetically and philosophically complex – may be addressed within an increasingly condensed and linear curriculum and to students who typically avoid close reading and careful analysis of such texts. As will be seen, a recent paper by Helen Brookman and Olivia Robinson on the use of original translation in the study of Old English poetry, which identifies translation as an act of interpretation that fuses critical judgements with creative thinking, offers both inspiration and complementary insights into this approach.[1]

Background

The principal challenge in engaging undergraduate students with Golden Age literature is often seen as a linguistic one, and more widely, one of literacy, by way of a mutually limiting lack of experience, skill, confidence and enthusiasm for reading.

In a world where everything is claimed and felt to be urgent, comprehension required and assumed to be instant, and memory regarded as increasingly redundant, it is no small challenge to find ways to promote the unhurried, detailed, incremental study of how meaning may be found in texts – and foreign-language ones at that – that were created in a world and at a time when people looked to the page and the stage rather than to screens of whatever size for compelling ways of passing their time, broadening their horizons, and developing their intellectual scope.

The meaning of words is so much harder to ascribe, of course, when we have scant or no familiarity with their referents in the material world, let alone within systems of thought or belief. Consequently, teaching programmes have for some time sought to bring the past closer to the present by making connections with the notable preoccupations of our own age: gender, race, nationalisms, religious conflict, new orthodoxies and the restriction of free speech among them. Activating these themes in the context of Golden Age studies reveals an area of study that is far from the remote, monolithic and impenetrable tabernacle of canonically sanctified imperial relics that some students might otherwise imagine.

An allied approach is to use the resources of the internet to emphasize the material culture of the Golden Age: the ever higher quality and greater

---

[1] Helen Brookman and Olivia Robinson, 'Creativity, Translation, and Teaching Old English Poetry', *Translation and Literature* 25/3 (2016), 275–97.

number of digital facsimiles of printed and manuscript texts provided by national libraries and international organizations; initiatives by museums and galleries to make available high-resolution digital reproductions of art-works; and universal tools such as Google Earth that provide the means to visualize, situate and relate monuments and locations graphically and geographically, all assist the student in visualizing elements of a text as they read it.

Visualization is commonly used as a technique in translation too. Somewhat in the manner of an actor interpreting a script, the translator creatively supplements the model for meaning derived from their research on the source text by drawing on their own experience to imagine a scene, a gesture, a mannerism, a tone of voice, and then seeks a form of words that expresses this in their target language.

This module will continue to evolve in response to students' interactions with it – the subject for a future paper. The scope of the present paper is thus to set out its methods and resources, without prescribing a particular sequence or weighting of activities.

A translational approach

This approach can be applied to the teaching of Golden Age texts. Instead of, or before, teaching the Spanish source text alongside a modern English translation, students can be asked to translate for themselves, initially with peer-support and then independently. There are several potential benefits to be derived from this. Investigating unfamiliar lexis and morphology develops a new flexibility in students' language skills that gives them greater confidence to deal with the previously unseen; and the translator's duty to understand in the source language before expressing in the target language motivates effective research, imaginative visualization, and empathy in characterization. As Brookman and Robinson put it: 'creative translation helps [students] to engage with and develop increased enthusiasm for the difficult and unfamiliar material, and to rise to the challenges of learning to interpret literary texts in their original languages'.[2]

---

2   Brookman and Robinson, 'Teaching Old English Poetry', 276.

Translation also obliges close reading: since each element of the source text must be considered, as the translator has to seek to understand meaning, purpose and effect at multiple levels. This is not simply for the sake of fidelity, but also because such an understanding gives them the flexibility to create a target text that is a re-creation and not merely a trans-codification of the source text. The creation of a target text through translation is a holistic process that involves understanding the concepts, interpreting the metaphors and re-writing of the source text. The work involved happens not just at a linguistic level but at every level.

The experience of translating poetry within an academic context is eloquently expressed by Poetry Professor Fiona Sampson, who describes it as 'a practice of interpretation' that is 'every bit as sophisticated as close critical reading', and who observes that in 'tracing the original poem's actual thought and music', she was engaging in 'the most precise, intimate reading' she had ever done.[3]

Furthermore, after working on extracts of the source text in this way, students are more willing and more able to engage with the text as a whole, and more likely to take an actively evaluative approach – by turns appreciative and critical – of texts by other translators. Moreover, through translational activity, the student shares in the creative processes of the author whose writings they interpret, as each makes innumerable interrelated choices in search of the representation that is at once most truthful and most compelling.

Limitations and opportunities

Recent changes in our curriculum have led to a radical reduction in the range of optional modules offered in Modern Languages, especially within Hispanic Studies, where many of these were literary. In consequence, a substantial number of early and early modern Spanish texts have been

---

[3] Brookman and Robinson, 'Teaching Old English Poetry', 275.

deleted from the syllabus. These include the anonymous *Auto de los Reyes Magos*, various *romances viejos* and *romances nuevos*, Calderón's *La vida es sueño* and *El gran teatro del mundo*, Cervantes's *Novelas ejemplares* and *La Numancia*, Juan de la Cueva's *El saco de Roma*, Juan del Encina's *Égloga de Plácida y Victoriano*, Lucas Fernández's *Auto de la Pasión*, Lope de Rueda's *Los engañados*, Bartolomé de Torres Naharro's *Comedia Himenea*, Gil Vicente's *Tragicomedia de don Duardos*, and three works by Lope de Vega: *La dama boba*, *El Caballero de Olmedo* and *Arte nuevo de hacer comedias*. Other previously taught works remain, but with less time allocated to them. Thus, *Lazarillo de Tormes* has undergone a 50 per cent cut from four hours to two; and the teaching of *Don Quijote* has been cut by 66 per cent from thirty hours to just ten. In the latter case, elements of Cervantes's masterpiece – chiefly those that concern its treatment of *morisco* Spain – are retained within a new co-taught module that goes under the title – somewhat ironically, given the circumstances, – of 'Histories of the Excluded'. Nevertheless, as the previous *Don Quijote* module involved introducing students to examples of chivalric and pastoral, and sentimental and picaresque novels, losses have been incurred there too.

There are a few new Golden Age additions to the syllabus, but the inclusion of these now depends on the extent to which a multi-disciplinary committee can be persuaded that undergraduate students will respond to them as accessible and relevant. Thus, *Lazarillo* clings on insofar as he represents the voice of the underclass, and by virtue of being short; whilst *Don Quijote* survives insofar as he is both iconic and subversive, and amenable to being served up in thematically selected chunks. Meanwhile, Lope's tenancy is renewed only at Calderón's expense, as *Fuenteovejuna*'s popular proto-feminist revolt unseats both Segismundo's philosophical transformation and Calderón's divine *teatrum mundi*. With the exception of some baroque *villancicos*, meanwhile, the remaining incomers are all from the realm of the visual arts: expressive in every way except verbally, a disconcerting observation in a language programme.

At the same time, however, our Translation Studies programme is growing, and creating room for new options in Year Four. On opportunity therefore exists to offer some teaching in Golden Age literature at this level. In addition to this, modules that foreground the development of skills in language on one hand and technology on the other are currently in favour with the driving forces of curriculum change, as well as being reasonably popular with students. As this paper will show, the technological resources for translators combine with those available to researchers in Hispanic studies to provide ample support for student learning.

Choosing a text

In designing this module, the first decision to take was what sort of text to focus on. The initial candidates were plays, *comedias* and *entremeses*, on account *inter alia* of their engagement with major religious, philosophical, and social themes, their ample stylistic and linguistic range, and the prominence of theatre and the theatrical within Spanish Golden Age culture; but also because good plays have the virtue of connecting with their audiences with unique immediacy.

Nevertheless, and arguably for these reasons, it seemed probable that Lope, Calderón and Tirso were effectively species of least concern in the undergraduate curricula of UK universities (although Stuart Davis's invaluable statistical investigation into this question indicates that in reality their situation is considerably more perilous), whereas the great poets of the period, Góngora, Quevedo, Garcilaso, to name just the most prominent, have been pushed to the verge of extinction.[4] This choice had a more positive aspect, too, drawing inspiration from Eavan Boland's description of Old English poetry as 'an archive of lost values and treasurable energies'.[5] The result of these deliberations was the selection of a poem: specifically Góngora's *romance* 'En un pastoral albergue'.

---

[4] See Stuart Davis's article 'The Golden Age in the Hispanic Studies classroom: The changing shape of what we teach our undergraduates in the UK' in this collection.

[5] Eavan Boland, 'On Translating Old English Poetry', in Greg Delanty and Michael Matto, eds, *The Word Exchange: Anglo-Saxon Poems in Translation* (New York: W. W. Norton, 2012), 525–6, 525, Cited in Brookman and Robinson, 'Teaching Old English Poetry', 276.

On the one hand, it offers the chance of playing some fashionable thematic cards: it depicts interracial relationships of love and hate, provocatively idealizes its female protagonist, presents a contrast between aristocratic expectations of privilege and the success of the marginalized, offers a geopolitical reading as the European Orlando contends with the African Medoro and obsesses about possessing the oriental Angelica, and may even be spun as a comment on Europe's role in the destruction of pristine natural environments. Beyond these particular issues, the appeal of the *romance* lay in its mediation between tradition and innovation, between familiar formulae and extraordinary novelty. In short, for all that it requires a knowledge of cultural and literary traditions, its value and its power lie in the way it obliges its reader to think differently. Simon Gaunt encapsulates this sense in his question: 'Shouldn't it in fact be *difficult* and *challenging* to access a different culture and isn't being confronted with the alterity of a strange language part of this process?'[6] Also striking was the intuition that the interpretative flexibility Góngora requires of his readers is akin to that required of the translator, who is similarly required first to anatomize and then to reassemble the source text in a process that reveals, generates and conveys meaning.

The module runs over one semester of ten teaching weeks, with two contact hours each week. When the module was first devised, it was assumed that this would prove to be more than enough time to introduce and practice the relevant resources and skills, and to build student's knowledge and understanding of the contexts and processes involved in the production, reception and translation of the *romance*, so a reserve of additional poems was selected in case the reach of the module needed to be extended and with a view to offering students a greater opportunity for independent study. These have yet to be used, but the next iteration of the module envisages accelerating the programme to create the space required for this activity.

---

6   Simon Gaunt, 'Untranslatable', in Emma Campbell and Robert Mills, eds, *Rethinking Medieval Translation: Ethics, Politics, Theory* (Cambridge: D. S. Brewer, 2012), 243–55, 254–5, cited in Brookman and Robinson, 'Teaching Old English Poetry', 277.

Objectives

Students taking the module are set the following objectives:

1. To engage imaginatively with unfamiliar poetic material from Spain's Golden Age.
2. To recognize the distinctive metrical features and poetic techniques used in the source text and to consider how they may be received by the reader.
3. To acquire a knowledge of the traditions within which the source text was created.
4. To evaluate previous translations from source-oriented and target-oriented perspectives.
5. To make a creative English-language translation of an early modern Spanish text.
6. To identify and deploy appropriate linguistic and scholarly resources.
7. To develop skills in creative and critical writing.
8. To reflect on the process of creating the target text, and to evaluate its success.
9. To work collaboratively and individually on achieving these objectives.

Methodology

The approach to the text comprises seven phases: induction, research, lexical analysis, collaborative translation, translation comparison, individual translation and a reflective essay. The first three of these phases also introduce students to a range of digital resources for researchers and translators.

Induction

From the outset, students are introduced to the principle that the translator should not translate anything they do not understand. The development of this understanding is mediated through the notion of translator competences. As well as the obvious 'language competence', recognized competences include something called 'information mining' – in which the translator identifies gaps in their knowledge or understanding and closes these through research – and 'technological competence' – in which the translator makes use of technological resources such as machine translation (MT) and online corpora to achieve this as efficiently and accurately as possible.[7]

To this end, students receive a presentation on these competences and on an initial set of technological resources to make them aware of their existence, what they can be used for, and how to use them. A second set is introduced later. The first set includes two types of resources: general and specialized. As regards the general resources, the objectives are to confirm that students know their way around the university library's catalogue via the Findit search engine, and to introduce them to Google Books, a form of search that many are not aware of. In respect of the specialized resources, students are guided through searches in the Internet Archive, the Biblioteca Nacional de España's Biblioteca Digital Hispánica, the Biblioteca Virtual Miguel de Cervantes (and its Góngora portal), and finally the *Todo Góngora* project created by José María Micó and his team at the Universitat Pompeu Fabra in Barcelona.[8] A specific objective here is to show students the texts

---

7   The range of competences that enable a professional translator to work successfully are discussed and tabulated with both thoroughness and clarity in a recent article on their applicability within the field of legal translation by Federica Scarpa and Daniele Orlando, 'What it takes to do it right: an integrative EMT-based model for legal translation competence', *The Journal of Specialised Translation* 27 (2017), 21–42.

8   Internet Archive (2018), <https://archive.org>; Biblioteca Nacional de España Biblioteca Digital Hispánica (2018), <http://www.bne.es/es/Catalogos/BibliotecaDigitalHispanica/Inicio/index.html>; Biblioteca Virtual Miguel de

on which modern editions are based, and the format in which its earliest readers could have encountered the poem. An additional benefit of visiting *Todo Góngora* is that it serves as evidence that Gongorine studies have an active online presence. This presentation and the supporting notes are available to students throughout the module via the Canvas Virtual Learning Environment (VLE).

Research

As soon as possible, however, students are given an active role, being organized into groups of two or three, each of which is assigned a modest research task on which to base a class presentation. Topics include: Góngora and *gongorismo*, the Angelica and Medoro episode in Ariosto's *Orlando furioso* (Book XIX, stanzas 16–37), the *Romancero nuevo* and Pastoral literature. Each assignment sets specific items to research, and specific sites and tools to use. Students are required to identify early and modern editions, to select critical studies for further reading, and to comment on the relative usefulness of the resources they have used. The members of each group use the VLE-hosted application Padlet to work collaboratively. Padlet is used for co-creating and sharing documents in a more user-friendly way than Google Docs. After the class the Padlet pages produced are linked to via Canvas for sharing and reference.

Lexical analysis

This phase moves on to the text of the poem itself and introduces students to a second series of online resources: this time for textual analysis, lexical reference and translation. These include some resources with which they are

---

Cervantes (2018), <http://www.cervantesvirtual.com>; *Todo Góngora*, Universitat Pompeu Fabra, Barcelona (2018), <https://www.upf.edu/todogongora>, all accessed 25 November 2018.

already familiar as language students, such as the comparative corpora of Linguee, Reverso and Wordreference, and the machine-translation (MT) engines of Google Translate and DeepL Translator, as well as two resources from the Real Academia Española that are generally unfamiliar to them: the monolingual *Diccionario de la Lengua Española*, and, even more importantly, the *Nuevo Tesoro Lexicográfico de la Lengua Española* (NTLLE), which provides uniquely extensive and flexible access to a comprehensive set of Spanish monolingual and bilingual dictionaries from the late fifteenth to the late twentieth century.[9]

The first resource to be used, however, is Voyant Tools.[10] This is an online suite of concordance tools, two of which fit our purposes: one that converts texts into word lists (Terms), and one (Cirrus) that can present these lists as word clouds in which each word is scaled and centred according to its frequency. Crucially, Voyant Tools enables the user to input a customized list of 'stopwords' that are then ignored by the program, allowing lexical elements whose frequency is higher than their semantic value, such as articles, pronouns, prepositions, and common verbs, to be screened out.

Terms tool is used to generate a word list for Góngora's poem, which is then copied to a Padlet page. Students work through this list individually, sorting terms into three categories: words they recognize, words they are unsure about, and words they do not know. After collating the results, items in the first two categories are discussed before terms from the third category are assigned to each group. Groups are then set the task of using NTLLE to find two pre-1800 definitions of each word in their section, choose the earliest one they found useful, write an English definition of their own, and add both to the Padlet page. This familiarizes them with using NTLLE and also alerts them to Spain's extraordinary lexicographical heritage.

Equipped with a better understanding of the lexis of the source text, the next tool used is Cirrus. Production of a word cloud leads into discussion of the relation between the frequency of a word's use and its significance.

9 RAE, *Diccionario de la Lengua Española* (2018), <http://dle.rae.es>; RAE, *Nuevo Tesoro Lexicográfico de la Lengua Española* (2018), <http://www.rae.es/recursos/diccionarios/diccionarios-anteriores-1726–1992/nuevo-tesoro-lexicografico>, both accessed 25 November 2018.
10 Voyant Tools (2018), <https://voyant-tools.org>, accessed 25 November 2018.

Cirrus lets the user manually adjust the weight given to each word, so each student is asked to look for lower-frequency words that they feel may be of equal or greater importance and to create their own version of the cloud to reflect this. Comparing the resulting clouds reveals interesting similarities and variations. Clouds are saved as jpeg images and shared via Padlet. Word clouds are not an end in themselves. By separating lexis from context and representing frequencies through position and scale, they facilitate reflection and prompt students to reconstruct the poem in their minds and rebalance the cloud accordingly.

Collaborative translation

The next step is to consider the translation of the *romance* as a text, and the balance between fidelity and accessibility. A reading task directs students to a selection of extracts from books and articles on the translation of literature and poetry and subsequent class discussion centres on the key questions of the different purposes and audiences the translation may have, and how the answers to these questions will affect the translation choices made. For example, is the English 'target text' meant to stand as a poem in its own right for a general reader of poetry, or as a simulacrum of Góngora's poem for a reader with a more focused interest, or as a guide to help students of Spanish literature meet the linguistic challenges of the poem? This leads into the question of what degree of ownership the translator may claim for the text they have created.

On the premise that the translation of a poem should be in verse, consideration is given to the comparative merits of different options: imitating the form of the Spanish octosyllabic and assonantal *romance* or adopting an established target-culture equivalent, such as the traditional English ballad measure, which would still feature quatrains and an ABAB scheme, but this time in full rhyme, with alternating tetrameter and trimeter, and with the option of an ABCB scheme. Conversely, a simpler solution may be preferred, raising the question of how much of the meaning of the source text lies in its form and what would be lost by subordinating form to image and narrative. In this way, the features of different verse forms can be identified and compared, and their effect considered. It will be apparent that the objective of translating the poem, and the practical and technological orientation that follows from this, are providing a pretext for the kind of close reading that was formerly a staple of literary study.

From this starting point, students are put into groups and asked to work on translating the first four quatrains of the *romance* whilst recording the principal problems they encountered and the ways in which they went about finding solutions to these, which they then present for discussion in class. They are encouraged to be as creative as they want, and to avoid thinking of the exercise as having a 'right answer'.

Translation comparison

Students are now introduced to the published translations of these stanzas made by Gamel Woolsey in 1951 (in Brenan) and by John Dent-Young in 2007, which are compared first with each other and then with the texts produced by the students.[11] These readings are then contextualized through consideration of a set of academic commentaries: Brenan and Dent-Young's introductions, extracts from relevant parts of Jones' (1966) edition, and material from the digital edition created by Carlos Ivorra of the Universidad de Valencia. Students prepare short presentations on these readings in which they are asked to assess how knowledge of this information may affect their translations.[12]

---

11   Woolsey's translations were created for Gerald Brenan's *The Literature of the Spanish People: From Roman Times to the Present Day* (Cambridge: Cambridge University Press, 1951).
12   John Dent-Young, ed. and trans., *Selected poems of Luis de Góngora: a bilingual edition* (Chicago: University of Chicago Press, 2007), 71–8; R. O. Jones, ed., *Poems of Góngora* (Cambridge: Cambridge University Press, 1966); Carlos Ivorra, *Todo Góngora*. <https://www.upf.edu/todogongora>, accessed 23 July 2018.

Individual translation and reflective essay

The remaining stanzas are divided between the students, who are required to produce their own translations and to write an essay reflecting on how the activities they undertook in the module helped them to complete the translation task. Both the translation and the essay are submitted as the summative assessment for the module, although the final mark is based solely on the essay.

Conclusion

The complexity of the process outlined above may seem disproportionate to the scale of the literary text at its heart – and the number of texts the approach is applied to is likely to be increased in future iterations – but a technologically assisted translational approach ensures that students engage closely with the content of the text selected for translation. The translational approach also ensures that students read actively instead of passively, and that they reflect on language and structure both within the source text and within the target text they are creating. This in turn helps them to engage with the cultural and intellectual dimensions of the source text.

As translators, students have to decide what each word, and each component of the text means and how it functions within the text, and they cannot afford to ignore or overlook anything. Nor can they leave gaps. They have to do it themselves, too, or in collaboration with the members of their group. They cannot leave it to the lecturer. Meanwhile, this more independent approach is supported by their new familiarity with an array of highly accessible and effective digital resources which can be usefully deployed in in all kinds of research and text production activities.

Through these activities, students can gain confidence and control, whilst activating essential skills for their personal development, independent learning and lifelong learning. As regards the technological element in this, the challenge is to ensure that functions as a practical toolkit for obtaining, evaluating and sharing information and a tool and does not become either an end in itself, or worse still, a barrier to understanding. The goal, after all, is to make it easier for students to focus on the imaginative and intellectual rewards of engagement with great literature.

PART III

Teaching poetry

KARL McLAUGHLIN

8 Meaningful parallels for students: Golden Age poetic production as examples of talent shows and celebrity spats

> I hear and I forget. I see and I remember. I do and I understand.
> — CONFUCIUS

ABSTRACT
Obstacles to effective engagement by university students with Golden Age texts include their knowledge deficit with respect to the historical, literary and cultural contexts underlying the texts. Poor understanding of content and context can lead to demotivation, thus decreasing the potential for learning. Establishing meaningful parallels between aspects of seventeenth-century Spanish culture and readily recognizable facets of contemporary culture can help speak to students more effectively. The present paper explores ways to harness students' familiarity with TV talent shows and social media squabbles between celebrities to connect them with analogous Golden Age phenomena, particularly literary academies/ poetry competitions and well-documented rivalries between famous figures. By helping students view the production of these key cultural phenomena through a prism to which they can relate more easily, a valuable foothold can be provided to stimulate their interest and encourage them to engage with Golden Age texts more actively and successfully.

Among the many experts who have succeeded in fostering a better understanding of the language and contexts of bygone periods is the British linguist and academic David Crystal, who is renowned for his methods for stimulating interest in Shakespeare among today's learners. As Crystal regularly emphasizes, Shakespeare is inconceivable for today's audiences without the Received Pronunciation accents of iconic actors such as Laurence Olivier, even if this is nothing like how such works were performed in their day. Successful strategies employed by Crystal to heighten student interest in The Bard and his period include, intriguingly, the revoicing of extracts with the pronunciation and accents in which the original plays would have been staged. In this way, students rediscover the original sounds of the playwright's work.[1] This type of learner-centred, rather than teacher-centred, learning – with a focus on what students do, rather than on what is being done to them – is the hallmark of effective learning.[2]

Part of the success of these and similar initiatives is passion for the subject and the ability to have students see things from a different and, even better, a surprising perspective. The manuals of inspirational teaching tell us much about this crucial aspect of education. As teachers, we always aim to display our passion and, hopefully, have that same passion motivate our students. We make our courses personal, demonstrating why we are interested in the subject matter and the research that underpins it. So far so good: the problem arises when students do not identify with that passion because the topic that inspires it in *us* seems remote and unconnected to *their* view of the world. This difficulty can be further compounded by the perception of a lack of direct applicability of the learning. Teachers and educators have grappled for years, particularly in the current climate of multiple competing interests, with the question of how to persuade students of the (joys and) benefits of learning about subjects they consider to be outmoded and of little practical use. Rather than read a course text before or in class, many students choose to devote their time to perusing updates on Facebook and other social media. Bridging the time and knowledge divides that separate today's immediacy-driven students from the periods they are required to study can therefore seem an insurmountable challenge.

---

1 On the history of academic interest in Shakespearean phonology, see David Crystal, 'Early Interest in Shakespearean Original Pronunciation', *Language and History* 56/1 (2013), 5–17. For a detailed insight into the potential (and challenges) of using popular modern-day resources such as YouTube for participatory Shakespeare teaching and learning, see Stephen O'Neill, *Shakespeare and YouTube: New Media Forms of the Bard* (London: Bloomsbury, 2014).

2 An interesting discussion of a recent international collaborative initiative to motivate young learners to engage with the literature of their own and others' countries, including through the creation of online comics, live videos and animations can be found in Geoff Walton, Mark Childs and Gordana Jugo, 'The creation of digital artefacts as a mechanism to engage students in studying literature', *British Journal of Educational Technology* 50/3 (2019), 1060–86.

Some preliminary words on motivation are appropriate at this juncture. As is commonly accepted, when faced with the opportunity to engage in a learning activity, a student determines, firstly, if the activity is one that is known to be interesting.[3] If it is, they engage in the activity. At the most basic level, to be intrinsically motivated means to complete a task because it is personally and internally rewarding, whereas to be extrinsically motivated means to complete a task for reward or to avoid punishment. Intrinsically motivated students work on tasks because they find them enjoyable. This intrinsic motivation can include, inter alia, a fascination with the subject, a sense of its relevance to life and the world, and a sense of accomplishment in mastering it. Among its many advantages, intrinsic motivation can be long-lasting and self-sustaining. Importantly, intrinsically motivated students are often deep learners who respond well when faced with a difficult and complex subject and are therefore a joy to teach. On the other hand, efforts at fostering such motivation can be slow to influence behaviour and usually require detailed and lengthy preparation.[4] The simple question 'What possible appeal might lie in Golden Age literature, beyond the appeal of getting a good mark?' is one that teachers of Spanish literature have pondered for years.[5]

At a very basic level, an obvious starting point – considering the gender make-up of a typical cohort of university students of Spanish – might be to devote more time to the study of female authors of the Golden Age. Yet by far the bulk of attention focuses on male authors, which is perfectly understandable if we bear in mind that 99 per cent of texts from the period were written by men.[6]

---

[3] See James A. Middleton, 'A Study of Intrinsic Motivation in the Mathematics Classroom: A Personal Constructs Approach', *Journal for Research in Mathematics Education*, 26/3 (1995), 255–7.

[4] On motivation, see, among others, Matt DeLong and Dale Winter, *Learning to Teach and Teaching to Learn Mathematics: Resources for Professional Development* (Mathematical Association of America, 2002), 163.

[5] See, for example, the special issue of *Calíope* on 'Teaching Golden Age Poetry', ed. Edward Friedman, 11/2 (2005).

[6] However, even scholars such as Barbara Mujica, who has done much to promote the cause of early modern women writers, acknowledge that a purely female focus would be a misrepresentation of the literature of the period and that there is no disputing the

Wolfgang Iser rightly draws the distinction between a contemporary reader, reading literature at the time it was written, and a historical reader, reading a text removed from the time it was written.[7] The task of engaging students therefore entails taking the text back to the time of writing to familiarize modern readers with the contexts in which it was produced. Clearly, dedicated Golden Age modules on undergraduate degree courses afford more time to stimulate interest and embed learning. However, an equally common scenario may be where the period, its literature and its culture have to be introduced in more general 'survey' modules. Needless to say, the approach will differ depending on the case.

One potentially useful way, in my opinion, would be not just to show what these contexts were but, where feasible, to draw comparisons with the real world or at least a world recognizable to our millennial students, one that includes talent shows, open mic evenings and, in general, 'putting oneself out there' using all available means. Was that so different to the seventeenth century? Could today's social media and similar phenomena prove the key to unlocking interest in a bygone age?

In essence, the question asked is 'What parallels, far-fetched or not, might be drawn to kindle student interest in Golden Age poetry?' For this, a cursory reflection on what captures young people's interest is needed. The ever-present TV in homes is an obvious starting point and a look at viewing figures for talent shows, coupled with the followings generated by associated social media spin-offs, indicates that such fascinations could be a valuable Trojan Horse.[8]

In terms of what drives wannabes to sign up to one or more of the current plethora of TV talent shows which adopt the same tried and tested formula across countless countries, various possible reasons have been advanced,

---

      value of maintaining the Golden Age canon: 'I do not envision undergraduate survey courses in which Leonor de Meneses replaces Cervantes or Angela de Azevedo supplants Calderón', in *Women Writers of Early Modern Spain. Sophia's Daughters* (New Haven, CT: Yale University Press, 2004), ix.

7   Wolfgang Iser, *The Act of Reading: A Theory of Aesthetic Response* (Baltimore, MD: Johns Hopkins University Press, 1978).

8   The metaphor is used here in the positive sense of a stratagem that causes a target to invite a 'foe' (the Golden Age, perceived as uninteresting) into its protected space.

including the performance experience, the desire to achieve industry exposure and the equally strong desire to build a fan base. Did similar motivations exist centuries ago? Granted, TV had not been invented but that is not to say there were no entertainment forums whose primary function was to uncover and showcase talent. Students brought up on a media-fuelled diet of talent shows would clearly have an interest in knowing which talent shows existed in seventeenth-century Spain.

Unequivocal evidence exists of the presence in towns and cities across Spain of established literary communities in the mid-seventeenth century. Poets interacted with other poets socially and intellectually, both in major cities and smaller locations. At a time when printing was still relatively rare and the amount of published poetry was much lower than the poetry that circulated in manuscript form, interaction often took the form of the direct sharing of verses among close friends.[9] Fast forward almost four centuries and we see a similar phenomenon, much more identifiable to the students of today, when only a small percentage of writings find their way into formal print. The 'labyrinth-like transmission flow' described by Frenk to refer to the ways in which Golden Age poetry passed from hand to hand can be likened to today's social media, with its restricted Facebook groups, not to mention Tweets and multiple retweets of words written by others.

There is every good reason to look at the lesser-known production of the day, particularly that generated by academies and poetry competitions, which were among the main talent show formats of Habsburg Spain, including Spanish dominions abroad. Authors such as Willard King and Jeremy

---

[9] 'El Siglo de Oro español fue una época de enorme actividad poética, una actividad que rara vez desembocaba en libros impresos y sí, frecuentemente, en manuscritos. El proceso de transmisión se ha venido describiendo así: garabateado por el poeta en un papel, el texto del poema era copiado por aficionados en papeles sueltos que, a su vez, volvían a copiarse y que eventualmente podían ir a dar, junto con otros, a un cartapacio y a un manuscrito de "Poesías varias de diferentes autores". Y este manuscrito, por su parte, servía para alimentar nuevas copias. En el curso de la transmisión el poema se desprendía casi siempre del nombre de su autor y circulaba anónimamente. Como casi nunca se conserva el texto original, lo que el editor moderno tiene frente a sí son los manuscritos y alguno que otro impreso, que manifiestan a las claras el laberíntico proceso de la transmisión'. Margit Frenk, 'Réplica a Antonio Carreira', *Acta poética* 34/1 (2013), 211–23.

Robbins, who have been instrumental in shedding light on the activities and popularity of Spain's literary communities of the century, have shown that many poets learned their trade by observing or taking part in academies and competitions, which saw a staggering amount of poetry produced to forge and maintain reputations.[10] As Carlos Gutiérrez reminds us, 'all writers pursuing social legitimacy in early modern Spain had first to fortify their social network, both in and out of the literary field'.[11] Cultivating social networks for status? Unheard of today!

The academies of Golden Age Spain adopted a wide range of forms, from sporadic and semi-permanent gatherings organized, in Robbins words 'wherever two or three poets were gathered together', to highly formalized literary circles sponsored by influential patrons.[12] To adapt the title of one of the most watched TV programmes in the United Kingdom, these events were very much a case of Strictly Come Versing.[13] Strict rules were imposed as regards verse forms, rhyme schemes and even grammatical rules (one academy, for example, obliged poets to end each line with an *esdrújula*). On many occasions, the exact wording of first and last lines of poems was determined by the organizers. Strict also were the topics, which ranged from the bloodletting of a lady's foot to more contrived and ridiculous situations which were outlined in the titles set.[14] Glosses, akin to some extent to personalized

---

10   Willard F. King, *Prosa novelística y academias literarias en el siglo XVII* (Madrid: R. A. E., 1967) and Jeremy Robbins, *Love Poetry of the Literary Academies in the Reigns of Philip IV and Charles II* (London: Tamesis, 1997).
11   Carlos M. Gutiérrez, 'The Challenges of Freedom: Social Reflexivity in the Seventeenth-Century Spanish Literary Field', in Nicholas Spadaccini and Luis Martín-Estudillo, eds, *Hispanic Baroques: Reading Cultures in Context* (Nashville, TN: Vanderbilt University Press, 2005), 137–61, 143.
12   Robbins, *Love Poetry of the Literary Academies*, 7.
13   *Strictly Come Dancing*, a British television dance contest featuring celebrity contestants, has been running for over fourteen years and draws weekly audiences of up to 13 million. Its Spanish counterpart, *¡Mira quién baila!*, has also been a major draw in Spain for many years in its different formats.
14   Robbins cites as an example the Hurtado de Mendoza ballad entitled 'Estando un caballero con una señora y una hija suya, avisaron que estaba allí un astrólogo, de que ella gustaba mucho, y fue necesario que se escondiese, y también la hija, y en la pieza a que se fue halló a la moza, que se ofendió de que hubiese entrado donde ella estaba', Robbins, *Love Poetry of the Literary Academies*, 86.

cover versions of well-known songs today, were also hugely popular.[15] The complicated rules imposed by academy and competition organizers tested wit and imagination to the limit through the thematic straightjackets established by the secretaries, often with the additional requirement that contributions address bizarre and even ludicrous situations.[16]

A favourite topic of academies was verse portraiture.[17] Given its rigid format and stock metaphorical associations, the *pintura* was an ideal test of a poet's wit and ingenuity. The published proceedings of academies of the period confirm the important place occupied also by burlesque variations of the portraits, which were even more popular as topics than their serious counterparts, often obliging participating poets to stretch their imaginations to resolve paradoxes or bizarre additional challenges set by the organizers.[18]

Just as in talent competitions, strict rules existed to ensure objectivity on the part of judges. Without going to present-day talent show extremes of having the judges turn their chairs around so as not to be influenced by anything other than participants' voices, careful steps were taken to ensure anonymity. The record of one academy held in the late seventeenth century to mark the canonization of St Francis Borgia offers an abundance of

15 Trevor J. Dadson, 'El arte de glosar: las "mudanzas" de Antonio Carvajal y la tradición barroca andaluza', in Trevor J. Dadson and Derek W. Flitter, eds, *La poesía española del siglo XX y la tradición literaria* (Birmingham: University of Birmingham Press, 2003), 125–53, 125–6.

16 'Within the academy, it is not only the poet's skill and ingenuity which is on show, but also that of the Academy secretary who has invented the topic', Robbins, *Love Poetry of the Literary Academies*, 72. Poets who failed to comply faithfully with the strict rules of the 'asunto' would often be named and shamed in the closing *vejámenes*.

17 For a detailed treatment of portrait verse in Spain, see Gareth Alban Davies, '"Pintura": Background and sketch of a Spanish seventeenth-century court genre', *Journal of the Warburg and Courtauld Institutes*, 38 (1975), 288–313.

18 For example, poets at the Academy in the home of Melchior de Fonseca de Almeida on 13 February 1661 were tasked with producing a 'Pintura de una dama hermosa, pintandola fea y dexandola hermosa', while the Academy hosted by Francisco de Borja y Aragón injected a local flavour into the proceedings by asking its members to come up with a 'Pintura de una fea, por apellidos de personas conocidas en Zaragoza'. See Aurora Egido, 'Las academias literarias de Zaragoza en el siglo XVII', in Manuel Alvar, ed., *La literatura en Aragón* (Zaragoza: Caja de Ahorros y Monte de Piedad de Zaragoza, Aragón y Rioja, 1984), 101–28, 121.

detail on all the arrangements, including the make-up of the judging panel and the rules for submission. These included the obligation to submit two unsigned copies (one for public display, one for the judges to consider), along with a third signed copy in a sealed envelope which was to be opened only when the judges had reached their decision.[19] The record of an earlier *justa* in honour of St Isidoro reveals that the names of the judges were not to be revealed in advance to prevent poets from trying to influence them ahead of the event.

It has been worth dwelling on the format and content of academies and competitions to draw out certain parallels which might to speak to the students of today. In general, the study of a representative sample of themes of academy verse could prove of interest as a means of encouraging engagement with Golden Age poetry and its contexts. Additionally, a cursory examination of a lesser-known academy would help establish the widespread popularity of these social and intellectual gatherings, while also revealing the degree to which poets in smaller locations were familiar with other academies, probably through travel or word of mouth.[20]

Having established potential parallels, the next question to address is how to bring these into the classroom. Here, multiple possibilities exist, including (bearing in mind the need to combine the acquisition of new knowledge with language learning and practice) the use of task-based learning

---

19 Ambrosio Fomperosa, *Días sagrados, y geniales, celebrados en la canonización de S. Francisco de Borja, por el colegio imperial de la compañía de Jesús de Madrid y la Academia de los más celebres ingenios de España* (Madrid: Francisco Nieto, 1672).

20 A section of Ms 17517 in the Biblioteca Nacional in Madrid contains 'Poesías Vurlescas a una academia de Plasencia', which are preceded by a lengthy request to the organizers by one of the participants. The manuscript record is valuable for the intertextual clues it provides concerning participants' awareness of the topics set for other academies, as evidenced by the humorous complaint to the academy president that one of the three topics chosen – 'A una dama que riyendose se le cayeron los dientes postizos' – had been doing the rounds for so long that half of it had been eaten up by woodworm. As the poetry of Anastasio Pantaleón de Ribera reveals, a fuller version of the topic was one of four set for a *certamen* organized by one of the most famous academies in Madrid, held at the home of Francisco de Mendoza in May 1626. Anastasio Pantaleón de Ribera, *Obras*, ed. Rafael de Balbín Lucas, 2 vols (Madrid: CSIC, 1944), II: 129.

approaches.²¹ After a small number of tutor-led seminars on general aspects of academies, *certámenes* and *justas*, students could be asked to imitate the style of the day and set *asuntos* – both serious and burlesque – for a fictitious academy. They could also judge poems from a real competition of the day, ranking the top three compositions in order and then matching their verdict with the actual results from published records of the gathering. They might even 'recreate' a seventeenth-century academy by performing the poems to an audience. More advanced groups could be tasked with composing short poems on a topic or completing missing lines from actual poems. *Pinturas* are also potential subjects of interest due to the present-day debate, driven largely by social media, surrounding the aesthetics of the female body and the beauty standards set for and by women. A study of a selection of Golden Age verse portraits offers an ideal opportunity to compare and contrast canons of beauty across periods and languages and, in passing, familiarize students with Petrarchan metaphor.

While some academies were regular affairs lasting considerable lengths of time, others were much shorter-lived, due in part to squabbles between rival poets.²² The concept of rivalry provides another useful angle through which to foster interest among today's students in the literature of the Golden Age, which was characterized by various high-profile feuds among renowned figures. Equally importantly, rivalry offers another Trojan Horse for the delivery of sessions on the main schools of poetic thought of the day. Everyone loves a scandal, a fondness that has remained unchanged down the ages. Turn any page of a popular newspaper or scroll down on any social media and one is guaranteed to see the latest developments in much-publicized quarrels between well-known figures. Katy Perry vs Taylor Swift, Lady Gaga vs Perez Hilton, Kim Kardashian vs Bette Midler, Russell Brand vs Donald Trump, Donald Trump vs Kim Jong Un … The list is endless.

Seventeenth-century Spain was no different, with considerable rivalry aired in private and in public between political figures. However, arguably the best-documented public squabble was of a literary nature and involved two

---

21   For an overview of the use of Task-based Learning, see Rod Ellis, *Task-based Language Learning and Teaching* (Oxford: Oxford University Press, 2003).

22   See, for example, Miguel Romera Navarro, 'Querellas y rivalidades en las academias del siglo XVII', *Hispanic Review*, 9 (1941), 494–9.

of the biggest names in the poetry of the age. As we all know – but students will not (yet) – the figureheads of two opposing aesthetic camps, Góngora and Lope de Vega, become embroiled in a long-running feud which went to the very heart of philosophies of poetry. Rather than approach the subject in a purely theoretical manner, with detailed lectures on the characteristics of *culteranismo* and *conceptismo*, or *populista* vs *elitista* forms of poetic composition, a fruitful way to embed the basic notions of each would be to focus on the actual feud and its ramifications. This might prove a stimulating avenue for students and even encourage self-study to establish the main figures in each camp. In addition, as we shall see, enmity and rivalry can be used to encourage exploration of other figures, including Cervantes.

Orozco Díaz's remark concerning Lope and Góngora – 'Cada uno se sentía observado por el otro y se mantenían así atentos a sus respectivas reacciones' – is an ideal starting point for a cursory look at an enmity that had poets and their patrons on the edge of their seats.[23] Although scholarship has moved beyond the binary classification of each as, respectively, the 'father of *comedia*' and 'father of *culteranismo*' (one representing *literatura mayoritaria* and the other *literatura de minorías*), and such pigeon-holing overlooks the numerous points of contact between the two, in terms of introducing students to Golden Age literature, the distinction can prove very helpful as a pretext for an overview of the two main schools of thought and of the importance attached to a debate that concentrated literary attention at the time.

Inaccurate as they may be, the aforementioned and simplistic antithetical oppositions are nonetheless useful if our aim is to provide brushstrokes for students on the essentials of a polarized debate. This is arguably better than muddying the waters for them by diluting the differences between the two poetic trends. Sweetening the pill of learning by focusing on sensationalism is, in this particular case, warranted. More importantly, if the content of a potentially dry subject has to be disguised in the form of polemic, so be it. As we shall see, it might even prove attractive to students in terms of encouraging additional work.

Just as Donald Trump and his North Korean counterpart escalated their political dispute to include attacks of a personal nature, the rivalry and

---

23   Emilio Orozco Díaz, *Lope y Góngora frente a frente* (Madrid: Gredos, 1974), 16.

mutual criticism between Góngora and Lope extended beyond purely literary aspects.²⁴ As is clear from the titles of several poems, little attempt was made to hide the identity of the enemy, an obvious example being Góngora's 'A la "Jerusalén conquistada" que compuso Lope de Vega'. In 'A la "Arcadia" de Lope de Vega Carpio', Góngora advises his rival to keep to what he is best at (theatre) and not engage with pastoral poetry, but the 'professional' attack is coupled with references also to Lope's adopted family crest and marriage to the daughter of a butcher.

Social media spats today indicate clearly the extent to which enemies monitor each other's posts and information closely. Similarly, the poetry of the seventeenth century reveals the detailed knowledge warring authors had of rivals' work. In some cases, a poet would include references to a rival's words in their own poem or even compose a parodic recreation (a form of satirical 'remake' today) of an enemy piece, inviting readers or, in oral performance contexts, listeners to compare the merits of each. A prime example is 'Ensíllenme el asno rucio' which pokes fun at Lope's 'Ensíllenme el potro rucio': the Góngora poem is only understandable with Lope's text uppermost in mind. In other words, such was the interdependence that they could not live without each other.

This, of course, was not the only rivalry between major literary figures of the day. Cervantes vs Lope was another well-known squabble. Here, students could be encouraged to engage in detective work to explore the reasons why close friends, said to have become acquainted in the home of Velázquez, became sworn enemies. A starting point would be to view the film by Manuel Huerga, *Cervantes contra Lope* (2016).²⁵ Students might also be tasked with identifying who cast the first stone in the dispute: was it Lope with his criticism of *Don Quijote* after being granted access to the work, as

---

24 Interestingly, Kim Jong-un's use of 'dotard' to describe his American adversary sparked a worldwide frenzy. Many rushed to consult the meaning of the term, which trended worldwide and spawned its own hashtag #dotard. An interesting exercise for students might to be trace the origins of terms used in poetic insult-trading in the Golden Age.

25 On the use of film and performance activities as a vehicle for kindling student interest in the drama of the period, see Charles Patterson, 'Lope on YouTube: Film Analysis and Amateur Video Production in a "Comedia"' *Hispania*, 98/3 (2015), 522–32. See also Duncan Wheeler, *Golden Age Drama in Contemporary Spain: The Comedia on Page, Stage and Screen* (Cardiff: University of Wales Press, 2012).

a friend, in advance of publication ('De poetas, muchos están en ciernes para el año que viene; pero ninguno hay tan malo como el Cervantes ni tan necio que alabe a Don Quijote')? Or was it Cervantes's displeasure at not having his *comedias* staged in Madrid, for which he blamed Lope's influence (hence his subtle jibe against *comedia* writers in *Don Quijote*)? Whatever the reason, the rivalry provides valuable material for an interesting study of clashing egos and of the transition from mutual praise to mutual hate. Parallels with contemporary swings in relationships, aired on social media, would be easy to establish and could be developed further through a student reconstruction of the insult-trading. Carrying out this activity using Twitter would add the extra (and very real-life) language challenge of condensing offences within a prescribed word limit.

To enable students to assume control of their learning, other task-based learning activities could be devised to further their knowledge of the literary contexts of rivalries. The opening lines of one of Quevedo's most scathing sonnets are ideal for an exercise in deciphering the malicious and belittling jibes, both personal and literary, hurled back and forward between poets. Just as today's spat-followers rush to check out the latest diatribes, followers of enemy poets would have been counting the days and hours to be able to access the latest instalments, including in manuscript form, of the war of words. These include the Quevedo sonnet, 'Receta para hacer Soledades en un día', which sets out all the ingredients needed to become a *culto* poet.[26] Additional ways of assisting with an understanding of the literary enmity and its various forms of manifestation would be to have students carry out further detective work and decipher the savage personal attacks in another famous Quevedo sonnet to his arch enemy, which opens with some of the best-known lines of the period's poetry:

> Yo te untaré mis obras con tocino
> porque no me las muerdas, Gongorilla,
> perro de los ingenios de Castilla,
> docto en pullas, cual mozo de camino.

---

[26] Such recipes may even strike a chord with a generation brought up on popular TV programmes such as *The Great British Bake Off*, which attracts weekly audiences of several million.

Meaningful parallels for students 153

Here, class exercises might consist of decoding the meaning of each line (the accusations of bad lineage, being a *converso*) and searching for evidence of anti-Semitism in the sonnet, including, of course, the 'nariz' of line 11, which provides a thematic link to other potential meaningful parallels for exploration.[27]

While fat shaming may not have been as popular as a phenomenon as it is today, particularly on social media such as Facebook and Instagram, public criticism of physical attributes in verse form was widespread in Golden Age Spain. Indeed, Góngora's aquiline nose featured much more prominently in another Quevedo poem, 'Érase un hombre a una nariz pegada', arguably his most famous burlesque sonnet. The witty piece provides ideal material for a creative class translation exercise, with individual or group renderings subsequently measured against the excellent version by Jorge Salavert, 'To a man with a big nose' (2008).[28] Belittling in seventeenth-century verse extended to physical stature also, with small men and women regularly targeted for attacks. The abundant examples in the poetry of the day make for interesting study, not just for the ingenious treatments of the popular topic, which was less a product of personal rivalry than a literary fashion practised in major cities and remote corners of the country, reflecting the pervasive nature of literary commonplaces, which was all the more impressive given the (by today's digital standards) slow forms of communication of the day.

A prime example of the conceptual wordplay deployed in such attacks is offered by a lesser-known author, the Extremaduran Catalina Clara Ramírez de Guzmán (1618–c. 1684), in a stylistically accomplished sonnet featuring abundant reversals of terms, compressed allusions and ingenious puns, all of which contribute to the goal of poking fun at the subject.

---

27   Examples include 'tocino' (l. 1), 'muerdas' (l. 2), 'perro' (l. 3), 'rabí', 'judía' (l. 10), 'escribas' (l. 13), 'sayón' and 'rebeldía' (l. 14).

28   The use of translation to help students focus on language and creativity can take multiple forms. A creative exercise (which also familiarizes students with verse forms, syllable counts and rhyme schemes) is to complete missing lines of a good English rendering of, for example, Lope's 'Un soneto me manda hacer Violante', of which multiple versions are accessible on Internet.

> Mirando con antojos tu estatura,
> con antojos de verla me he quedado
> y, por verte, Felicio, levantado,
> saber quisiera levantar figura.
> Lástima tengo al alma que, en clausura,
> la trae penando cuerpo tan menguado.
> Átomo racional, polvo animado,
> instante humano, breve abreviatura,
> di si eres voz, pues nadie determina
> dónde a la vista estás, tan escondido
> que la más perspicaz no te termina,
> o cómo te concedes al oído.
> En tanto que la duda se examina,
> un sentido desmiente a otro sentido.[29]

A second sonnet in the manuscript containing this piece (BNM Ms 3917, fol. 386r) by an unnamed author on the very same topic (and the same man, Francisco de Arévalo) constitutes a strong indication that the theme may well have been a topic set for a competition or academy context. The subject of tiny men and women was a particular favourite in academy poetry. The Academy held in the home of Melchor de Fonseca in Madrid (1663) included one on the subject of 'Un hombre pequeño de cuerpo', with submissions including a burlesque ballad by Antonio de Espinosa beginning 'Liendre metida en calçones'. The man's tiny size enables him to shelter from the sun in the shadow of a fly, with the author adding further 'No has sido mala yerba / porque no has crecido nunca'.[30]

The tiny man theme extended also to epitaphs, another important but understudied characteristic of baroque poetry and an equally fertile area to

---

29 For a recent edition of this author's verse, see Catalina Clara Ramírez de Guzmán, *Obra Poética*, eds Aránzazu Borrachero Mendíbil and Karl McLaughlin (Mérida: Editora Regional de Extremadura, 2010). As noted above, given the gender profile of a typical cohort of students of Spanish, an increased presence of female authors may help counter the perception of a male-dominated portfolio of literary figures studied.

30 *Academia que se celebró en casa de Don Melchor de Fonseca de Almeida, en cuatro de febrero, siendo Presidente él mismo, Secretario Don Juan de Montenegro y Neira, y Fiscal Don José Berné de la Fuente, Aposentador de su Majestad, en la real Junta de Aposento* (Madrid: Francisco Nieto, 1663), fol. 35r.

Meaningful parallels for students 155

kindle interest among modern-day students.[31] Examples that spring to mind include Jacinto Alonso Maluenda's 'Epitafio a un hombre muy pequeño', which opens 'Tilde con alma imagino / que fuera la enana figura / que ocupa esta sepultura / más corta que un vizcaíno'.[32] Here, parallels with English poetry could be drawn to assist with student learning. As Claire Bryony Williams reminds us, 'epitaphs, some originally copied from tombstones, some composed solely for the page, also appeared in large numbers in printed poetry miscellanies suggesting that 17th-century readers wanted to read epitaphs alongside other popular forms such as the sonnet and the epigram'.[33]

Needless to say, obscure poets were a popular target of witty epitaphs, with arguably the most famous of all such epitaphs being Quevedo's *silva* against Góngora, which brings us back once again to the rivalry that conditioned much of poetic production in the period:

> Este que, en negra tumba, rodeado
> de luces, yace muerto y condenado,
> vendió el alma y el cuerpo por dinero,
> y aun muerto es garitero; [...]
> Éste a la jerigonza quitó el nombre,
> pues después que escribió cíclopemente,
> la llama jerigóngora la gente. [...]
> Fuese con Satanás, culto y pelado:
> ¡mirad si Satanás es desdichado!

Here too it is not difficult to imagine possibilities for active student engagement, for example, by identifying the attacks, both direct and veiled, on Góngora in the epitaph or, at a more advanced level, composing an epitaph in the style of the seventeenth century and beginning 'Aquí yace'.[34]

---

31   Sagrario López Poza, 'El epitafio como modalidad epigramática en el Siglo de Oro (con ejemplos de Quevedo y Lope de Vega)', *Bulletin of Hispanic Studies*, 85/6 (2008), 821–38.
32   Jacinto Alonso Maluenda, *Bureo de las musas del Turia en prosa y en verso* (Valencia, 1631).
33   Claire Bryony Williams, 'Manuscript, Monument, Memory: the Circulation of Epitaphs in the 17th Century', *Literature Compass* 11/8 (2014), 573–82.
34   Again the poetry of Alonso Maluenda offers an excellent model in the shape of his 'Epitafio a un poeta culto' (beginning 'Yace aquí un versificante'), which features in a number of anthologies of satirical verse.

Capitalizing further on student interest in put-downs, a return to the academy contexts discussed earlier would allow exploration of a little-studied aspect of these popular literary gatherings: the closing *vejamen*. In its widest sense, the term meant any form of satire publicizing a person's physical and moral shortcomings. However, it had another, very specific meaning also: by the seventeenth century, the *vejamen* had become a formal component of academies and poetry competitions. In this eagerly awaited last piece of business on the agenda, a poet of reputed wit would deliver an oral satire on the participants and even on the academy itself. British and American students brought up on the blunt and controversial criticisms levelled at contestants in popular talent shows such as *American Idol* and *Britain's Got Talent* will readily identify with seventeenth-century Simon Cowell figures expertly proclaiming their scant regard for lacklustre performers.[35] The records of poetic competitions are replete with humorous attacks that would bring a smile to Cowell's face today. The attacks could refer to the quality of the poets' work, their reputation, their physical appearance, or a combination of all three, as the humorous put-down by Jerónimo Cáncer in his published *vejamen* of a 1640s Madrid Academy indicates.[36]

To sum up, as this contribution has endeavoured to illustrate, various aspects of Golden Age poetry which tend to receive less attention on university degree programmes offer multiple opportunities for creative, stimulating study by students, whether on dedicated Golden Age modules or as part of more general approaches to Spanish literature. The extensive possibilities offered by the richest period in Spain's literary history can and should be seized to encourage students to engage more actively with their learning. While standard lecture approaches are crucial for providing structured

---

35 Similar figures identifiable by Spanish students include the scathing Risto Mejide on shows such as *Tú sí que vales* and *Got Talent España*.

36 'Vimos junto a nosotros un hombre tan feo que nos atemorizó; y mi camarada, que hasta entonces no había hablado palabra, dijo: ¡Jesús sea conmigo, y qué cosa tan infernal! ¿Quién es ese hombre tan feroz? – Este es D. Juan de Zabaleta, le respondí yo; es excelente poeta y ha escrito muy buenas comedias, aunque le sucedió un desmán en la comedia de *Aún vive la honra en los muertos*, que fue tan mala como esta redondilla dirá el suceso de aquel día: 'Al suceder la tragedia / Del silbo, si se repara, / Ver su comedia era cara, / Ver su cara era comedia'. Juan Carlos González Maya 'Vejamen de D. Jerónimo de Cáncer. Estudio, edición crítica y notas', *Criticón* 96 (2006), 87–114.

content and academic analysis of canonical authors and major themes, these can be complemented by additional thinking-outside-the-box strategies to stimulate interest, including seeking meaningful parallels capable of capturing the imagination of student cohorts hooked on present-day phenomena, including social media. Learning by doing through varied, creative and non-mechanical tasks can prove highly productive in retaining enthusiasm for subjects that, at first glance, may seem remote and of little value.

Transmission and performance of verses in the form of academies and competitions; rivalries and squabbles in lines as opposed to on-line; belittling satires and epitaphs; female participation, etc.; all can be included in novel approaches to the study of the period's poetry in a stimulating way to demonstrate to students the wealth of learning to be gained by spending time on a subject that may not hold much appeal initially but which, on closer inspection, constitutes a rewarding investment of time and effort. The published works of authors appearing on reading lists of literature courses are but the tip of an iceberg compared to the actual verse production of the century. Connecting old materials with the interests and realities of today's learners through meaningful parallels can prove an effective way of encouraging them not just to dip their toes in the water of Golden Age poetry but to take the plunge and explore aspects below the icy surface to gain a surprisingly refreshing experience. As the approach and examples outlined above seek to demonstrate, bringing unfamiliar perspectives to familiar themes enables us to offer a more accurate picture of early modern poetry and the contexts in which it was penned.

ANTONIO CARREÑO-RODRÍGUEZ

9 Golden Age 'diss tracks': Teaching Baroque poetry and polemic through rap

> En Andalucía la imagen popular llega a extremos de finura y sensibilidad maravillosas, y las transformaciones son completamente gongorinas.
> — FEDERICO GARCÍA LORCA, 'La imagen poética de don Luis de Góngora'

ABSTRACT
Much has been made of the rivalry between Baroque poets Luis de Góngora, Lope de Vega and Francisco de Quevedo. This personal antagonism and literary feud was fuelled further by reciprocal poetic insults and a heated debate over the relative merits of *cultos* and *llanos*. This paper presents this polemic from the perspective of contemporary popular music, where personal and aesthetic clashes are often distilled in so-called 'diss tracks', songs primarily intended to disrespect antagonists via satire and parody. This trend, already present in the music of John Lennon and Paul McCartney, following the controversial breakup of the Beatles in 1970, has become increasingly common in hip-hop since the 1990s. Music by NWA, Tupac Shakur, Ice Cube, Nas and Jay-Z will be analysed and discussed as a pedagogic point of entry to the presentation of seventeenth-century poetry and poetics.

The study of early modern Spanish literature, culture and language demands that students step outside of their preconceived notions of meaning and, instead, submit themselves to a set of historical realities, aesthetic and political criteria that are often unfamiliar. For this reason, it is essential to situate the specific texts under scrutiny within a historical, philosophical, and social framework. No less important in this regard is to encourage students to consider the normative contexts out of which their own worldviews are formed, and to experiment with a wide range of interpretive approaches. Such efforts not only open their minds to new cultures and ideas, but also offer them multiple vantage points from which to reflect upon their own. In the process, they are challenged to explore the relevance of critical inquiry and the value of dialogue across cultures and academic disciplines. In each of my classes I strive to bring the language of literary and cultural analysis to life by emphasizing the real-world applications of the concepts and issues we study. To this end, I work to provide examples learners can easily grasp and consistently urge them to seek opportunities for similar application in their lives outside the classroom. In the introduction to literary and cultural analysis that is a prerequisite for upper-division courses, I ask students to use the narrative techniques present in traditional comedy, tragedy and romance to interpret contemporary films and television shows, and to consider the consequences of such shifts in content and context. Similarly, traditionally rarefied subjects such as poetics and metrics are considered in the scrupulous analysis of canonical literary works, to be sure, but also in the music of contemporary pop artists. For the purpose of introducing rhetorical figures, I ask them to look for brand name products and advertisements that employ such devices. The range of examples provided by my students for synesthesia (an air freshener named 'Light Touch', a nail polish called 'Mountain Air', and the house paint 'Icy Wind') attests to the success of such endeavours. My objectives here are to dissolve traditional notions of high and low cultures, advance their intellectual engagement with cultural and literary texts of all types, and to encourage them to think perceptively about the world they inhabit.

Likewise, when discussing the intense rivalries that existed among Spanish Baroque poets, dramatists and novelists, the various personal and aesthetic considerations that divided them, as well as the satirical pieces these feuds elicited, I ask students to draw parallels between these specific textual and contextual circumstances with hip-hop's numerous rap wars or 'beefs'. As occurred in seventeenth-century Spain, these modern-day quarrels are often distilled textually, publically, in so-called 'diss tracks', songs primarily intended to disrespect one's adversary.[1] Such references are often more

---

[1] '*Dis*, once an exclusive term of hip-hop language, has become entirely mainstream, even used by candidates for public office and sexagenarian talk show hosts. This word, while derived from standard English terms in which *dis-* functions as a negative prefix (e.g., *disrespect, dismiss,* etc.), gathered its meaning in the social context of interpersonal rejection, or what another generation might have referred to as "putting someone down"', Imani Perry, *Prophets of the Hood: Politics and Poetics in Hip Hop* (Durham, NC: Duke University Press, 2004), 26.

accessible to students and serve to impress upon them the basic contemporaneity of texts that might otherwise seem chronologically and culturally remote.[2] Yet, beyond mere gimmick seeking to enthuse young learners, a comparative approach of this kind, which crosses languages, genres, periods, and national lines, generates scrutiny that might otherwise be neglected by more traditional methodologies. Indeed, the analysis of early modern Spanish lyrical production alongside that of American hip-hop, from the perspective of rivalry and polemic, offers an excellent entrée into oft-overlooked themes and practices common to both traditions: the kinship between music and lyric, the influence of literary and musical circles upon individual creativity and regional identity, the significance of competitive orality, and the interdependence between homophobic and misogynistic discourse and masculine self-fashioning. More commonly broached topics in Golden Age seminars, such as intertextuality, imitation, parody, anti-Semitism, and the use of poetic masks, are also cast in new light by means of this cross-cultural, inter-epochal approach.

An initial point of entry into such an examination might be the study of tropes in lyrical composition. In this regard, we can design and compile a corpus of Spanish Golden Age texts that, alongside their hip-hop counterparts, display satire and parody. This series might be comprised of poems that pit Baroque masters against one another in rich intertextual relations that reference and often openly exhibit differences of style, technique, and creative personality: the works of Lope de Vega, Francisco de Quevedo and the so-called Castilian School, for example, as well as those of Luis de Góngora and his numerous '*nueva poesía*' followers, on the peninsula and

[2] Luis Avilés reminds instructors of the pitfalls associated with drawing anachronistic parallels across epochs and cultures. He suggests that recognizing the differences that separate us from the culture and time period we scrutinize is also an invaluable tool for learning, in 'Poesía y diferencia cultural: prácticas para el estudio de textos poéticos de los Siglos de Oro', *Calíope* 11/2 (2005), 7–19, 16. Edward H. Friedman challenges us to make the material interesting and relevant, while respecting the historical contexts, in 'Teaching Golden Age Poetry: The Old and The New', *Calíope* 11/2, 2005, 59–68. These two articles appear in the volume *Calíope* dedicated in 2005 to *Teaching Golden Age Poetry* 11/2, which included several other thought-provoking essays that have helped delimit the scope of our essay. Our intention here is to build upon the theoretical foundations and pedagogical strategies outlined in this volume.

in the colonies.³ The hostile polemic that ensued following the publication of the Cordoban's *Fábula de Polifemo y Galatea* in 1612 and his *Soledades* a year later, were distilled in personal and aesthetic terms, in both prose and verse: in *dedicatorias*, rhetorical treatises, commentaries, and epistles; in ballads, *letrillas, silvas, canciones, décimas*, and sonnets.⁴ Among the most ardent detractors of this new poetics as practised by Góngora and his acolytes, were the advocates and poetic practitioners of a more classical, less embellished, Petrarchan style (*estilo llano*): Lope, Quevedo and the brothers Argensola, Lupercio Leonardo and Bartolomé Leonardo.⁵ Additional genres, authorial

3   Among Góngora's early devotees and apologists, José García Salcedo Coronel, the erudite editor of a 3-volume tome of the *Polifemo* (1629), is worthy of note. Also José Pellicer, the author of *Lecciones solemnes a las obras de don Luis de Góngora y Argote* (1630), and Cristóbal de Salazar Mardones who wrote *Ilustración y defensa de la fábula de Píramo y Tisbe* (1636). Gabriel Bocángel, Pedro Soto de Rojas, Anastasio Pantaleón de Ribera, Francisco de Trillo y Figueroa, Salvador Jacinto Polo de Medina, Miguel Colodrero de Villalobos and don Juan de Tassis y Peralta, the Count of Villamediana, were also followers of this aesthetic. In Aragon, Juan de Moncayo was its great champion; in Mexico, Sor Juana Inés de la Cruz; and in Peru, Juan de Espinosa Medrano. *Culteranismo* also influenced the theatre of Calderón de la Barca and the religious oratory of Hortensio Félix Paravicino.
4   For Maria Grazie Profeti, the satirical sonnet constitutes a 'micro-genre' of Baroque literature, comparable to the amorous sonnet, the *carpe diem* sonnet, or the funerary sonnet. The satirical modality was often employed in the two bitter disputes regarding literary modernity: 'la de la comedia nueva a la manera de Lope y la de la "nueva poesía" según la fórmula de Góngora', 'El micro-género de los sonetos de sátira literaria y Quevedo', *La Perinola* 8 (2004) 375–95, 375. The satirical sonnets of Lope and Góngora were gathered and analysed by Joaquín de Entrambasaguas in 'Góngora y Lope o examen de un desprecio y de una admiración', *Punta Europa* 65 (1961), 40–59 and Emilio Orozco Díaz, *Lope y Góngora frente a frente* (Madrid: Gredos, 1973), 96–139; 312–81. On Lope and Quevedo's personal, ideological and literary affinities, see Antonio Carreño-Rodríguez, 'Leyendo a Quevedo: Lope', *La Perinola* 14 (2010), 197–220, and Antonio Sánchez Jiménez, 'Quevedo y Lope (poesía y teatro) en 1609: patriotismo y construcción nacional en la *España defendida* y la *Jerusalén conquistada*', *La Perinola* 17 (2013), 27–56. More recently, Lindsay G. Kerr has studied the poetics of parody in Góngora and Lope in *Luis de Góngora and Lope de Vega: Masters of Parody* (Woodbridge: Tamesis, 2017).
5   María Cristina Quintero notes that, 'modern criticism has rectified the traditional critical opposition between *gongorismo* (or *culteranismo*) and *conceptismo*', *Poetry as Play: 'Gongorismo' and the 'Comedia'* (Amsterdam: John Benjamins, 1991), 78.

attributions and other participants, could further extend this complex web of contextual and intertextual relations.⁶

The most notorious hip-hop rivalry drawn along geographical lines, and which produced scathing lyrics reminiscent of those exchanged between *culteranos* and *conceptistas*, was the infamous East Coast–West Coast feud of the mid- to late 1990s. Though the focal points of this rap war gravitated around West Coast-based Tupac Shakur (aka 2Pac) and East Coast rapper the Notorious B. I. G. (aka Biggie Smalls or simply Biggie), both ill-fated artists were, like their early modern predecessors, part of wider, regional creative circles, represented by musicians associated with their record labels: Sean 'Puffy' Combs' New York-based Bad Boy Records, and Dr Dre's Los Angeles-based Death Row Records. At stake in this coastal rivalry was an issue of style and content, in short, aesthetics. Hip-hop's rugged New York roots, founded upon DJs scratching old soul or funk records while the emcee improvised or recited lyrics in a dark, confessional mode, was now being challenged by a new subgenre emerging from California: *Gangsta rap*. Consisting almost

---

Within the traditional view, Menéndez Pelayo, went so far as to claim that there was 'nada más opuesto entre sí', *Historia de las ideas estéticas en España* (Madrid: Centro de Investigaciones Científicas, 1994 [1940]), vol. 2, 325. Later critics, such as Dámaso Alonso and Alexander Parker, maintained that wordplay, wit, and verbal conceit underlie all poetic practice during the Baroque. Though this facile categorization may have become obsolete for critical purposes, Carlos M. Gutiérrez reminds us that there is still no denying the existence of a personal and poetic rivalry between two opposing literary circles, personified in the figures of Góngora and Quevedo: 'Este consenso actual de la crítica de que existía una *homogeneidad* de base en la poesía de ambos no ha de llevarnos a negar que existieran diferencias poéticas entre ellos ni a negar lo que efectivamente *dicen* determinados textos', *La espada, el rayo y la pluma: Quevedo y los campos literario y de poder* (West Lafayette, IN: Purdue University Press, 2005), 63.

6 The Gongorine polemic elicited all manner of literary and critical responses, as attested by the rich semantic field of titles, in favour, against, and impartial: *examen, comentario, ilustración, anotación, lecciones, censura, apología, defensa, parecer, escrutinio*, etc. Both Robert Jammes, 'Apéndice II: La polemica de las *Soledades*, 1613–66' in Luis de Góngora, *Soledades* (Madrid, Castalia, 1994), 607–719 and Mercedes Blanco, 'La polémica en torno a Góngora, 1613–30. El nacimiento de una nueva conciencia literaria', *Mélanges de la Casa de Velázquez. Nouvelle série* 42/1 (2012), 49–70, provide extensive catalogues of texts involved in the anti-Gongorine polemic, which lasted from 1613 to 1666.

entirely of rolling bass-lines and drums, this new poetics featured themes and lyrics that generally celebrated the gangster lifestyle of South-Central Los Angeles. It also portrayed racial profiling and police brutality in a raw, unsparing fashion. Many, if not most, rap artists of this tendency openly boasted of their associations with various street gangs as part of their image, the Bloods and Crips being the most commonly represented. In the wake of NWA's 1988 debut studio album, *Straight Outta Compton*, the West Coast became the dominant region in hip-hop, prompting the envy and animosity of the East, as reflected in the virulent lyrics of New York rapper Tim Dog's 'Fuck Compton,' the original diss track that precipitated the feud: 'Take your jheri curls! Take your black hats! / Take your wack lyrics and your bullshit tracks! / Now you're mad and you're thinkin' about stompin'? / Well, I'm from the South Bronx; fuck Compton!'[7]

The creation of an early modern Spanish corpus, then, might include the seventeen lyrical compositions José Manuel Blecua gathered under the heading *Sátiras personales* in his edition of Quevedo's poetry.[8] To this anti-Gongorine inventory, we might also add the *décima* 'Dice don Luis que me ha escrito' with its clear echoes of Martial's epigram on Cinna as well as the celebrated sonnet 'Érase un hombre a una nariz pegado', though here the reference to his rival is remote, at best.[9] In addition to alluding to Góngora's

---

7   Song lyrics were accessed via Genius.com, though spelling and punctuation are often amended to more faithfully render the original.

8   Francisco de Quevedo, *Obra poética*, ed. José Manuel Blecua (Madrid: Editorial Castalia, 1999), vol. 3, 227–49. Jammes was the first to cast doubt regarding Quevedo's production of this corpus, a topic subsequently treated by others. María José Tobar Quintanar enumerates the numerous problems associated with establishing firm authorship and with dating this corpus in 'Los poemas antigongorinos de Quevedo: defensa de Lope y ataque al estilo *ad personam* de Góngora', *Castilla. Estudios de Literatura* 4 (2013) 177–203.

9   Francisco de Quevedo, *Obra poética*, IV, *Teatro y traducciones poéticas*, ed. José Manuel Blecua (Madrid: Castalia, 1985). In her philological analysis of this corpus, Tobar Quintanar summarizes Quevedo's critique of Góngora's new poetic language as follows: 'Su portentoso dominio de las técnicas conceptistas permitió a Quevedo decir también en verso lo que él mismo y otros manifestaron en prosa: el fracaso de la obra grave del cordobés, la confusión y oscuridad de su nuevo lenguaje, su ininteligibilidad, la vaciedad de su contenido, la simpleza de su composición, su ruptura de la poética

inattention to his responsibilities as a man of the cloth, to his weakness for card-playing and gambling, a distinguishing rhetorical feature that typifies Quevedo's verbal assault on Góngora is, of course, the latter's association with a *Converso* lineage. Thus in the sonnet that begins, 'Yo untaré mis obras con tocino / porque no me las muerdas, Gongorilla, / perro de los ingenios de Castilla, / docto en pullas, cual mozo de camino' (ll. 1–4). Angry at the Cordoban's derision of his *Anacreón castellano*, Quevedo contemptuously quips at his rival's alleged Jewish ancestry: '¿Por qué censuras tú la lengua griega / siendo solo rabí de la judía?, / cosa que tu nariz no lo niega. // No escribas versos más, por vida mía; / aunque aquesto de escribas se te pega, / por tener de sayón la rebeldía' (ll. 9–14). Arellano, Profeti and Tobar Quintanar link such anti-Semitic accusations with the prevalence of scatological and homophobic allusions associated with the anus, excrement, the dilogy *puerco*, and related semas that evoke dirtiness, darkness, stickiness.[10] This rich lexical field serves also to identify Góngora with sodomy (sonnets 826, 828, 836, 837, 841) and, by extension, the *culter-ano* with heresy, as this neologism is a composite of the words *culto* and *luterano*.

Homophobia and anti-Semitism also feature prominently in Ice Cube's controversial 1991 diss track 'No Vaseline', aimed at former NWA bandmates Eazy-E, Dr Dre, MC Ren and DJ Yella, and their long-time manager Jerry Heller. The song's vindictive and ferocious lyrics accuse co-founders of Ruthless Records, Easy E and Heller, of exploiting the group's naiveté and swindling their profits, represented lyrically as homosexual rape: '[You] tried to diss Ice Cube; it wasn't worth it! / 'Cause the broomstick fit your ass so perfect / Cut my hair? Naw, cut them balls, / 'Cause I heard you like giving up the drawers! / Gang-banged by your manager fella / [who's] getting money out your ass like a mothafuckin' Ready Teller'. And again, later, when referencing an NWA track that had previously labelled Ice Cube a traitor:

---

clásica y su consideración como vicio que los jóvenes poetas deberían aborrecer', 'Los poemas antigongorinos', 186.

10   See Ignacio Arellano, 'El soneto de Quevedo "Sulquivagante pretensor de Estolo": ensayo de interpretación', in Sebastian Neumeister, ed., *Actas del IX Congreso de la Asociación Internacional de Hispanistas* (Frankfurt am Main: Vervuert, vol. 1, 1989), 331–40; Profeti, 'El micro-género de los sonetos', 392–4 and Tobar Quintanar, 'Los poemas antigongorinos', 196–9.

'Ay, yo, Dre, stick to producing! / [You] calling me [Benedict] Arnold, but you "Bent-a-Dick": / Eazy-E saw your ass and went in it quick! / You got jealous when I got my own company, / But I'm a man and ain't nobody humpin' me!' In addition to accusing the group of 'selling out', that is, of abandoning their urban roots and hardcore aesthetic for the sake of greater profit and white, middle-class respectability, Ice Cube depicts the relationship between Heller and Eazy as that of plantation master and house slave, the latter willingly conspiring with his owner to exploit his peers: 'Now I think you a snitch; / [Y'all should] Throw a house nigga in a ditch! / Half-pint bitch, fucking your homeboys, you little maggot!: / Eazy-E turned faggot, / With your manager fella / Fuckin' MC Ren, Dr Dre, and Yella!' Intertextual references to Alex Haley's *Roots* and to Kunta Kinte's brutal transformation into Toby by means of a vicious whipping serve to further associate band members with emasculated field slaves and loss of identity. The suggestion that they revolt against their oppressors, by lynching Easy E and murdering their 'White Jew' manager, sparked outrage amongst anti-defamation groups.

Lope, who unlike Quevedo – and Ice Cube – tends to avoid invective and *ad hominem* attacks, might correspondingly be represented in our corpus by a handful of poems that satirize the new style by means of parody: 'Inés, tus bellos ya me matan, ojos', plays upon the Gongorine penchant for hyperbaton, while the sonnets 'Pululando de culto, Claudio amigo', 'Conjúrote, demonio culterano', 'Cediendo a mi descrédito anhelante', '– Pluma, las musas, de mi genio autores' and '– Boscán, tarde llegamos. ¿Hay posada?', all ridicule the unintelligibility of the *cultos*' verse as well as their widespread use of ornate neologisms.[11] In the latter poem of this series, Boscán and Garcilaso, the Castilian founders of the harmonious, Petrarchan lyrical mode, are received at an inn by a gibberish-talking maidservant, presumably bitten by the *culterano* bug. Upon hearing her abstruse speech, the two weary travellers deduce that they must have lost their way and now find themselves astray in the Basque Country: '– Boscán, perdido habemos el camino; / preguntad por Castilla, que estoy loco / o no habemos salido de Vizcaya'

---

11   Profeti highlights the salient features of Lope's satirical sonnets: parodic imitation of the *culteranos*' extravagant vocabulary and syntax, intertextual references to rival poems, and the frequent use of dialogue, 'El micro-género de los sonetos', 387.

(ll. 12–14). In 'Conjúrote, demonio culterano', an exorcism is performed upon a possessed youth whose communication has been corrupted by a *culterano* demon. When commanded to exit the delirious boy ('– ¡Habla cristiano, perro!', l. 12), the evil spirit spits out a series of incoherent utterances that betray his heathen origins. The lyrical voice of Burguillos (Lope's burlesque alter ego) rouses his indolent quill to transcribe the 'versos sencillos' of his muses' dictation in '– Pluma, las musas, de mi genio autores'.[12] Upon realizing that his instrument has become rebellious and will only write in the fashion of Góngora's *Polifemo* ('rimas sonoras', l. 4), the poet threatens him with 'tijeras y cuchillos' (l. 6). The quill's refusal to bend to his master's will in the final tercet stages the irresolvable opposition of the competing poetics.

The sonnet 'Livio, yo siempre fui vuestro devoto', constitutes a metaliterary statement on Lope's poetics of clarity by juxtaposing the disparate temperaments that underlie the prevailing aesthetics of *llanos* and *cultos*: 'vos, en amor, como en los versos, duro, / tenéis el lazo a consonantes roto. // Si vos imperceptible, si remoto, / yo blando, fácil, elegante y puro; / tan claro escribo como vos escuro; / la Vega es llana y intrincado el soto'.[13] Orozco attributes to Lope the response sonnet which begins 'Pues en tu error impertinente espiras', in which the poetic voice describes an ailing, senile Góngora, 'padre de los cultos desvaríos' (l. 13).[14] If 'Seas capilla, plumas o bonete' also belongs to *el Fénix*, as this scholar contends, it would constitute

---

12   For Profeti, 'la escisión del sujeto poético es funcional en la polémica anti-cultista de Lope', 'El micro-género de los sonetos', 386.
13   Lope de Vega, *Obras completas. Poesía II: Rimas, Rimas sacras, Rimas humanas y divinas del licenciado Tomé de Burguillos*, ed. Antonio Carreño-Rodríguez (Madrid: Fundación José Antonio de Castro, 2004), 638. The opening lines of this sonnet appear to reflect a sentiment similar to that which Lope expresses in his *Respuesta* to the *Papel que escribió un señor de estos reinos a Lope de Vega Carpio en razón de la nueva poesía*, published in *La Filomena* (1621). Though at first the celebrated playwright praises Góngora's early verse 'en aquel estilo puro', he appears to regret somewhat the Cordoban's transition toward a new poetic language: 'Mas no contento con haber hallado en aquella blandura y suavidad el último grado de la fama, quiso … enriquecer el arte y aun la lengua con tales exornaciones y figuras cuales nunca fueron imaginadas ni hasta su tiempo vistas', Lope de Vega, *Obras completas. Poesía IV: La Filomena, La Circe*, ed. Antonio Carreño-Rodríguez (Madrid: Fundación José Antonio de Castro, 2004), 311–12.
14   Emilio Orozco Díaz, *Lope y Góngora frente a frente* (Madrid: Gredos, 1973), 328.

his most scathing verbal assault on the Cordoban, labelled 'bellaco, picarón, amujerado' (l. 11) and, along the lines of Quevedo's numerous homosexual and anti-Semitic indictments, 'cornudo y puto por la quinta especie / y por la ley antigua chamuscado' (ll. 13–14).[15]

The rap genre is most often auto-biographical in nature and realist in mode. Yet, as Imani Perry reminds us, we must not conflate life and art: 'artists tell about their lives, and it is the task of the critic to avoid making one-to-one correlations between music and the artists, to avoid a venture into some strange brand of artistic determination'.[16] This brings to mind yet another literary convention that links these two corpora rhetorically: the poetic mask or persona. Lope's numerous alter egos (Pánfilo de Luján, Belardo, Zaide, Jacinto, etc.) and pseudonyms (Tomé de Burguillos) often serve to conceal autobiographical reference within specific generic modes: the pastoral, the Moorish, the courtly, the burlesque.[17] Similarly, the violent, hyper-masculinist, underworld character types portrayed by some emcees in their lyrics (the gangster, the hustler, the dealer or pusher, the player or pimp) function as symbolic images of skill, courage, power, and control. Dwayne Michael Carter, Jr, better known professionally as Lil Wayne, has crafted dozens of monikers to this effect: 'Tommy Gun Tunechi, Trigga Man, the Warden, Weezy the Don, Young Pimpin', to name but a few.

Rap pseudonyms can also signal a deliberate reshaping of one's creative identity. Tupac Shakur's transformation from 2Pac to Makaveli, on the posthumous *The Don Killuminati: The 7 Day Theory* album, for example, reflects the rapper's newfound political intent following his 1996 release from prison. The son of prominent Black Panther leader Afeni Shakur, who named him after eighteenth-century Peruvian revolutionary Túpac Amaru, the artist's appropriation of Italian humanist and political thinker Machiavelli reflects

---

15   Orozco, *Lope y Góngora*, 111.
16   Imani Perry, *Prophets of the Hood: Politics and Poetics in Hip Hop* (Durham, NC: Duke University Press, 2004), 91.
17   On the dangers of resorting to biographical fallacy in order to reveal the intentions and veiled references behind Lope's many lyrical masks, see Antonio Sánchez Jiménez, *Lope pintado por sí mismo: Mito e imagen del autor en la poesía de Lope de Vega Carpio* (Woodbridge: Tamesis, 2006).

his latest attempt at propagating a 'Thug Life' mentality within the Black community. Extending the Panther's Ten-Point Program, Makaveli's lyrics in tracks like 'White Man'z World' seek to galvanize the inner city, overcome senseless gang violence, and unite the Black nation against their racist oppressors: 'Proud to be Black, but why we act like we don't love ourselves? / [...] Know what it means to be Black, [...] / We still strugglin' in the White man's world. / [...] can't you see that we under attack?'

Finally, we must include within our corpus of Baroque texts the series of scathing poems attributed to Góngora that explicitly lampoon Quevedo, Lope, as well as the latter's works and admirers. In the sonnets 'Anacreonte español, no hay quien os tope' and 'Cierto poeta, en forma peregrina', classical, geographical, and religious references, cloaked in sarcastic wordplay, serve to mock Quevedo's excessive drinking, trademark glasses, false erudition, and clubfoot. In addition to personal invective, references to Lope in Góngora's poetry are also often intertextual. As Quintero observes, in his burlesque sonnets Góngora 'establishes himself as an astute and informed reader of Lope's works'.[18] The sonnet 'Vimo, señora Lopa, su Epopeya' blatantly profanes Lope's *Jerusalén conquistada* under the guise of false praise. A favourable reception of this religious epic on the Third Crusade is placed in the mouth of a Portuguese-speaking African slave whose mixed speech and wild associations are farcical in the extreme. In 'A cierto señor que le envió *La Dragontea* de Lope de Vega', the lyrical voice suggests that Lope's epic on the life and death of Sir Francis Drake falls short of its lofty intentions: 'para ruido de tan grande trueno / es relámpago chico: no me ciega' (ll. 5–6). Couching the poetic rivalry in geographical terms that opposes 'la musa castellana' (l. 9) with Andalucía (represented metonymically by the Roman name for the Guadalquivir), the poet invokes Apollo in the last tercet, that the Greek god of artistic creation might rouse him from his indolence and inspire colorful verse: '¡Oh planeta gentil, del mundo Apeles, / rompe mis ocios, porque el mundo vea / que el Betis sabe usar de tus pinceles!' (ll. 12–14). In 'Patos de la aguachirle castellana', the poet equates Lope and his followers to a coarse flock of quacking ducks from the backwaters of

---

18 Quintero, *Poetry as Play*, 56.

Castile.[19] When exhorted to bow before the more sophisticated quills of the *culto* swans and their Attic verse, the vulgar birds dart away, seeking to plunge back into the stagnant waters from which they came.

Hip-hop's first rap 'beef', the so-called 'Bridge Wars' of the mid- to late 1980s, arose from a dispute regarding the true birthplace of the genre, pitting the South Bronx's Boogie Down Productions, led by lead rapper KRS-One, against the Juice Crew, hailing from Queensbridge. In the series of diss tracks prompted by this inter-borough feud, rap emcees, like Lope and Góngora, occupied self-proclaimed positions as representatives of their community, neighborhood, or crew, often emphasizing the importance of defending the honour and integrity of one's home turf, of 'repping,' that is, 'representing one's hood'. In this regard, *XXL* columnist Brendan Frederick reminds us that hip-hop was once a local phenomenon: '[m]ore than just a voice of the ghetto, hip-hop at its best [was] the voice of specific blocks, capturing the distinct tone and timbre of an artist's environment.' The feud began with Marley Marl and MC Shan's track 'The Bridge,' which recited the praises of their home borough and some of its earlier rap crews, later taken by KRS-One and his crew to imply that Queens was where hip-hop had begun. In response, BDP released the track 'South Bronx', which sang the praises of their 'hood' and made the argument for it being the real birthplace of hip-hop. The track also directly threatened MC Shan with lyrics like: 'the rhymes you wrote was wack, / So you think that hip-hop had its start out in Queensbridge?, / If you popped that junk up in the Bronx, / you might not live!' A follow-up track, 'The Bridge is Over' employs homophobic epithets inflected by a Jamaican accent to emasculate their rivals and further qualify their style as weak: 'Because Shan and Marley Marl dem-a-rhymin' like dey gay / pickin' up the mic, mon, dem don't know what to say: / Saying that hip-hop started out in Queensbridge!'

In the sonnet 'Por tu vida, Lopillo, que me borres,' Góngora mocks *La Arcadia*'s pretentious bookcover, with its exaggerated family crest emblazoned

---

19   Joaquín de Entrambasaguas suggests the anonymous author of 'Patos de la aguachirle castellana' is, in fact, Cervantes, *Estudios sobre Lope de Vega* (Madrid: CSIC, 1946), vol. I, 115. For the sonnet's attribution to Góngora, see Orozco, *Lope y Góngora*, 124–6. The *soneto de cabo roto* that begins 'Hermano Lope, bórrame el soné-' has also been attributed to both Góngora and Cervantes, undoubtedly because of the latter's felicitous execution of this irregular form in the preliminary verses of *Don Quijote*.

with umpteen turrets, and pleads with the celebrated playwright to abandon the lofty mode of pastoral verse and return to his popular, low-brow theatre: 'vuelva a su oficio, y al rocín alado / en el teatro sáquenle los reznos' (ll. 10–11). The poem ends by punning on Lope's pitiful aristocratic pretensions and his most recent marriage to Juana de Guardo, the daughter of a wealthy meat purveyor: 'No fabrique más torres sobre arena, / Si no es que ya, segunda vez casado, / Nos quiere hacer torres los torreznos' (ll. 12–14). Góngora again sarcastically puns on Lope's self-interested relationship with Juana in 'A ti, Lope de Vega, el elocuente'. This time he maliciously conflates her father's trade in the slaughterhouse with *el Fénix*'s prolific virtuosity and commercial impulse: 'repentino poeta acelerado, / morador de la fuente del mercado / sustentado con sangre de inocente. // Hanme dicho que dices de repente, y que de tu decir estás pagado' (ll. 2–6). Apollo and the lofty Muses deny the plebeian Lope their praise in 'Después que Apolo tus coplones vido'. Following Clio's flight from the poet's substandard attempt at satire, the lyrical voice urges him to forsake courtly verse and return to the common stage: 'Deja las damas, deja a Apolo y tente; / pide perdón al pueblo que enojaste' (ll. 9–10). In the sonnet '"¡Aquí del Conde Claros!", dijo, y luego' a Homeric catalogue of Lope's major works summons an assemblage of unsophisticated devotees: *cien rapaces, un ciego, un lanudazo lego, dos dueñas incapaces, tres monjas locuaces, un fray borrego, un cura de aldea, un idiota*, etc.

Góngora's 'Embutiste Lopillo, a Sabaot' parodies and, in fact, improves upon Lope's awkward rhyme scheme based on exotic Old Testament names in the sonnet 'Alfa et Omega, Jehová'. But where Góngora best displays his mastery of the parodic mode is in the *romance contrahecho* 'Ensíllenme el asno rucio', a burlesque re-writing of Lope's Moorish ballad that begins 'Ensíllenme el potro rucio'. As in his sonnets, the Cordoban derides *el Fénix*'s urbane pretensions to cultivate courtly lyric by degrading – carnivalizing in Bakhtinian terms – the original text: in place of Lope's majestic colt of the first verse, Góngora substitutes a lowly ass; the valiant Moorish knight Azarque becomes the lowborn mare-breeder Galayo; and the highborn lady, Adalifa la de Baza, gives way to the rustic Teresa la del Villar. Facile homonyms and platitudes abound while erotic and scatological references serve to debase the original poem's idealism and refined chastity.[20]

20   Orozco cites both ballads in full and offers a biographical interpretation of each, *Lope y Góngora*, 30–9. See also Robert F. Ball, 'Góngora's Parody of Literary Convention'

In the diss track's predilection for ego assassination, the humiliation of one's opponent and oeuvre is combined with a demonstration of an emcee's cleverness and verbal dexterity. Often this is displayed through parody and pastiche. In the context of the infamous East Coast–West Coast feud of the mid-1990s, the release of LA-based Tha Dogg Pound's 'New York, New York' (1995) triggered a response song, not unlike Góngora's 'Ensíllenme el asno rucio'. Indeed, the refrain in Capone-N-Noreaga's 'LA, LA' (1996) reproduced several of the original song's lyrics, mimicking also its rhyme scheme, cadence, delivery and flow. The chorus in 2Pac's 'Hit 'em Up', which repeats the phrase 'Take Money!', spoofs that of rival Junior M. A. F. I. A's, featured in their first single, 'Player Anthem': 'Make money!'

Reference to other artists and to their songs constitutes a signature feature of hip-hop's intertextuality, particularly within the context of a 'beef'. During their much- publicized battle, Jay-Z attacked his former mentor Nas in a celebrated composition titled 'Takeover'. Alluding to the disparate quality of the poet from Queensborough's scanty production, he pleads with his cross-town rival to: 'Use your brain! You said you've been in this for ten? / I've been in it five. Smarten up, Nas! / Four albums in ten years, nigga? I could divide: / That's one every ... let's say two; two of them shits was doo, / One was "nah", the other was *Illmatic*. / That's one-hot-album-every-ten-year average. / And that's so ... lame!' Nas responded in kind, in 'Ether', by mockingly imitating Jay-Z's earlier, quick-tongue delivery, prominent amongst emcees in the early 1990s, and by accusing his protégé of stealing his rhyme style: 'I rule you. *Before, you used to rap like the Fu-Schnickens. / Nas designed your Blueprint, who you kidding? / Is he 'H to the izz-O, M to the izz-O'? / For shizzle*, you phony, the rapping version of Sisqo. / And that's for certain: you clone me!'

Nas' last line reflects hip-hop's preoccupation with creative originality and authenticity. In NWA's 'Real Niggaz', released following Ice Cube's departure, the group denounces their ex-band member's perpetuation of their aesthetic: 'But, how the fuck you think your rap would last, / With your ass saying shit that is said in the past? / Yo, be original; you're shit is

(PhD dissertation. New Haven, CT: Yale University, 1976), 256–386, and Robert Jammes, *La obra poética de Luis de Góngora y Argote*, trans. M. Moya (Madrid: Castalia, 1987), 121–5.

sloppy. / Get off the dick, you motherfucking carbon copy!' It also targets would-be-imitators of the *gangsta* genre they helped develop: 'All these niggas with the gibber gabber, / But couldn't kill a fly with a motherfuckin' sledge hammer. / Gangsters in black are out there, / But only because, yo, it's the shit that we wear! / [...] Trying to be like us, sound like us, dress like us ...' 2Pac's 'Hit 'em Up', which contains explicit insults aimed at several East Coast rappers, accuses Shakur's former friend turned rival, the Notorious B. I. G., of appropriating his self-indulgent, sumptuous image: 'Now it's all about Versace: you copied my style!' In 'Doe Rae Me' Eminem joins the 50 Cent/Ja Rule beef, by berating the latter. He imagines the moment Ja's record label, Def Jam, created a new image for him following the murder of rap icon Tupac: 'You's a motherfuckin' actor, / slash 'Pac, impersonating rapper. / [...] How it happen? / Artist and repertoire, saw him in action: / Pac assassination; Def Jam grabbed him, told him: "Reenact him, you'll go platinum!" [...] // You Mockeveli; get your own identity!'

A similar concern expressed by Lope within the context of the Gongorine polemic reveals the limits of the Renaissance practices of *imitatio* and *aemulatio* and reflects a shift, perhaps, toward more modern notions of originality and artistic creativity. In his *Respuesta* to the *Papel que escribió un señor de estos reinos ... en razón de la nueva poesía*, published in *La Filomena* (1621), Lope laments the ignorant abuse of Góngora's imitators: 'a muchos ha llevado la novedad a este género de poesía, y no se han engañado, pues en el estilo antiguo en su vida llegaron a ser poetas, y en el moderno lo son el mismo día; porque con aquellas trasposiciones, cuatro preceptos y seis voces latinas o frasis enfáticas, se hallan levantados a donde ellos mismos no se conocen, ni aun sé si se entienden'.[21] Citing the case of Justus Lipsius' new Latin imitators, which undoubtedly must have classical rhetoricians Cicero and Quintillian turning in their graves, 'así, los que imitan a este caballero producen partos monstruosos, que salen de generación, pues piensan que han de llegar a su ingenio por imitar su estilo'.[22]

It is important to note that the satirical and parodic tradition within early modern Spanish verse is not born of personal animosity and competing

---

21   Lope de Vega, *Obras completas. Poesía IV*, 313.
22   Lope de Vega, *Obras completas. Poesía IV*, 313.

poetics alone. Indeed, the lyrical feuds propelled by the *nueva poesía* polemic are part of a much broader cultural and poetic spirit of competition that emerges out of the Late Middle Ages in the *jochs partits* of the troubadours, and that is later expressed and codified in the *cancioneros*, a tradition within which Lope and Góngora actively participated.[23] The *gallos universitarios o vejámenes de grado* of academic circles along with the more popular and democratic *certámenes* or *justas poéticas* are also part of this dynamic scene in which Lope acted as one of the latter's principal promoters.[24] These communal spaces and cultural practices share numerous affinities with the emcee battles of early hip-hop talent shows. The early modern practice of composing poetry spontaneously or *de repente*, often in the form of a *glosa* or *décima espinela*, has its modern day analogue in music sampling and the improvisational nature of freestyle rap.[25] Indeed, as in the battle or diss song

23 See the assemblage of *canciones* attributed to Góngora and Lope compiled and studied respectively by Miguel Querol Gavaldá in *Cancionero musical de Góngora* (Barcelona: Consejo Superior de Investigaciones Científicas, Instituto Español de Musicología, 1975) and *Cancionero musical de Lope de Vega* (Barcelona: Consejo Superior de Investigaciones Científicas, Instituto Español de Musicología, 1986–91). On Lope's presence in the *cancionero*, see also Rafael Ramos Nogales, 'Lope de Vega en el "Cancionero del Barón de Claret"', *Anuario Lope de Vega* 5 (1999), 199–212.
24 In *Quevedo y su tiempo: la agudeza verbal* (Barcelona: Crítica, 1992), Maxime Chevalier describes several rhetorical devices associated with the *vejamen* employed by Quevedo in his satire, principally equivocation and caricature based on nickname. Entrambasaguas studies Lope's participation in the *Justas* celebrated in Toledo and Madrid in 'Lope de Vega en las Justas poéticas toledanas de 1605 y 1608', *Revista de literatura* 32/63–4 (1967), 5–104 and 33/65–6 (1968), 5–52. María Soledad Carrasco Urgoiti analyses the importance of the *vejamen de academia* within early modern literary culture in 'Notas sobre el vejamen de academia en la segunda mitad del siglo XVII', *Revista Hispánica Moderna* 31 (1965), 97–111. Luis Miguel Godoy Gómez studies the emergence and growth of *Justas poéticas* in Seville in *Las Justas poéticas en la Sevilla del Siglo de Oro* (Sevilla: Diputación de Sevilla, 2004), while Aurora Egido considers their celebration in Aragon and their relationship with writing, 'Literatura efímera: oralidad y escritura en los certámenes y academias de los Siglos de Oro', *Edad de Oro* 9 (1988), 69–87. Juan Delgado provides a useful, albeit outdated, bibliography on *Justas poéticas* in 'Bibliografía sobre justas poéticas', *Edad de Oro* 7 (1988), 197–207.
25 This consideration brings to mind Don Quijote's lucid conversation with don Diego de Miranda's son, the Salmantine student don Lorenzo, concerning the strict rules of the poetic gloss and the biased nature of academic judging (II, 18).

(or its precursor, the African-American folk practice of playing the dozens), the *decimero* often would satirize an adversary extemporaneously, challenging the target to respond in kind, thereby setting up a song duel that tested the originality and wit of contending composers. This tradition lives on in Latin America.

Lastly, the transition from the ephemerality of oral performance to the permanence of mechanical reproduction are equally distinguishing features of both traditions. Indeed, like early Spanish lyric, hip-hop as an art form lies at the crossroads of literature and music. And while the development of the printing press led to widespread production, distribution and circulation of poetic texts in sixteenth-century Spain, advancements in recording technology (i.e. eight-track tape, compact audio cassette, and vinyl record) had a similar effect on the early dissemination of rap songs in the 1980s. Also germane is, of course, the consuming public. The *flores, cancioneros, romanceros,* and *silvas* of the sixteenth and seventeenth centuries, crafted and printed with a well-to-do readership in mind, contrast with the more inexpensive and widely diffused *literatura de cordel* tradition and the *pliegos sueltos*. In today's music industry, albums, anthologies, collections, and compilations, produced by a prominent record label and in studio, differ widely from the early hip-hop practice of lending or peddling mixed tapes on the street.[26]

One might consider framing the juxtaposition of these varied corpora within the cultural turn in the Humanities and the historical development of cultural studies as an interdisciplinary enterprise within the academy; the work of Richard Hoggart, Raymond Williams, E. P. Thompson and Stuart Hall is seminal. Yet one need not abandon the Hispanic tradition in order to find theoretical formulations that challenge hierarchical notions of culture and aesthetics. In his 1926 conference on 'La imagen poética de don Luis de Góngora', Federico García Lorca rejects the formalistic parameters of traditional literary study and its elitist distinction between high and low culture. Desiring to recover Góngora's much-maligned second phase, Lorca knocks the Cordoban's poetry off its 'high art' pedestal by associating

---

26   See María Cruz García de Enterría, *Sociedad y poesía de cordel en el Barroco* (Madrid: Taurus, 1973) and Antonio Rodríguez-Moñino, Arthur Lee-Francis Askins and Víctor Infantes de Miguel, *Nuevo diccionario bibliográfico de pliegos sueltos poéticos, siglo XVI* (Madrid: Editora Regional de Extremadura, 1997).

his extravagant language with popular, Andalusian wit and verbal acuity: 'Buey de agua y lengua de río son dos imágenes hechas por el pueblo, y que responden a una manera de ver ya muy cerca de don Luis de Góngora'.[27] Here Lorca anticipates one of the cornerstones of the Birmingham School's legacy: the scrutiny of both canonical and non-canonical objects in a *relational* rather than a *hierarchical* fashion. This is what we have attempted to do by analysing early modern Spanish poetry, its academic and court circles, alongside contemporary rap songs, in its origins the product of a subordinated 'youth subculture'. Students, particularly those marginalized by the values of the dominant culture, surely benefit from a comparative approach that promotes close reading, critical thinking and the continuous reflection of their own conditions of existence. Finally, this model need not limit itself solely to lyric. Arguably, the greatest rivalry of the Golden Age was fleshed out in the pages of the three *Quijotes*: Cervantes, that 'old school' advocate of Aristotle's *Poetics* versus the irreverent, new darling of the Spanish stage. Of course Lope, considered a 'sell-out' by several of his contemporaries, had a formidable crew. Think Avellaneda.

---

[27] Federico García Lorca, 'La imagen poética de Luis de Góngora', *Obras completas* (Madrid, Aguilar, 1972), 62–85, 63.

RUBÉN CRISTÓBAL HORNILLOS

10 La poesía clásica a través de canciones actuales

[Teaching classic poems through contemporary songs]

ABSTRACT
The present chapter explores the use of contemporary songs from a broad range of genres including pop, rock, rap, reggae and reggaeton as a bridge to connect students with well-known and lesser-known texts from early Spanish literature. It draws on work conducted for a doctoral thesis at the University of Zaragoza, where an innovative project was developed to harness the literary content of songs in order to create a genuine dialogue that helps students identify new intertextuality-based relationships, thus increasing their motivation to engage with older materials. In class, the songs are discussed initially using the 'Tell Me' approach (Chambers, 2007) before proceeding to a detailed analysis of their literary content and a comparison with a range of Early Modern texts. Of fifteen interactive teaching units used in a successful literary education pilot scheme with Polish secondary school students of Spanish, two specific examples of how mystical poetry can be approached through reggaeton and pop are outlined briefly.

Introducción

Los alumnos de literatura española no parten de la nada, sino que conocen, leen y, sobre todo, escuchan fuera del aula muchos textos que componen su universo cultural y estético. Un canon adolescente que vinculamos en esta propuesta con la tradición literaria para que comprendan y, sobre todo, aprecien todo lo que comparten con esta: desde el lenguaje hasta los temas, motivos y recursos poéticos, es decir, la literatura.

La música contiene literatura. Las canciones pop, rock, rap, reggae o reggaetón que escuchan los jóvenes se componen de métrica, rima, temas, tópicos literarios y figuras poéticas que proceden de la tradición literaria.

Grupos y cantantes como Nach, Macaco, El Kanka, Dani Martín, Wisin y Ozuna, Enrique Iglesias, Juanes, Alejandro Sanz, Bebe, La oreja de Van Gogh y Rozalén, entre muchos otros, beben de autores como Jorge Manrique, Garcilaso de la Vega, Santa Teresa de Jesús, Fray Luis de León, San Juan de la Cruz, Quevedo, Góngora, Lope de Vega, Calderón de la Barca y Sor Juana Inés de la Cruz.

Objetivos

Esta propuesta responde a la necesidad de buscar vías metodológicas alternativas para la educación literaria tanto en los niveles de Educación Secundaria Obligatoria como universitarios, especialmente en lo que se refiere a la introducción de la literatura clásica.

El objetivo de esta propuesta didáctica consiste precisamente en explotar didácticamente los contenidos literarios que comparten las canciones y las obras clásicas para facilitar a los alumnos un diálogo que amplíe su sentido estético y su competencia literaria. Dicho de otra manera, conectar los gustos y conocimientos previos de los alumnos con la literatura española del currículo académico. De este modo, se puede aprovechar todo lo que comparten las canciones que escuchan los jóvenes como un 'potente enganche' con la tradición literaria para conectar los gustos y los conocimientos de los alumnos con el currículo de literatura.

Metodología

La educación literaria basada en canciones introduce los contenidos literarios de la poesía española clásica a través de las canciones que escuchan los alumnos (métrica, rima, esquemas, temas, tópicos literarios, vocabulario y recursos literarios).

Se trata por tanto de una metodología intertextual y multidisciplinar que se fundamenta en los principios del aprendizaje significativo de Ausubel, que propone usar la realidad y los conocimientos previos del alumno como puente cognitivo de los contenidos académicos, y en la educación literaria según Colomer y López y Encabo.[1] Este aprendizaje propone conectar la obra literaria con otras manifestaciones artísticas a través del intertexto del lector según Mendoza Fillola.[2] Es necesario también, aprovechar la dimensión emocional de la música y el mundo interior del alumno.[3]

Partimos para ello de la teoría del aprendizaje significativo de Ausubel, que propone asentar cualquier proceso de aprendizaje en los conocimientos previos y los intereses de los alumnos con el objetivo de relacionar el contenido nuevo que se presenta de una manera no arbitraria (plausible, razonable y no azarosa) y no literal (sustancial, relevante y lógica) con las ideas existentes en la estructura cognitiva del individuo. Según Ausubel, el alumno asimila mejor los contenidos nuevos que le son expuestos, en nuestro caso unos contenidos literarios concretos, si se vinculan con contenidos previos mediante un 'puente cognitivo', también llamado 'organizador previo', y que para nosotros serán precisamente las canciones.

En esta línea, y dentro ya del área de la didáctica de la literatura, Colomer Martínez ha abogado en las últimas décadas por una educación literaria que

---

1   David Paul Ausubel, Joseph D. Novak y Helen Hanesian, *Educational psychology: a cognitive view* (New York: Holt, Rinehart & Winston, 1968) y Ausubel, *The Acquisition and Retention of Knowledge* (Dordrecht: Kluwer Academic, 2000); Teresa Colomer Martínez, 'De la enseñanza de la literatura a la educación literaria', *Comunicación, Lenguaje y Educación* 9 (1991), 21–31, <https://dialnet.unirioja.es/servlet/articulo?codigo=126236>, consultado 13 noviembre 2018; Amando López Valero y Eduardo Encabo Fernández, *Fundamentos didácticos de la lengua y la literatura* [versión Kindle] (Madrid: Editorial Síntesis, 2013).

2   Antonio Mendoza Fillola, *El intertexto lector. La Educación lingüística y literaria en Secundaria. Materiales para la formación del profesorado* (Murcia: Consejería de Educación y Cultura de la Región de Murcia, 2006), vol. 2, 93–124.

3   Marta Sanjuán Álvarez, *La dimensión emocional en la educación literaria* (Zaragoza: Prensas de la Universidad de Zaragoza, 2013) y 'Leer para sentir. La dimensión emocional de la educación literaria,' *Impossibilia* 8 (2014), 155–78, <https://dialnet.unirioja.es/servlet/articulo?codigo=5372192>, consultado 10 mayo 2018; Ken Robinson and Lou Aronica, *Creative schools: Revolutionizing education from the ground up* (New York: Viking Penguin, 2015).

se basa en explotar y desarrollar los gustos y conocimientos del alumnos como puente hacia el placer estético que genera la obra literaria y que se opone a la enseñanza de literatura tradicional basada en un enfoque historicista y de análisis textual.

Mendoza Fillola destaca en el mismo sentido la necesidad de buscar nuevos procedimientos y enfoques en la didáctica de la literatura que partan del intertexto lector, es decir, de los conocimientos, inferencias y saberes implícitos de los lectores, 'a través de un aprendizaje significativo y, a la vez multicultural, que ponga de manifiesto la actividad receptora del lector/espectador y las conexiones entre diversas artes'.[4] Como señala este autor, las conexiones culturales entre distintas manifestaciones artísticas pueden referirse a la forma (componentes y rasgos estilísticos, estructura, tipología textual y de géneros, etc.) o al contenido (temas, tópicos, variantes y recursos semánticos).

Además, como señalan Bordons y Díaz-Plaja, este planteamiento intertextual posibilita al lector 'establecer pasarelas que le lleven más allá en su competencia lectora gracias al cruce de géneros literarios, niveles lingüísticos y distintas artes (pintura, escultura, música, etc.), rompiendo los comportamientos estancos literarios que muchas veces lastran una auténtica educación lectora'.[5]

En este mismo sentido, López Valero y Encabo Fernández consideran que la educación literaria debe buscar estrategias didácticas intertextuales y significativas que permitan desarrollar el placer, el conocimiento y el sentido crítico del alumno.[6]

Sanjuán Álvarez invita para ello a encontrar nuevos métodos orientados a transformar la enseñanza de la literatura en una educación literaria mediante una serie de vínculos emocionales profundos entre los contenidos temáticos del texto, sus valores éticos y sociales, los conflictos o situaciones concretas

---

4   Antonio Mendoza Fillola, 'El concepto de intertextualidad en los textos literarios y en las artes visuales: una reflexión didáctica sobre la contigüidad cultural', en *III Simposio Internacional de la Sociedad Española de Didáctica de la Lengua y la Literatura* (La Coruña: Universidad de La Coruña, 1993), 333–42, 333, <http://ruc.udc.es/dspace/handle/2183/9236>, consultado 13 mayo 2018.

5   Gloria Bordons y Ana Diaz-Plaja, 'Peces: un tema universal como pasarela entre diversas literaturas', *Lenguaje y Textos* 28 (2008), 43–74, 46.

6   López y Encabo, *Fundamentos didácticos*, capítulo 1.4.

en la que estos se encuentra, su concepción de la realidad social y sus pautas de comportamiento, sin renunciar a tratarlos en relación con las características estéticas de las obras literarias: 'Solo si favorecemos experiencias gratas de lectura conseguiremos sentar las bases para la construcción de lectores literarios'.[7] Esta autora defiende recuperar la perspectiva humanista de la educación literaria, entendida como la puerta a la cultura, la emancipación individual y social y propone partir de los recursos propios del alumno, 'su experiencia pasada con la vida y con el lenguaje literario, sus necesidades y preocupaciones actuales, un estado de ánimo específico y otros elementos', presentes en obras más cercanas al público juvenil, aunque puedan tener una menor calidad literaria, que es lo que sucede también con las canciones que escuchan los jóvenes, para tender puentes hacia lecturas de más calado.[8] Una visión que se integra en lo que Robinson y Aronica denominan 'aprendizaje creativo', como proceso flexible y creativo para conectar cualquier materia de estudio, en este caso la literatura, con las habilidades personales y la realidad que los estudiantes viven fuera del aula.

Nuestra propuesta de educación literaria basada en canciones viene a conciliar así los postulados de la educación literaria, la intertextualidad y la significatividad cognitiva y emocional a través de la explotación didáctica de los contenidos literarios presentes en la música actual, concretamente de los contenidos intertextuales que comparten estas con las obras literarias clásicas, entendiendo estos, de acuerdo a Mendoza Fillola, como 'las conexiones culturales implícitas o explícitas en la producción literaria, compartidas tanto en la forma (componentes y rasgos estilísticos, estructura, tipología textual y de géneros), como en el contenido (temas, tópicos, variantes y recursos semánticos) con otras manifestaciones artísticas'.[9] Gracias a los cuales, según señala el mismo autor, el alumno 'integra, selecciona y activa significativamente el conjunto de saberes, estrategias y recursos lingüístico-culturales para facilitar la lectura de los textos'.[10]

---

7   *La dimensión emocional*, 165.
8   Marta Sanjuán Álvarez, 'De la experiencia de la lectura a la educación literaria. Análisis de los componentes emocionales de la lectura literaria en la infancia y la adolescencia', *Ocnos* 7 (2011), 85–100, 94, <https://www.revista.uclm.es/index.php/ocnos/article/view/ocnos_2011.07.07>, consultado 13 mayo 2018.
9   'El concepto de intertextualidad', 334.
10 Mendoza Fillola, *El intertexto lector*, 105.

Descripción de la propuesta didáctica

Esta propuesta didáctica consta de quince unidades en cada una de las cuales se conecta una canción actual con una obra clásica de la Edad Media, el Renacimiento y el Barroco tal como se ilustra en su portada (ver Figura 10.1) y en la introducción (ver Figura 10.2) del curso disponible en la web de la Universidad de Zaragoza (<https://ocw.unizar.es/ocw/course/view.php?id=50>). Las canciones se han escogido en función de los gustos de los adolescentes en general y de los alumnos en particular, pero también en función de los contenidos literarios que nos proponemos trabajar a través de los textos literarios clásicos seleccionados.

Figura 10.1. Portada ilustrativa del material didáctico. Fuente: elaboración propia.

Unidades didácticas de educación literaria basada en canciones

Presentación	Unidad 8. El amor carnal. Del reggaeton a la poesía mística
Unidad 1. El motivo del destierro. Del rock alternativo al Cantar del Cid	Unidad 9. Los vicios humanos. De 'No sopor, no sopor' de Sabina a la picaresca
Unidad 2. La descripción de Granada. De Rosa López al romance de Abenámar	Unidad 10. El amor eterno. De Enrique Iglesias a Francisco de Quevedo
Unidad 3. La búsqueda del buen amor. De Carlos Ponce al Arcipreste de Hita	Unidad 11. El Carpe Diem. De Juanes a Luis de Góngora
Unidad 4. La vida y la muerte. De Nach a Jorge Manrique	Unidad 12. La descripción del amor. De Alejandro Sanz a Lope de Vega.
Unidad 5. El 'tempus fugit'. De Macaco y Fito a Garcilaso de la Vega	Unidad 13. La violencia de género. De 'Ella', de Bebé, a 'Fuenteovejunta', de Lope
Unidad 6. El 'beatus ille'. Del Canto del Loco a Fray Luis de León	Unidad 14. La vida como sueño. De 'Soñaré', de la Oreja de Van Gogh, a Calderón
Unidad 7. El lamento vital. Del Kanka a Santa Teresa de Jesús	Unidad 15. El despecho y la discriminación. De Rozalen a Sor Juana Inés de la Cruz

Figura 10.2. Índice de la propuesta didáctica. Fuente: elaboración propia.

Parte de este material fue elaborado para su publicación en formato plano, el cual fue ampliado y rediseñado para su uso online durante el curso 2017–18 dentro de un proyecto de innovación de la Universidad de Zaragoza.[11] Así, las unidades cuentan con actividades interactivas siguiendo los estándares educativos IMS, SCORM y HTML, que son compatibles con la plataforma Moodle y adaptables para su uso en diferentes dispositivos (móviles, tablets, ordenador, pizarra digital, etc.).

Estructura de cada unidad

Cada unidad didáctica se divide en tres apartados, que explicamos a continuación y representamos mediante un dibujo en la Figura 10.3.

---

11   Rubén Cristóbal Hornillos, *Diez canciones para conectar con los clásicos* (Madrid: MECyD, 2016), <https://sede.educacion.gob.es/publiventa/diez-canciones-actuales-para-conectar-con-los-clasicos-literarios/ensenanza-lengua-espanola/21346>, consultado 11 mayo 2018.

Figura 10.3. Secuenciación de una unidad didáctica. Fuente: elaboración propia.

1) Introducción de contenidos a partir de la canción. Empezamos conversando sobre las canciones siguiendo el enfoque 'Dime' con preguntas del tipo: ¿Qué es lo que más y lo que menos te gusta de la canción?, ¿qué te ha sorprendido? o ¿qué conexiones encuentras con otras canciones, obras literarias o tu vida diaria?, para facilitar que el alumno debata y reflexione de forma guiada y gradual sobre aspectos interesantes, curiosos y controvertidos de las canciones.[12] A continuación guiamos al alumno mediante cuestiones más complejas para que identifique en la canción los temas y recursos literarios que construyen el sentido de la obra, para terminar con cuestiones relacionadas con el ritmo, la métrica y la rima de ésta.

2) Conexión de la canción y el texto literarios. En el segundo apartado conectamos de una forma intertextual los contenidos vistos en la canción con los mismos contenidos presentes en un poema clásico para que el alumno pueda identificarlos de una forma más auténtica para él, ampliando de

---

12 Aidan Chambers, *Dime: Los niños, la lectura y la conversación* (México: Fondo de Cultural Económica, 2007).

La poesía clásica a través de canciones actuales 185

este modo su competencia literaria y ayudándole a caracterizar los textos desde un punto de vista estético y sociocultural.
3) Profundización y contextualización. Por último, profundizamos en aquellos aspectos literarios que consideramos más interesantes del texto clásico en relación con su autor, corriente y época literaria, aunque sin olvidar tampoco la canción inicial.

La mística a través del reggae y la canción de autor

Como ejemplo desglosamos dos unidades que introducen dos poemas de poesía mística a través de música actual. Concretamente se trata del poema 'Noche oscura del alma' de San Juan de la Cruz a partir de la canción de reggaeton 'Escápate conmigo' de Wisin y Ozuna; y el poema 'Que contiene una fantasía contenta con amor decente', de Sor Juana Inés de la Cruz, a partir de la canción '80 veces', de Rozalén.

En las dos unidades didácticas empezamos conversando sobre las canciones de acuerdo al enfoque 'Dime' ya mencionado con preguntas del tipo: ¿Qué es lo que más y lo que menos te gusta de la canción?, ¿qué te ha sorprendido? o ¿qué conexiones encuentras con otras canciones, obras literarias o tu vida diaria? Facilitamos así que el alumno debata y reflexione de forma guiada y gradual sobre motivos literarios de las canciones, como el 'locus amoenus', la huida amorosa, el despecho o el olvido, pero también temas controvertidos, como el culto al cuerpo y la cosificación de la mujer, para profundizar en estos desde una perspectiva crítica.

En la primera canción, 'Escápate conmigo', de Wisin y Ozuna, planteamos al alumno que analice de una forma crítica el género del reggeaton, uno de los más seguidos en la actualidad por los jóvenes pero también uno de los más cuestionados. Para ello debatimos sobre aspectos habituales en la música y en la literatura, como los tópicos amorosos, la atracción sexual, la huida amorosa o el secreto, que aparecen también de una forma simbólica en la 'Noche oscura del alma'. Esto nos permite vincular ambas obras de una forma auténtica a pesar de los siglos que las separan, como vemos en la Figura 10.4.

🎵 'ESCÁPATE CONMIGO', WISIN Y OZUNA   📖 'NOCHE OSCURA DEL ALMA', SAN JUAN DE LA CRUZ

Cuenta oficial youtube / wisinofficialVEVO. *Escápate conmigo*. *Wisin y Ozuna* (Licencia estándar de youtube)

INTEF/Margarita Irene (CC BY-NC-SA)

1. Será la magia que tienen tus ojos, *11A*
2. esos truquitos para enamorar, *11B*
3. tú me seduces a mi antojo *9A*
4. y de tu hechizo no puedo escapar. *11B*
5. Que ganas tengo de buscarte *9C*
6. y de volverte a besar *8B*
7. por más que traten de alejarte, *9C*
8. baby conmigo hoy te vas. *8B*

1. En una noche oscura
2. con ansias en amores inflamada,
3. ¡oh dichosa ventura!,
4. salí sin ser notada
5. estando ya mi casa sosegada.

6. A oscuras y segura
7. por la secreta escala, disfrazada,
8. ¡oh dichosa ventura!,
9. a oscuras y en celada,
10. estando ya mi casa sosegada.

Figura 10.4.   Comienzo de la unidad 8 con los textos encarados.
Fuente: elaboración propia.

La canción de '80 veces', de Rozalén, se conecta con un soneto de Sor Juana Inés de la Cruz a través del motivo central de la entrega amorosa y el despecho, que encontramos en ambos textos, aunque en el caso del poema místico se refiera simbólicamente a Dios (ver Figura 10.5). Además de trabajar las conexiones temáticas que presentan ambos textos, en el apartado de profundización buceamos en la vida de Sor Juana Inés de la Cruz a través de varios estudios y de la serie titulada 'Juana Inés', centrándonos en dos aspectos controvertidos de su figura en el México del siglo XVII: los sacrificios que tuvo que asumir para poder dedicarse al estudio y a la escritura y la posible relación que mantuvo con la virreina de Nueva España. Dos cuestiones que confrontamos con la realidad actual a través de una entrevista de Rozalén a la revista Shangay, en el que alude a la lucha social del colectivo LGTB.

Así mismo, al igual que en el resto de unidades, en ambos casos guiamos al alumno para que identifique – primero en las canciones y luego en los poemas – los campos semánticos y recursos literarios que enriquecen el

"80 VECES" ('CON DERECHO A'), 2013, MARÍA ROZALÉN, CANCIÓN DE AUTOR

Cuenta oficial de youtube / rozalenVEVO. *80 veces*, Rozalén (Licencia estándar de youtube)

1 Hoy me he preguntado 80 veces *10*
2 que por qué sigo queriéndote, *9*
3 que por qué sigo pensando, *8*
4 que eres tú quien me hará feliz, *9A*
5 si no me aportas nada, no te importo nada, *13*
6 en lo único que piensas es en ti. *12A*

"QUE CONTIENE UNA FANTASÍA CONTENTA CON AMOR DECENTE", SOR JUANA INÉS DE LA CRUZ

Anónimo. *Retrato de Juana de Asbaje a los quince años de edad, cuando entró a la corte virreinal y antes de coger los hábitos. Posiblemente anacrónico.* (Dominio público)

1. Detente, sombra de mi bien esquivo,
2. imagen del hechizo que más quiero,
3. bella ilusión por quien alegre muero,
4. dulce ficción por quien penosa vivo.
5. Si al imán de tus gracias atractivo
6. sirve mi pecho de obediente acero,
7. ¿para qué me enamoras lisonjero,
8. si has de burlarme luego fugitivo?

Figura 10.5. Comienzo de la unidad 15 con los textos encarados.
Fuente: elaboración propia.

sentido de las obras (la metáfora, la sinécdoque, la hipérbole, la antítesis, la paradoja, el epíteto, la anáfora, la apóstrofe, el hipérbaton o el encabalgamiento) y que analice su rima y métrica.

Conclusiones y evaluación

El trabajo de los textos literarios a través de canciones confirma, tal como señala Mendoza, que 'el planteamiento comparatista permite concretar una serie de objetivos y pautas de intervención didáctica'.[13] Podemos concluir así que esta propuesta:

---

13 Antonio Mendoza Fillola, 'Leer y comparar: notas sobre las posibilidades del comparativismo en el aula de educación secundaria', *Lenguaje y Textos* 28 (2008), 19–41, 31.

1) Pone de relieve la posibilidad de tender puentes entre los gustos de los adolescentes de hoy en día y la literatura clásica.
2) Activa, aprovecha y amplía el intertexto del lector, además de las habilidades y estrategias del alumno, lo que le permitirá establecer en el futuro nuevas relaciones basadas en su intertextualidad y su inclusión en un contexto cultural.
3) Potencia la competencia literaria del alumno, entendida como la capacidad de comprender una obra literaria y disfrutar de esta, así como su capacidad para reconocer, comprender y conectar las características literarias de distintas obras.
4) Favorece que el alumno acepte de forma positiva la diversidad cultural e identifique las coincidencias y las diferencias entre producciones culturales de distinta época y tipología.
5) Ayuda al alumno caracterizar los textos desde un punto de vista artístico, estético y sociocultural, sin dejar por ello de valorar y apreciar las conexiones que comparten.

Esta propuesta fue sometida a una evaluación dentro de una investigación doctoral desarrollada entre los cursos 2012–13 al 2014–15 en un contexto de Aprendizaje Integrado de Contenidos y Lenguas Extranjeras (AICLE), dentro la sección bilingüe de español del liceo José Martí de Varsovia.[14]

La intervención central se desarrolló durante el curso 2013–14 y consistió en un cuasi-experimento, que siguió un modelo de grupo no equivalente con pretest y postest, según lo denomina Campbell y Stanley.[15] Dicha investigación nos permitió comprobar que los alumnos que siguieron esta metodología redujeron su amotivación un 16,7 por ciento más que los que siguieron una metodología convencional y aumentaron su motivación intrínseca un 21,5 por ciento más que estos. En el mismo sentido, sus resultados sobre los contenidos trabajados superaron en un 15,4 por ciento a los alumnos del grupo de control.

---

14   Rubén Cristóbal Hornillos, *Impacto de la educación literaria basada en canciones*, tesis doctoral (Granada: Universidad de Granada, 2017), <http://digibug.ugr.es/handle/10481/44882#.WgrTCNLiYiI>, consultado 11 mayo 2018.
15   Donald T. Campbell y Julian C. Stanley, *Diseños experimentales y cuasi-experimentales en la investigación social* (Buenos Aires: Amorrortu editores, 2007).

La propuesta ha sido sometida posteriormente a distintos ciclos de revisión y aplicación, como en el proyecto de innovación de la Universidad de Zaragoza del curso 2017-18 dirigido al alumnado universitario del Máster en Profesorado de Educación Secundaria Obligatoria.

Los resultados nos permitieron revalidar la perspectiva teórica transformadora que había guiado la investigación y que habíamos puesto a prueba, es decir, la educación literaria basada en canciones. Pero sobre todo, nos permitió corroborar que los contenidos literarios del currículo de secundaria o enseñanza superior no están tan alejados de los alumnos como parece desprenderse de los enfoques historicistas y de análisis textual que siguen predominando en las aulas, lo que hace posible, como muestran los resultados anteriormente mencionados, un proceso de enseñanza y aprendizaje más significativo.

Mediante esta metodología partimos así de los conocimientos previos (plano cognitivo) y gustos (plano emocional o afectivo) del alumno, y ordenamos el proceso de aprendizaje siguiendo los principios ausubelianos de diferencia progresiva, reconciliación integradora, organización secuencial y de revisión-consolidación. Una vez actualizados los contenidos particulares del alumno y abstraídos los contenidos más generales e inclusivos de estos, es decir los contenidos literarios que contienen, las nuevas ideas se anclan a un subsumidor o idea de anclaje ya presente en la estructura cognitiva del alumno, el cual queda a su vez modificado gracias a la incorporación de los significados adicionales de estas.

De este modo, los elementos de la estructura cognitiva se reorganizan y adquirieren nuevos significados, reconciliándose e integrándose con los conceptos nuevos cumpliendo con el principio de reconciliación integradora. Es decir, rescatamos los subsumidores intertextuales que el alumno ya posee para consolidarlos y enriquecerlos con los nuevos.

PART IV

Teaching theatre

AROA ALGABA GRANERO AND SARA SÁNCHEZ-HERNÁNDEZ

11   El proyecto de innovación docente *TAAULA.*
     El teatro áureo en el aula de Filología

     [*TAAULA. El teatro áureo en el aula de Filología*:
     A Teaching Innovation Project]

ABSTRACT

The Teaching Innovation Project known as *TAAULA: El teatro áureo en el aula de Filología* centres on the use of modern-day performances of Golden Age drama as a classroom tool for the acquisition of competency in the reading of Spanish plays. The present paper outlines the teaching methodology developed during the current academic year by four lecturers from the Faculty of Philology and implemented in two subjects on the undergraduate degree in Hispanic Philology which focus fully or partly on theatre. The authors covered in the project are canonical names from the Spanish Renaissance and Baroque: Juan del Encina, Lucas Fernández, Gil Vicente, Lope de Rueda, Juan de la Cueva, Juan de Vergara, Miguel de Cervantes, Lope de Vega, Calderón de la Barca and Tirso de Molina.

Introducción

El Proyecto de Innovación Docente *El teatro áureo en el aula de Filología (TAAULA)*, insertado dentro del *Plan Estratégico 2013–18* de la Universidad de Salamanca, ha planteado el empleo de las representaciones teatrales áureas presentes en la escena española actual como herramienta en el aula para la adquisición de la competencia lectora de textos dramáticos españoles.[1] En

1   Este trabajo ha sido financiado por la beca Formación del Profesorado Universitario (FPU) del Ministerio de Educación, Cultura y Deporte, actual Ministerio de Educación

nuestro trabajo hemos pretendido mostrar las metodologías educativas que hemos comenzado a desarrollar cuatro profesores de la facultad en este curso académico en dos asignaturas del Grado en *Filología Hispánica* relacionadas, total o parcialmente, con el teatro del Siglo de Oro.[2] Los autores en los que se ha centrado el proyecto han sido los canónicos del Renacimiento y Barroco españoles: Juan del Encina, Lucas Fernández, Gil Vicente, Lope de Rueda, Juan de la Cueva, Juan de Vergara, Miguel de Cervantes, Lope de Vega, Calderón de la Barca y Tirso de Molina.

En la era de las TICs y de la informatización de la educación, los docentes tenemos la responsabilidad de ayudar a los estudiantes a adquirir el mayor número de 'Competencias para el siglo XXI', recogidas por el *World Economic Forum*.[3] Este proyecto ha pretendido contribuir a que los alumnos adquieran y refuercen las *Foundational literacies*, las *competencies* y las *character qualities*.[4]

Más específicamente, se ha pretendido:

1. Conocer y analizar los textos teatrales del Siglo de Oro desde una perspectiva no solo textual, sino también escénica, ampliando los límites tradicionalmente adoptados por la filología a los estudios dramáticos.
2. Desarrollar las capacidades de expresión oral y de comprensión y expresión lectora.
3. Implicar al alumnado de forma activa en el estudio del teatro clásico, elaborando tanto trabajos individuales como grupales.
4. Aprender a utilizar instrumentos de análisis diferentes, como las nuevas tecnologías, con grabaciones teatrales o bases de datos que puedan servir

---

    y Formación Profesional y por la Junta de Castilla y León, a través de la Consejería de Educación, y por el Fondo Social Europeo, Programa Operativo de Castilla y León.

2   Los dos restantes son Javier San José Lera (coordinador del proyecto y Catedrático de Literatura Española) y Alba Agraz Ortiz.

3   World Economic Forum, <https://widgets.weforum.org/nve-2015/chapter1.html>, consultado 29 octubre 2018.

4   Esto es, las habilidades que sirven como base sobre la cual los estudiantes podrán adquirir las competencias más avanzadas y específicas (*character qualities*). Se trata, por tanto, de fortalecer las habilidades definidas como de *literacy, numeracy, scientific literacy, ICT literacy* y *cultural and civic literacy* <https://widgets.weforum.org/nve-2015/appendices.html#appendix1>, consultado 29 octubre 2018.

para su futuro profesional, ya sea en el desarrollo de la práctica escénica, de la investigación o de la enseñanza.

Creemos, no como acto de fe, sino de razón comprobada y de años de estudio y devoción al teatro, que esta forma literaria 'gozosamente impura' se ha de enseñar con su dualidad intrínseca de texto y espectáculo a los alumnos de Filología y lo hemos puesto en marcha con nuestro proyecto de innovación docente TAAULA. *El teatro áureo en el aula de Filología* (ID2017/087).[5]

En este siglo en el que los *Performance Studies* son cada vez más prolíficos y también la investigación del teatro áureo con las puestas en escena y las humanidades digitales han cobrado cada vez más importancia a través de proyectos (Seliten@t, TC/12, TESAL16, etc.), tesis doctorales dedicadas a ellas (puestas en escena de Calderón, de la CNTC, de *Don Quijote*, de *La Celestina*, de *Pedro de Urdemalas*, etc.), monografías y artículos de investigación o recursos digitales cada vez más accesibles (Centro de Documentación Teatral Teatroteca, hemerotecas digitales, grabaciones de YouTube, etc.), hemos considerado que la docencia de la literatura dramática debía abrirles los ojos de las tablas al alumnado, combinando el conocimiento histórico-literario del teatro dramático con la perspectiva escénica.[6]

---

[5] Miguel Martínez, Emilio de, 'Del teatro y su enseñanza en clases de literatura', en Germán Vega García-Luengos, Héctor Urzáiz Tortajada y Pedro Conde Parrado, eds, *El patrimonio del teatro clásico español: actualidad y perspectivas: homenaje a Francisco Ruiz Ramón: Actas selectas del Congreso del TC/12: Olmedo, 22 al 25 de julio de 2013* (Olmedo: Ayuntamiento de Olmedo; Valladolid: Ediciones Universidad de Valladolid, 2015), 165–72, 166.

[6] Sergio Adillo Rufo, *Catálogo de representaciones del teatro de Calderón de la Barca en España (1715–2015)* (Madrid: Fundación Universitaria Española, 2017); María Fernández Ferreiro, *La influencia del Quijote en el teatro español contemporáneo. Adaptaciones y recreaciones dramáticas quijotescas (1900–2010)* (Alcalá de Henares: Universidad de Alcalá, 2017); María Bastianes, *La Celestina en escena (1909–2012)* (Madrid: Universidad Complutense de Madrid, 2016 [Tesis que será publicada próximamente en la serie Spanish Golden Age Studies de Peter Lang]); Alejandro González Puche, *Pedro de Urdemalas, la aventura experimental del teatro cervantino* (Vigo: Editorial Academia del Hispanismo, 2012); Duncan Wheeler, *Golden Age Drama in Contemporary Spain: The Comedia on Page, Stage and Screen* (Cardiff:

El panorama de la pedagogía del teatro áureo es amplio y cada vez más profesores son conscientes de la necesidad de que, como señalaba Calderón, el que lea las obras 'haga en su imaginación composición de lugares'. Así Diane E. Sieber indica que emplea la estructura 3D del corral de Almagro en sus clases, Dale J. Pratt y Valerie Hegstrom emprenden el proyecto de representar con alumnos de grado y posgrado *La dama duende* o los *Entremeses* cervantinos, César Oliva incide en la mezcla de la teoría y la práctica en el aula, o Robert Lauer convierte a sus estudiantes en jueces y abogados de los distintos personajes de *La vida es sueño*.[7]

University of Wales, 2012). Otras publicaciones que merecen mención en este contexto: María Bastianes, Esther Fernández y Purificació García Mascarell, eds, *Diálogos en las tablas. Últimas tendencias de la puesta en escena del teatro clásico español* (Kassel: Reichenberger, 2014); Alba Carmona, Purificació García Mascarell y Gastón Gilabert, 'La escena y la pantalla. Lope hoy', *Anuario Lope de Vega* 24 (2018), 1–9; Susan L. Fischer, *Reading Performance: Spanish Golden Age Theatre and Shakespeare on the Modern Stage* (Woodbridge: Tamesis, 2009); Daniel Madrid, 'Técnicas de innovación docente en Didáctica de la Lengua Inglesa', en Catalina González Las y Daniel Madrid, eds, *Estrategias de innovación docente en Didáctica de la Lengua y la Literatura* (Granada: Grupo Editorial Universitario, 2005), 91–120; Emilio de Miguel Martínez, *De teatro: la preparación del espectador* (Kassel: Edition Reichenberger, 2013) y Anita K. Stoll, 'Teaching Golden Age Drama: Metatheater as Organizing Principle', *Hispania* 75/5 (1992), 1343–7.

7   Dianne E. Sieber, 'The Digital *Comedia*: Teaching Golden Age Theater with New and Emerging Technologies', en Laura R. Bass y Margaret R. Greer, eds, *Approaches to Teaching Early Modern Spanish Drama* (New York: Modern Language Association of America, 2006), 198–205, 213; Dale J. Pratt y Valerie Hegstrom, 'Mentoring environments and Golden Age Theatre Production', en Laura Bass y Margaret R. Greer, eds, *Approaches to Teaching Early Modern Spanish drama* (New York: Modern Language Association of America, 2006), 198–205, 202–3; César Oliva, 'La teoría y la práctica teatral en las aulas', en Germán Vega García-Luengos, Héctor Urzáiz Tortajada y Pedro Conde Parrado, eds, *El patrimonio del teatro clásico español: actualidad y perspectivas: homenaje a Francisco Ruiz Ramón: Actas selectas del Congreso del TC/12: Olmedo, 22 al 25 de julio de 2013* (Olmedo, Ayuntamiento de Olmedo; Valladolid: Ediciones Universidad de Valladolid, 2015), 173–6, 176; Robert A. Lauer, 'Trials: Teaching the Spanish Baroque *Comedia* in the Twenty-First Century', en Laura R. Bass y Margaret R. Greer, eds, *Approaches to Teaching Early Modern Spanish drama* (New York: Modern Language Association of America, 2006), 189–97, 193.

El proyecto de innovación docente TAAULA

Recursos empleados

La procedencia de los materiales audiovisuales seleccionados por el equipo docente con los que tanto el alumnado como los profesores trabajaron es diversa (ver Tabla 11.1). La primera fuente de extracción de grabaciones de representaciones teatrales ha sido Teatroteca, una plataforma digital de préstamo de vídeos teatrales que aloja grabaciones realizadas por el Centro de Documentación Teatral del INAEM; un segundo método de recopilación de grabaciones fue el sitio web YouTube, que aloja en abierto este tipo de materiales. También se recurrió a grabaciones que las propias compañías teatrales pusieron a disposición del profesorado, y, finalmente, se emplearon DVDs de películas y de series televisivas. Otro tipo de actividad empleada fue la asistencia a representaciones teatrales en directo. Este recurso depende de la programación de teatros cercanos en la comarca salamantina o en Madrid de funciones de interés para la materia de estudio.

Tabla 11.1. Recursos empleados en *TAAULA*.

Material	Fuente
Cervantes, Miguel de, *El cerco de Numancia*, Dir. Manuel Canseco, Compañía teatral Manuel Canseco, 1998.	Teatroteca
Cervantes, Miguel de, *Entremeses*, Dir. José Luis Gómez, Teatro La Abadía, *La cueva de Salamanca*, *El viejo celoso* y *El retablo de las maravillas*, 1996 y 2015.	
Cervantes, Miguel de, *Maravillas de Cervantes*, Dir. Joan Font, Compañía Nacional de Teatro Clásico, 2000.	
Encina, Juan del, *Triunfo de Amor a partir de textos y músicas de Juan del Enzina*, Dir. Ana Zamora, Nao d'amores, 2016.	
Fernández, Lucas, *Farsas y églogas*, Dir. Ana Zamora, Nao d'amores, 2012.	
Vega, Lope de, *El caballero de Olmedo*, Dir. José Pascual, Fundación Siglo para la CNTC, 2003.	
Vega, Lope de, *El perro del hortelano*, Dir. Eduardo Vasco, Compañía Nacional de Teatro Clásico, 2011.	
Calderón de la Barca, Pedro, *El alcalde de Zalamea*, Dir. Eduardo Vasco, Compañía Nacional de Teatro Clásico, 2010.	

(*Continued*)

Table 11.1. (*Continued*)

Material	Fuente
Calderón de la Barca, Pedro, *La vida es sueño*, Dir. Calixto Bieito, Compañía Nacional de Teatro Clásico, 2000.	
Molina, Tirso de, *El burlador de Sevilla*, Dir. Miguel Narros, Compañía Nacional de Teatro Clásico, 2003.	
Moreto, Agustín, *El lindo don Diego*, Dir. Carles Alfaro, Compañía Nacional de Teatro Clásico, 2003.	
Rueda, Lope de, *El Deleitoso y otras delicias*, Teatro Guirigai, 2009.	
Rueda, Lope de, *Sobre Ruedas*, Dir. Fernando Urdiales, Teatro Corsario, 1987. Textos de *La tierra de Jauja*, *Los linajes* y *La generosa paliza*.	La compañía
The Borgias, 'celebración de las bodas de Lucrezia Borgia y Giovanni Sforza', fragmento de *The Borgias*, serie de televisión creada por Neil Jordan, 2011.	
The Tudors, 'Enrique VIII conoce a Ana Bolena', fragmento de *The Tudors*, serie de televisión, creada por Michael Hirst, 2007.	DVD
Lope, 'El Corral de Madrid. Lope siente la seducción del teatro', fragmento de la película *Lope*, dirigida por Andrucha Waddington, España, 2010.	
Calderón de la Barca, Pedro, *La vida es sueño*, Compañía de Titiriteros de la Universidad Nacional de San Martín, 2011.	
Calderón de la Barca, Pedro, *La vida es sueño*, Dir. Helena Pimenta, Compañía Nacional de Teatro Clásico, 2012.	
Jornadas Festival de Teatro Olmedo Clásico. Diálogo VII, 'Sobre *El perro del hortelano*, de Pilar Miró, Jornadas Festival Olmedo Clásico 2017', *YouTube*, 22 de agosto de 2017. Web. 6 de marzo de 2018.	
Ministerio de Educación, Cultura y Deporte, Canal Cultura, 'Helena Pimenta. La vida es sueño (2012), primera obra de dirige para la CNTC. "Figuras" 2016. CDT', *YouTube*. 20 de octubre de 2016. Web. 8 de mayo de 2018.	YouTube
Molina, Tirso de, *El burlador de Sevilla*, Dir. Dan Jemmet, La Abadía, 2008.	
Molina, Tirso de, *El burlador de Sevilla*, Dir. Darío Facal, Teatro Español, 2015.	
Ron Lalá. *Cervantina*, Ron Lalá-CNTC, 2016.	
Tato, Álvaro. 'Álvaro Tato en Atención Obras', *YouTube*, 14 de noviembre de 2016. Web. 27 de marzo de 2018.	

El proyecto de innovación docente TAAULA

Material	Fuente
Vega, Lope de, *Fuenteovejuna*, Ksec Act, 2009.	
Vega, Lope de, *El caballero de Olmedo*, Dir. Fernando Urdiales, Teatro Corsario, 2009.	
Vega, Lope de, *El caballero de Olmedo*, Dir. Mariano de Paco, Secuencia 3, 2013.	
Vega, Lope de, *El perro del hortelano*, película Dir. Pilar Miró, 1996.	
Vega, Lope de, *El perro del hortelano*, Dir. Magüi Mira, Vania y Focus, 2002.	
Vega, Lope de, *El perro del hortelano*, Dir. Helena Pimenta, Compañía Nacional de Teatro Clásico, 2016.	

El proyecto *TAAULA*

El proyecto *TAAULA* se ha aplicado a dos asignaturas: *El teatro renacentista: de la herencia medieval a la creación de la comedia nueva* y *Literatura Española de los Siglos de Oro II* (ver Tabla 11.2). La naturaleza diversa de las mismas ha determinado que los medios utilizados sean distintos en una y otra. A pesar de ello, los docentes hemos ejecutado un mismo plan de trabajo con ligeras modificaciones.

Tabla 11.2. Asignaturas de *TAAULA*.

El teatro renacentista: de la herencia medieval a la creación de la comedia nueva	Literatura Española de los Siglos de Oro II
Optativa	Obligatoria
Tercero y cuarto curso de Filología Hispánica	Tercer curso de Filología Hispánica
Primer cuatrimestre	Segundo cuatrimestre
Dieciséis alumnos	Ciento veintiséis alumnos

La primera de las asignaturas, *El teatro renacentista: de la herencia medieval a la creación de la comedia nueva*, se impartió en el primer cuatrimestre del curso académico 2017/2018 y que contó con dieciséis alumnos matriculados. El desarrollo del temario de la asignatura se dividió en tres grandes bloques (ver Tabla 11.3).

Tabla 11.3. Temario de la asignatura.

Tema 1. El género teatral	Texto teatral y dramaturgia. El texto literario del teatro renacentista: diálogo y didascalias. Los subgéneros dramáticos: Auto, Coloquio, Comedia, Égloga, Farsa, Representación, Tragedia, Tragicomedia. Los espacios del teatro en el siglo dieciséis.
Tema 2. El teatro renacentista en la primera mitad de siglo	Juan del Encina y su *Cancionero*. Las *Farsas y Églogas* de Lucas Fernández. Bartolomé de Torres Naharro y su *Propalladia*. El teatro de Gil Vicente.
Tema 3. El teatro en la segunda mitad de siglo	Lope de Rueda, *Comedia Eufemia*, *Pasos* y la invención del entremés. Juan de Vergara y su *Coloquio de Selvagia*. *Los siete infantes de Lara* de Juan de la Cueva. *Entremeses* de Cervantes y *La tragedia de Numancia*.

En el primer bloque, desarrollado en septiembre y octubre, los profesores impartieron clases magistrales relativas a las características del género dramático orientadas a los problemas del estudio del teatro en el siglo dieciséis. Para la evaluación de esta primera parte, los alumnos realizaron una tarea individual, consistente en el comentario de tres fragmentos de vídeo que mostraban la práctica escénica de varias épocas, desde finales de la Edad Media, con pasajes relacionados con el mundo de la corte europea, hasta fines del siglo dieciséis; así, el alumnado pudo poner en práctica los conceptos clave y la materia aprendida en esta primera parte. Se propuso el visionado de tres breves vídeos extraídos de dos series y una película: las danzas y representaciones teatrales en esponsales cortesanos, en *Los Borgia*, los momos en la corte inglesa, en *Los Tudor*, y la fascinación por el corral de comedias del primer Lope de Vega, en la película *Lope*.

En el segundo bloque, desarrollado en noviembre, los profesores ejecutaron un desarrollo histórico del teatro en la primera parte del siglo dieciséis. Se estudió a Juan del Encina, a Lucas Fernández, a Torres Naharro y el teatro castellano de Gil Vicente. Las explicaciones teórico-prácticas fueron acompañadas, en la medida en que fue posible, con el visionado de fragmentos de

El proyecto de innovación docente TAAULA

montajes teatrales de estos autores. Para el caso de Encina, se seleccionaron materiales audiovisuales de *Triunfo de amor*, espectáculo teatral montado por la compañía Nao d'amores. En este sentido, se realizó un análisis de dos de sus obras, intercalando fragmentos de texto con el visionado de segmentos de grabaciones de dicha representación, de manera que los alumnos pudieran establecer concomitancias y diferencias entre teatro escrito y teatro representado, y la importancia de algunos recursos teatrales como el disfraz, la música y el baile en escena. También se visualizó una escena representada por la compañía Laboratorio Escénico Univalle.

Para el teatro de Lucas Fernández, se seleccionaron escenas finales de sus obras navideñas puestas en escena por la citada compañía Nao d'amores en las que se podía apreciar el empleo de elementos litúrgicos, como los retablos, que bien pudieron haberse empleado en su época. Finalmente, y como actividad complementaria de esta segunda parte de la asignatura, se realizó una práctica de campo, que consistió en la asistencia al espectáculo teatral *Triunfo de amor* que Nao d'amores representó en noviembre en Peñaranda de Bracamonte. Al siguiente día, se programó un coloquio en clase sobre la representación teatral.

El tercero y último bloque, desarrollado en diciembre, se dedicó al teatro de la segunda mitad del siglo dieciséis (ver Tabla 11.4), se estudió a Lope de Rueda, Juan de Vergara, Juan de la Cueva y Miguel de Cervantes. Esta parte de la asignatura fue desarrollada por los propios alumnos. Ellos tenían que explicar, mediante siete exposiciones grupales, el autor y obra seleccionados al resto de compañeros, mediante un análisis dramático de los textos teatrales. Los dos primeros trabajos grupales estuvieron dedicados a Lope de Rueda. El primero analizó los *Pasos* 'La carátula', 'Cornudo y contento' y 'La Tierra de Jauja'. De este último, se empleó la grabación del espectáculo *Sobre ruedas* representado por la compañía Teatro Corsario cuyo cartel tienen proyectado.

Un tercer grupo estudió a Juan de Vergara y su *Coloquio de Selvagia*. Ante la falta de representaciones modernas de la pieza, se recurrió a la existencia de una lectura dramatizada de dicha obra, realizada en el teatro de la propia universidad. Las últimas clases estuvieron dedicadas a Cervantes. Uno de los grupos analizó *El cerco de Numancia*. La existencia de la grabación de una representación moderna de la pieza, dirigida por Manuel Canseco, permitió visualizar algunos fragmentos del espectáculo. Los dos grupos restantes analizaron los *Entremeses* 'La cueva de Salamanca', 'El juez de los divorcios', 'El viejo celoso' y 'El retablo de las maravillas', montado por Morfeo Teatro.

De los otros entremeses emplearon grabaciones de montajes de La Abadía, Th3atre Mad y La Espiral Teatro.

Tabla 11.4. Grupos de trabajo.

Grupos	Obra	Autor
1.	*Pasos* La carátula Cornudo y contento La Tierra de Jauja	Lope de Rueda
2.	*Comedia Eufemia*	Lope de Rueda
3.	*Coloquio de Selvagia*	Juan de Vergara
4.	*Los siete infantes de Lara*	Juan de la Cueva
5.	*El cerco de Numancia*	Miguel de Cervantes
6.	*Entremeses* La Cueva de Salamanca El juez de los divorcios	Miguel de Cervantes
7.	*Entremeses* El retablo de las maravillas El viejo celoso	Miguel de Cervantes

Para evaluar los resultados de la implementación del proyecto *TAAULA* y su incidencia en la mejora del aprendizaje, se realizó una encuesta de diez preguntas en Moodle (ver Tabla 11.5). Once de los dieciséis alumnos matriculados efectuaron la encuesta al finalizar el cuatrimestre. Las ocho primeras preguntas eran en Escala Likert, y los alumnos debían seleccionar su valoración, entre un rango que iba del uno al cinco, siendo uno la menor puntuación y cinco la mayor. Las otras dos preguntas restantes eran abiertas, y los alumnos podrían expresar por escrito su opinión acerca de lo que se les consultaba. Así, las primeras cuatro preguntas eran de carácter más general, mientras que, en el segundo bloque de la encuesta, de otras cuatro preguntas, se consultaba sobre el uso de grabaciones de representaciones modernas, tanto para las clases magistrales como para las exposiciones grupales, y también sobre la asistencia al espectáculo teatral *Triunfo de amor*. De los resultados pudo observarse que la aplicación del proyecto fue beneficiosa para el aprendizaje y para la adquisición de las competencias específicas de la asignatura.

El proyecto de innovación docente TAAULA

Tabla 11.5. Preguntas y resultados de la encuesta.

Preguntas en escala Likert	Resultados (del uno al cinco)
1. Tras cursar la asignatura, conozco elementos que integran la historia del teatro del siglo XVI en España	4.4
2. Tras cursar la asignatura, mi competencia lectora de los textos teatrales del siglo dieciséis ha mejorado	4.3
3. ¿Considera que los profesores han explicado los contenidos con claridad y han respondido a las dudas que se han planteado?	4.7
4. En términos generales, ¿ha aprovechado y disfrutado de la asignatura?	4.7
5. La visualización de vídeos en clase resulta útil para comprender la materia	4.5
6. La asistencia a la representación de *Triunfo de amor* ha resultado interesante y fructífera	4.2
7. La tarea de comentario de vídeos resulta adecuada y útil	3.9
8. El visionado de vídeos para la exposición de clase ha sido útil para entender el texto	4.0

En el último apartado de la encuesta, se interpeló al alumnado, mediante dos preguntas abiertas, acerca de la adecuación de los contenidos de la materia y sobre si tenían algún comentario o crítica hacia la asignatura. En la primera de ellas, se preguntó al alumnado sobre si los contenidos de la asignatura fueron adecuados, así como si deseaban añadir o suprimir alguna cuestión en futuros cursos académicos. En general, las respuestas mostraron la conformidad de los alumnos en cuanto a la materia impartida, ninguno de ellos manifestó ningún cambio al respecto, aunque uno de ellos pidió que los profesores reforzaran los contenidos de la parte que los propios alumnos debían desarrollar mediante las exposiciones orales, cuestión que se tendrá en cuenta en el futuro.

En la última pregunta se pedía al alumnado que manifestara sus sugerencias, críticas hacia la asignatura o hacia el profesor, así como sugerencias de mejora. La mayoría de los alumnos comentaron que han disfrutado mucho de la asignatura y que el desarrollo del temario ha sido adecuado. No obstante, se detectó que las exposiciones orales son algo problemáticas para algunos alumnos, por lo que en el futuro se va a reflexionar sobre ello para mejorar.

En vista de las opiniones vertidas por los alumnos, parece que, en general, la aplicación del proyecto de innovación y mejora docente fue provechosa.

Literatura española de los Siglos de Oro II

En la asignatura obligatoria de *Literatura española de los Siglos de Oro II*, debido a la organización de la asignatura en su totalidad, con otros tres bloques temáticos (los lunes se han dedicado al bloque de historia literaria y la cultura del siglo diecisiete y los miércoles se enfocaron a estudiar la novedad de la novela, a partir de la lectura de *Don Quijote*) y al número de alumnos matriculados (ciento veintiséis), la estructura de las clases fue en parte diferente a la de *El teatro renacentista: de la herencia medieval a la creación de la comedia nueva*. Se prescindió de las exposiciones orales, ya que eran inviables en un grupo tan numeroso de estudiantes.

Se dedicaron al teatro las clases de los martes, dividiendo en dos bloques los contenidos. El primer bloque lo formaron cuatro clases introductorias sobre el teatro del siglo diecisiete. Las tres primeras sesiones se utilizaron para aportar unos conceptos generales sobre el teatro del Siglo de Oro: las unidades aristotélicas, los géneros más utilizados, los condicionantes externos como espacios escénicos o compañías de actores; las claves del *Arte nuevo de hacer comedias en este tiempo*, de Lope de Vega; los elementos propios del espectáculo teatral del diecisiete, con las partes del corral o la escenografía barroca. En relación con todos estos conceptos y elementos se añadieron a la plataforma virtual de la asignatura distintos recursos, como artículos de consulta, acceso al portal de Teatro Clásico Español, referencias gráficas a los corrales de comedias y sus partes.

La cuarta sesión introdujo a los alumnos a la perspectiva doble del teatro como texto y como espectáculo, proponiendo, a través del estudio de las didascalias explícitas, implícitas, los tipos de diálogo y las categorías fundamentales de tiempo, espacio y personaje, un estudio textual que incentivara la construcción de una puesta en escena imaginando aspectos como escenografía, iluminación, música o efectos sonoros, vestuario, maquillaje, atrezo o tramoya. Previamente a la clase, se subió a la plataforma una serie de ejemplos de *El alcalde de Zalamea, Fuenteovejuna, El lindo don Diego* y *Cervantina*, de Ron Lalá (obra que combina distintos textos de Cervantes) y dos vídeos de YouTube (de *Cervantina* y la puesta en escena de *Fuenteovejuna* de la compañía japonesa Ksec Act), animándoles a reflexionar sobre la teatralidad de estos. Así, pudimos insistir en el aula en el papel esencial de la música como caracterización de personajes en *Cervantina* o la simbología del cromatismo en el vestuario de la compañía japonesa para contrastar la violencia del comendador (rojo) con la sumisión del pueblo (blanco, beige).

Las siguientes clases que formaron el segundo bloque, se centraron en el análisis de los textos teatrales y de las puestas en escena de estos. Concretamente, se estudiaron *El caballero de Olmedo* y *El perro del hortelano*, de Lope de Vega, *El burlador de Sevilla*, de Tirso de Molina, y *La vida es sueño*, de Calderón de la Barca. En el aula virtual, además de los materiales comentados en clase, se les proporcionaron reseñas de los montajes, enlaces a entrevistas a directores o dramaturgos o diálogos con actores y estudiosos para completar su formación en el ámbito de la producción y recepción escénicas.

Primeramente, tras leer *El caballero de Olmedo* y antes de la clase, se añadió a la plataforma virtual una serie de escenas para el comentario y unas preguntas sobre esta que unos cuantos alumnos respondieron oralmente al hilo de la explicación en clase. Pusimos a disposición de los estudiantes en la plataforma virtual vídeos de YouTube con los montajes de Secuencia 3 y Teatro Corsario, con diferentes perspectivas, iluminación, caracterización de personajes, etc. Asimismo, empleamos en el aula escenas de la CNTC de 2003 de la Teatroteca que nos permitieron ahondar en la función del vestuario, la iluminación o los efectos sonoros con carga trágica.

Las dos sesiones siguientes se enfocaron a *El perro del hortelano*, como texto y como espectáculo. En la clase de texto se fueron desarrollando las claves de la obra, que se iban especificando mediante ejemplos del texto. En la clase dedicada a las puestas en escena de *El perro* incidimos en la violencia de Diana y en su vertiente más erótica, dando la posibilidad a los alumnos de ver distintos clips de montajes de YouTube (de Helena Pimenta y de Magüi Mira, a la vez que dos vídeos de la galardonada película de Pilar Miró).

En el aula se utilizaron escenas de la versión de la CNTC de 2011, de Eduardo Vasco, de forma que los alumnos comprobaron cómo la distribución del espacio escénico y la proxémica entre personajes era relevante para reflejar las desigualdades o la caracterización de las relaciones. Del mismo modo, algunos alumnos, muy participativos, se mostraron asombrados con el montaje de Magüi Mira y resaltaron la diferencia de vestuario, gama cromática y la sensualidad de Diana frente a las decisiones escénicas de Vasco, mucho más comedidas. Ante esta situación, pudimos debatir sobre la atemporalidad de los conflictos de amor y poder, la hipocresía social, el erotismo, etc.

En la clase dedicada al texto teatral de *El burlador de Sevilla*, nos enfocamos en los textos en los que se podían observar los distintos ambientes, la caracterización de don Juan y las didascalias que se traducían en significativos efectos escénicos. Utilizamos para la clase de puestas en escena de *El burlador* montajes diversos y controvertidos, como el de Darío Facal (con micrófonos en escena, un vestuario muy sensual y recursos audiovisuales), y el de Dan Jemmet (con una escenografía de barra de bar y un don Juan paródico, viejo, calvo y con bastón). Les pedimos que los visualizaran en YouTube con anterioridad a la clase para comentar, junto a cuatro escenas de la CNTC (2003) dirigida por Miguel Narros que les proyectamos en el aula, la recreación de los ambientes mediante la escenografía, la caracterización de personajes según el vestuario, atrezo o tono y la visión paródica o enaltecedora del mito del don Juan.

Respecto a la clase de *La vida es sueño*, se empleó una sesión para texto y otra para espectáculo, siguiendo el planteamiento habitual. Se eligieron varias escenas de la obra para comentar aspectos teatrales, de lenguaje y temáticos. En la clase de puesta en escena de *La vida es sueño* se comentaron varias escenas del montaje de la CNTC de Calixto Bieito (2000). Con los vídeos y las imágenes correspondientes a estas y otras dos puestas en escena (la de la CNTC de Helena Pimenta y la de la Compañía de Titiriteros UNSAM), pudimos profundizar en cuestiones como la escenografía (espejo, velo, trono, arena), la proxémica (que marcaba relaciones entre Segismundo y sus subordinados o su padre), las didascalias del texto con las que había correspondencias en escena y con las que no, los recursos para expresar las dudas de Segismundo o la fragilidad de otros personajes (kinésica, vestuario o desnudez, etc.).

Además, cabe destacar tres actividades complementarias: la asistencia el 22 de marzo a la puesta en escena de *El caballero de Olmedo* en el Teatro de la Comedia de Madrid (montaje de la compañía Noviembre Teatro), la proyección completa de la versión dirigida por Eduardo Vasco para la CNTC de *El perro del hortelano* el día 20 de abril y el coloquio 'Humor, teatro clásico y teatro contemporáneo: de Cervantes a *Cervantina*', que tuvo

El proyecto de innovación docente TAAULA

lugar el 26 de abril con el dramaturgo, adaptador y actor Álvaro Tato, que trabaja con la compañía Ron Lalá y la CNTC, adaptador de obras clásicas y creador de versiones novedosas como *Cervantina*, con el que los alumnos pudieron comunicar sus percepciones sobre teatro clásico y plantear sus dudas sobre el tema.

En cuanto a la evaluación del proyecto *TAAULA* en este bloque de teatro de la asignatura *Literatura Española de los Siglos de Oro II*, hemos seguido el mismo procedimiento que en *El teatro renacentista: de la herencia medieval a la creación de la comedia nueva*, elaborando una encuesta de satisfacción al final del cuatrimestre sobre los contenidos y los métodos de enseñanza utilizados. Se propusieron once preguntas, de las cuales nueve siguen la escala Likert, con el mismo esquema de puntuación que en la asignatura optativa. Las otras dos eran de respuesta libre, para que los estudiantes expusieran sus opiniones y sugerencias de cambios (ver Tabla 11.6).

Aunque solo respondieron treinta alumnos de ciento veintiséis, las respuestas sirvieron para proporcionarnos una visión de su perspectiva respecto a la asignatura. Así, las cinco primeras preguntas eran de carácter más general. Las cuatro siguientes preguntas se dedicaron a cuestiones más concretas de los vídeos, las actividades complementarias y el glosario. En general, fueron positivas, aunque teniendo en cuenta el resultado del glosario, nos planteamos modificar la actividad o cambiar los criterios. No cabe duda que el tamaño de la asignatura no facilitó una eficaz aplicación de novedades docentes significativas.

Tabla 11.6. Preguntas y resultados de la encuesta.

Preguntas en escala Likert	Resultados (del uno al cinco)
1. En términos generales ¿has aprovechado y disfrutado del proyecto *TAAULA* (El teatro áureo en el aula de Filología)?	3.6
2. Tras cursar la asignatura, mi competencia lectora de textos teatrales del siglo diecisiete ha mejorado	3.7
3. ¿Consideras que los profesores han explicado los contenidos con claridad y han respondido a las dudas que se han planteado?	3.5
4. ¿Te parece adecuada la incorporación de un bloque de clases dedicado al teatro del siglo diecisiete?	4.1

(*Continued*)

Table 11.6. (*Continued*)

Preguntas en escala Likert	Resultados (del uno al cinco)
5. Las clases introductoras de los martes (contexto histórico, géneros dramáticos, elementos del espectáculo teatral) me han resultado útiles para las clases posteriores dedicadas al análisis de espectáculos teatrales	3.3
6. La tarea de elaboración de una entrada de diccionario de teatro del Siglo de Oro me ha ayudado a comprender mejor la dimensión teatral	2.2
7. La visualización de vídeos en clase resulta útil para comprender el texto teatral estudiado	3.7
8. La asistencia a la representación de *El Caballero de Olmedo* ha resultado interesante y fructífera	3.8
9. Si participaste en el encuentro con Álvaro Tato, valora la actividad	3.0

En las dos últimas preguntas, en las que el alumnado podía expresar su opinión de forma desarrollada sobre los contenidos y sugerir modificaciones, también se obtuvo normalmente un buen grado de satisfacción por parte de los estudiantes, que consideraron adecuadas las lecturas propuestas e innovadora la inclusión de grabaciones de puestas en escena de las obras estudiadas en clase. No obstante, se tuvo en cuenta sus propuestas de cambio para futuros cursos (la supresión de alguna obra por el volumen excesivo de trabajo, más dedicación al comentario de textos, la inclusión de dramaturgas o la proyección de más puestas en escena completas).

Las conclusiones que se han podido extraer de la aplicación del proyecto en el bloque de teatro son que los estudiantes han podido acceder a las obras del Siglo de Oro desde la doble perspectiva del teatro, no solo como texto, como suele suceder en la enseñanza filológica, sino también como espectáculo. Así, se desarrollaron los objetivos de mejora de comprensión y expresión oral y lectora y el manejo de las TICs en el aula virtual que se propusieron en el proyecto inicial.

Una parte de los estudiantes participó muy activamente en clase a través de las preguntas que se iban proporcionando con anterioridad. Además, un grupo de ellos asistió a las actividades optativas mencionadas (proyección de *El perro del hortelano*, asistencia a *El caballero de Olmedo*, en Madrid, y encuentro con Álvaro Tato).

Conclusiones

En la era de lo audiovisual que es el siglo veintiuno, parece que el uso de recursos audiovisuales con carácter docente resulta beneficioso para el aprendizaje activo del alumnado en el sentido de que estos, habituados como lo están al visionado continuo de vídeos, estaban predispuestos a recibir ese tipo de estímulo con un fin docente.

De los objetivos específicos expuestos al inicio, se cumplieron todos en mayor o menor medida:

- Mejora de las habilidades comunicativas y destrezas orales necesarias para su futuro laboral.
- Innovación en los métodos de estudio y de acceso a la obra teatral, considerando el género desde su dualidad textual y espectacular. De esta forma, el estudiante ha desarrollado las habilidades prácticas necesarias para enfrentarse a un texto teatral y para saber comentarlo con capacidad crítica y reflexiva.
- Comprensión de la modernidad y repercusión del teatro de los Siglos de Oro en nuestros días. Se ha incentivado el estudio de épocas literarias tan ricas y complejas como el Renacimiento y el Barroco facilitando la adquisición de conocimientos y destrezas del alumnado a través de los medios audiovisuales, que conectan con las necesidades de la sociedad de las nuevas tecnologías.
- Ampliación de la cantidad de obras teatrales estudiadas en otros cursos académicos.
- Fomentar la creatividad del estudiante al utilizar un sistema de evaluación distinto a la tradicional repetición de contenidos.
- Impulso del trabajo en equipo, la colaboración y puesta en común de conocimientos, capacidades necesarias en el mundo laboral.

Más allá de los datos objetivos y los resultados obtenidos, con nuestro proyecto hemos tratado de acercar al filólogo en ciernes a un territorio de confluencia entre el papel y la ficción en pie que es el teatro, descubriéndoles que los autores áureos y sus preocupaciones no se alejan tanto de sus propias inquietudes actuales. Hemos buscado, por tanto, huir de la repetición de contenidos y despertar el interés en el análisis detallado de los textos a través de métodos comparativos, animar a los estudiantes a acudir a obras de teatro clásico sin prejuicios falsos, convertirlos no solo en lectores, sino también en espectadores con sensibilidad y juicio crítico. Y, por supuesto, también hemos tratado de juzgarnos a nosotros mismos, concediéndole la voz al alumnado para ayudarnos en la labor, siempre en proceso de construcción y mejora, de ser buenos docentes.

GEMA CIENFUEGOS ANTELO

12 Escenas para el aula de E/LE: el personaje femenino en el teatro del Siglo de Oro

[Scenes for the Spanish as a Foreign Language classroom: Female characters in Golden Age theatre]

ABSTRACT

This chapter describes an approach for teaching Spanish Golden Age Theatre using a selection of scenes and related texts centred on female characters. It begins by offering a brief critical overview of literature teaching in Spain, reviewing the place occupied by literature in the curriculum and the teaching methodologies followed, from traditional modes to literary education. It then outlines the theoretical framework underpinning the proposed approach and argues that the difficulties of teaching Golden Age Theatre to undergraduate students of Spanish can be attenuated by adopting a transversal (as opposed to a historicist) focus coupled with basic principles of literary education such as the experience of the literary text, writing workshops, etc. The suggested methodology combines analysis (reception of a given text) and construction (production of a created text), with the teacher transmitting the codes required for student understanding and interpretation.

Ayer y hoy de la enseñanza de la literatura

En los años 1990 hubo un conato de rebelión por parte de un grupo de intelectuales dedicados a la creación literaria y a la docencia en contra de algunas de las reformas incluidas en la entonces novedosa ley de enseñanza (la llamada LOGSE), concretamente contra la notable pérdida de horas lectivas dedicadas la literatura y, por tanto, a lectura guiada en las aulas.[1] Emilio Barón, profesor en la Universidad de Granada, clamaba con ironía:

> Corren rumores acerca de la supresión de la Literatura como asignatura con carácter obligatorio en la carrera de Filología Hispánica. [...] Si esta barbaridad se lleva a cabo, los burócratas de turno habrán dado un paso más (¡y qué paso!) para eliminar de los planes educativos españoles la enseñanza de la Literatura. Porque el asunto no es de hoy: ya tiene su historia. Y su razón de ser: el poder, cualquier poder, siempre ha mirado con recelo al escritor, a la obra literaria, a ese foco de pensamiento crítico y de posible disidencia.[2]

Y es que, llovía sobre mojado: ya en el año 1974, en el contexto de la Ley General de Enseñanza, Fernando Lázaro y Emilio Alarcos publicaban los resultados de una encuesta realizada a insignes escritores y maestros de la filología, como Antonio Muñoz Molina, Dámaso Alonso, Andrés Amorós, Juan Manuel Rozas o Francisco Rico, que daba cuenta de su generalizado pesimismo sobre el estado, los objetivos y la metodología de la enseñanza de la literatura en todos los niveles educativos.[3]

Si bien en su momento los más críticos pronosticaron efectos perversos desde una óptica ideológica, los sucesivos recortes que en los planes de estudios vienen sufriendo las materias de humanidades en la etapa secundaria, han tenido sobre todo un impacto nocivo en la competencia comunicativa de los estudiantes.[4] Arrinconar la literatura en un lugar ínfimo del currículum supone ignorar que la lectura literaria nos prepara para leer, comprender e

---

1 Ley Orgánica 1/1990, de 3 de octubre, de Ordenación General del Sistema Educativo. *Boletín Oficial del Estado* 238, de 4 de octubre de 1990.
2 Emilio Barón Palma, 'La lectura y el comentario en la enseñanza de la literatura: algunas reflexiones', *Cauce. Revista de Filología y su Didáctica* 13 (1990), 219–38, 221.
3 Fernando Lázaro Carreter y Emilio Alarcos Llorach, *Literatura y Educación* (Madrid: Castalia, 1974) y 'La enseñanza de la literatura', en Jesús González Terrón y José Manuel González Calvo, eds, *Actas de las I Jornadas de Metodología y Didáctica de la Lengua y la Literatura Españolas* (Cáceres: Universidad de Extremadura-ICE, 1991), 11–32.
4 Desde hace décadas, la literatura y, más recientemente, la filosofía. Una panorámica más exhaustiva a este respecto puede consultarse en María Isabel Alférez Valero, 'Educación literaria y currículum en España desde 1970', *Glosas didácticas* 17 (2008), 103–10; Ricardo Moreno Castillo ofrece una visión crítica de tales reformas señalando causas y efectos en *De la buena y mala educación* (Barcelona: Los Libros del Lince, 2008) y

interpretar mejor otros discursos sociales o académicos, dado que supone un entrenamiento en una forma discursiva más compleja. Así lo explica Bombini:

> Una retórica específica, el predominio de las funciones poética y metalingüística, la apropiación y uso de los mecanismos de connotación, los préstamos intertextuales, el particular modo de trabajar la referencia, las particularidades del sistema de enunciación literaria.[5]

El hecho es que en los estudios universitarios los profesores constatamos en cada nueva promoción de estudiantes los efectos del abandono de la literatura, que se traducen de forma inmediata en un déficit en el nivel de comprensión lectora, incluso en planes como Educación (anterior Magisterio), Humanidades o Estudios Hispánicos a los que acceden principalmente estudiantes que han cursado opciones de Bachillerato de Ciencias Sociales, o bien de Humanidades.[6] Un estudio reciente de Yubero y Larrañaga refleja con preocupación el escaso hábito lector que un alto porcentaje de estudiantes universitarios manifiestan:

> Suele entenderse erróneamente que los alumnos universitarios ya poseen hábito lector y tienen las competencias lectoras necesarias para desarrollar con eficacia sus estudios. Es algo que resulta al menos paradójico cuando se analizan los datos de hábitos lectores de estos estudiantes y se observan niveles que, aun siendo superiores a la población general, se quedan muy por debajo de lo que se debería suponer.[7]

La deficiente competencia lingüístico-literaria que presenta buena parte de los estudiantes que por su opción de estudios superiores vuelve a cursar

---

La conjura de los ignorantes. De como los pedagogos han destruido la enseñanza (Madrid: Pasos Perdidos, 2016).

5   Gustavo Bombini, 'Sujetos, literatura y currículum', en Carlos Battilana y Gustavo Bombini, eds, *Voces de un campo problemático. Actas del Primer Congreso Nacional de Didáctica de la lengua y la literatura* (La Plata, Argentina, 1997), 137–58, 140.

6   No pretendemos soslayar que existen factores de cambio social que evidentemente inciden en el descrédito de las humanidades, como la supremacía de otras materias de estudio del ámbito experimental o científico o el impacto de las nuevas tecnologías en los tiempos de ocio de los escolares, entre otros.

7   Santiago Yubero y Elisa Larrañaga, 'Lectura y Universidad: hábitos lectores de los estudiantes universitarios de España y Portugal, *El profesional de la información* 24/6 (2015), 717–23, 719.

asignaturas de literatura en la universidad, obliga al profesorado a buscar nuevos modos de acceso al texto literario, tanto más en el caso de los textos clásicos cuyo nivel de complejidad requiere buscar formas innovadoras para enseñar a leerlos y apreciarlos en su cualidad de clásicos.

La pedagogía del *contagio* de la literatura

Recordemos que aquellos maestros *en rebelión* no solo se manifestaron contra la merma de los estudios de humanidades, sino que también subrayaban las deficiencias de la praxis docente más extendida, errática en cuanto a la definición del objeto de estudio (qué) y su finalidad en cada nivel de enseñanza (para qué), así como en la metodología aplicada en el aula (cómo). Miguel Ángel Garrido ofrece un análisis clarividente de la cuestión:

> La literatura es, antes que cualquier otra consideración, el texto literario; su enseñanza ha de ir, pues, encaminada al entusiasmo de descubrir la aventura de leer. El alumno aprenderá así que la literatura es vida, pero vida intensificada connotativa y simbólicamente a través del lenguaje; por tanto, habrá de ser fundamentación y adquisición de experiencias antes que acarreo de datos 'sin sentido'. Éste sería el verdadero conocimiento y la adecuada finalidad, en la escuela, del hecho literario: descubrir, conocer e interpretar el mundo por medio de la creación literaria.[8]

En ese sentido, parece que algo se ha avanzado al asumirse en el currículum la educación literaria como corriente metodológica en la que fundamentar la práctica docente durante las etapas obligatorias de la educación. Sin embargo, la realidad generalizada, al menos en las aulas de secundaria, continúa lastrada por el enfoque historicista, un canon cerrado de lecturas sometidas a examen y la pervivencia del comentario de texto en sus diferentes modalidades, con lo cual en el reducido espacio lectivo asignado a la materia el docente se queda sin tiempo para invertir en facilitar al alumno una verdadera experiencia estética de la literatura y guiarle en el entrenamiento fructífero de la recepción literaria.

---

[8] Miguel Ángel Garrido, *Nueva Introducción a la Teoría de la Literatura* (Madrid: Síntesis, 2001), 343.

La percepción que en la actualidad tenemos algunos profesores universitarios de literatura es que un objetivo prioritario en nuestra materia ha de ser subsanar o reescribir en la medida de lo posible la experiencia de la 'clase de literatura' de una mayoría de alumnos que manifiestan haber perdido el gusto por la lectura en el instituto. De modo que, en nuestra práctica docente hemos de mantener una perspectiva tridimensional: 1) literaria, centrada en el lector (recepción y goce estético); 2) pedagógica, centrada en los contenidos y en el alumno-docente en formación; 3) constructivista, es decir, centrada en los procesos cognitivos de interpretación y dotación de sentido a un texto.

'Antes que enseñar literatura, hay que educar la sensibilidad. La sensibilidad no se enseña: más bien se contagia', dijo en una ocasión Luis Landero, autor de hermosísimos relatos y durante muchos años profesor de literatura en institutos de secundaria.[9] La frase, reducida a 'la literatura no se enseña, se contagia', se ha convertido en una especie de mantra para aquellos profesores e investigadores de la literatura (y de su didáctica) convencidos de que esta materia de estudio posee una suerte de virtud inherente que – rebasando la máxima horaciana – vendría a ser la de 'educar entusiasmando', convencidos además, de que el *modus operandi* del profesor es un factor determinante para lograr el ansiado contagio lector de los educandos.[10] La afortunada metáfora de Landero, a nuestro modo de ver, abandera un punto de inflexión en la más reciente historia de la enseñanza de la literatura. Sánchez Corral concreta los fundamentos del cambio metodológico en ámbitos precisos de la teoría de la literatura:

> Si aspiramos, desde nuestra perspectiva didáctica, a que la práctica de la literatura en el aula empiece a ser considerada como una situación comunicativa que le reporta al alumno las ventajas específicas de construir significados a través de la experiencia estética, entonces hemos de acudir a fundamentar nuestra actividad educativa en los modelos derivados de las diversas corrientes literarias enmarcadas en la *poética de la lectura*. De ahí que los nuevos enfoques didácticos pongan el acento en la formación

---

[9] Luis Landero, 'Experiencia pedagógica de un escritor', *Cuadernos de Literatura Infantil y Juvenil* 63 (1994), 26–34, 28.

[10] Manuel Abril, 'Enseñar literatura, tal vez soñar', *Comunicación, Lenguaje y Educación* 18 (1993), 91–9; Federico Altamirano Flores, 'El contagio de la literatura: otra mirada de la didáctica de la literatura', *Dialogía* 7 (2013), 227–44.

de hábitos de lectura y, en consecuencia, se le otorgue importancia al placer que han de procurar los textos tanto en la infancia como en la adolescencia.[11]

Teresa Colomer, una de las principales impulsoras del cambio metodológico en la enseñanza de la literatura, señala algunos procedimientos básicos, los cuales se hallan emparentados con nuestra propia propuesta:

> Han empezado a abrirse caminos integradores de la producción y recepción de textos literarios al servicio de los nuevos objetivos de formación. Los proyectos de trabajo, la renovación de las prácticas de traducción o de paráfrasis, la utilización de la intertextualidad como método de contraste o algunos intentos de renovar el eje cronológico con criterios actuales se hallan tanteando nuevas formas de potenciar la construcción del sentido a través de la literatura.[12]

Nuestra propuesta de método, válida también para los estudiantes extranjeros de literatura española, se enmarca en ciertas líneas de innovación que derivan de estos fundamentos teóricos (*poética de la lectura*).

Contagiar la literatura en el aula de E/LE

A la luz de lo expuesto hasta aquí, las dificultades que encuentra un estudiante universitario del siglo veintiuno al enfrentarse a un texto clásico en su lengua materna (en este caso, español) ya no parecen acaso tan distintas ni tan distantes de las que pudiera topar un estudiante extranjero, cuyo plan de estudios hispánicos le exige un nivel alto de dominio del español, pero que aún le resulta insuficiente para una construcción plena del sentido de un texto literario clásico. Si bien sus estrategias de aprendizaje serán lógicamente diferentes, en ambos casos, el método del profesor habrá de centrarse en el

---

[11] Luis Sánchez Corral, 'De la competencia literaria al proceso educativo: actividades y recursos', en Antonio Mendoza, ed., *Didáctica de la lengua y la literatura* (Madrid: Prentice Hall, 2003), 319–48, 325.

[12] Teresa Colomer, 'La enseñanza de la literatura como construcción de sentido', *Lectura y vida. Revista latinoamericana de Literatura* 22/4 (2001), 2–19, 16.

proceso de recepción, facilitando la implicación del alumno-lector, es decir, convirtiéndole en un receptor activo y motivado.

En los estudios superiores debemos añadir la apreciación del discurso literario, es decir, la consideración del estilo y del contexto de producción de la obra, pero no privilegiaremos, sino que subordinaremos estos niveles de aproximación a los textos a la recepción personal. Por otra parte, dado que la competencia lingüística del aprendiz de literatura en una L2 puede presentar cierta insuficiencia, la función del profesor no ha de ser la de un traductor del texto ni la de un instructor sobre el texto, sino que ha de llevar al aula una vivencia del texto que posibilite (*contagie*) la emoción de su lectura. Así pues, constituyen procedimientos básicos desde nuestra perspectiva metodológica la experimentación y la interpretación del texto. A nuestro modo de ver, si no logramos esa conmoción (en sentido etimológico), restaremos capacidad y motivación a los alumnos para la adquisición de lo instructivo nocional del arte literario y de los elementos contextuales de producción de las obras.

En parte, nuestro modelo se basa en unos trabajos ya veteranos de Cleanth Brooks y Roben P. Warren, que surgieron como producto de un movimiento estadounidense de renovación de los estudios literarios, el *New Criticism*, en la primera mitad del siglo veinte.[13] Nos fijamos en dos de los aspectos clave de su manual de referencia, *Understanding Poetry*. En primer lugar, en el hecho de que *experimentar* y *entender* tienen la consideración de sinónimos y, en segundo, en que su método de estudio de la poesía facilita integrar el aprendizaje y ejercicio de la lengua meta (entendida esta en su variedad diacrónica y estilística de una producción literaria concreta).

A nuestro modo de ver, *Understanding Poetry* propone una experiencia del texto poético que es idónea para su aplicación a los textos dramáticos áureos escritos en verso. Como explica el profesor Luis Galván:

> *Understanding Poetry* es un despliegue de la analogía con el drama. La 'situación dramática' (capítulo 1) es una escena o una historia que el hablante contempla o en la cual participa; las imágenes y el lenguaje analógico (capítulos 2 y 4) son medios para presentar la situación; el estado de ánimo y la actitud (capítulo 2) son los del hablante;

---

13   Brooks, Cleanth y Robert Penn Warren, eds, *Understanding Poetry* (New York: Holt, Rinehart and Winston, 1976) and *Instructor's Manual for Understanding Poetry* (New York: Holt, Rinehart and Winston, 1976).

el 'tono' (capítulo 3) es su tono de voz, el particular acento que da a su discurso; el significado (capítulo 5) es una propiedad del poema como un todo, y no solo de la situación presentada o los sentimientos expresados.[14]

Así pues, el teatro barroco nos ofrece un campo idóneo de aplicación de nuestra propuesta, fundamentada como hemos explicado, en las teorías de la recepción, semiótica y pragmática. La premisa más importante es la selección de textos por series, siguiendo los postulados de *Understanding Poetry*: agrupaciones homogéneas o heterogéneas (de distinto género o época) con un criterio de afinidad que permita un recorrido transversal y/o diacrónico por distintas obras. Un ejemplo: si en la programación de la asignatura los contenidos contemplan una ordenación histórica desde la Edad Media al Siglo de Oro, podríamos escoger para su recepción y trabajo en el aula poemas, cuentos y escenas dramáticas con un criterio de afinidad temático en torno al amor y la imagen/respuesta de la mujer amada.[15] Esta es solo una posible selección de textos que incluye variedades formales y tonales:

1) Uno de los cuentecillos en tono de burla de *El libro de buen amor*, como el 'Enxiemplo de lo que contesçió a don Pitas Pajas, pintor de Bretaña' (vv. 474–92), cuya primera estrofa anuncia:

> Del que olvidó la muger te diré la fazaña
> si vieres que es burla, dime otra tal mañana;
> era don Pitas Pajas un pintor de Bretaña
> casose con muger moça, pagábase de compaña.[16]

2) Un pasaje de *La cárcel de amor* donde se aprecie el tópico del amor cortés: por ejemplo, la primera carta de Leriano a Laureola, que comienza así:

---

14 Luis Galván Sánchez, 'Lectura de poesía en la educación literaria: apuntes de método', *Revista de Literatura* 68/135 (2006), 41–75, 44.

15 Ambos períodos de la historia de la literatura suelen constituirse en asignatura única en los planes de estudios renovados (Grado en Español o Filología Hispánica, Grado en Humanidades; también en los estudios de Español de las universidades de ámbito europeo y norteamericano).

16 La mayoría de los textos citados se encuentran disponibles en la Biblioteca Virtual Cervantes (en adelante, BVC: <http://www.cervantesvirtual.com>). Para no incurrir en reiteraciones incómodas solo daremos la ubicación de los textos en caso de que se encuentren en otros sitios web y facilitamos el comienzo de los textos y/o la numeración de los versos para su rápida localización dentro de la obra.

'Si tuviera tal razón para escribirte como para quererte'

3) Una escena amoroso-erótica de *La Celestina*. Acto XIX, el diálogo entre Calisto y Melibea en el huerto, que empieza de este modo:

'MELIBEA – ¿Qué quieres que cante, amor mío? ¿Cómo cantaré, que tu deseo era el que regía mi son y hacía sonar mi canto?'

4) El soneto *Amor constante más allá de la muerte* de Quevedo:

'Cerrar podrá mis ojos la postrera'[17]

5) Escena de la Jornada I de *La dama boba* de Lope en la que Laurencio, el galán protagonista, habla del amor a Finea en términos platónicos, y ésta, que no le entiende, responde cómicamente:

'Agora/ conozco, hermosa señora' (vv. 746–807)[18]

6) Dos fragmentos de *Don Quijote* en que contrastan el retrato idealizado de Dulcinea, concebido en la imaginación de Don Quijote ('– Yo no podré afirmar si la dulce mi enemiga gusta o no de que el mundo sepa que yo la sirvo.', Don *Quijote*, I, 23), y el paródico-realista imaginado por Sancho ('– Todo eso no me descontenta; prosigue adelante – dijo don Quijote –. Llegaste, ¿y qué hacía aquella reina de la hermosura?', *Don Quijote*, I, 31).

Escenas para el aula de E/LE

En nuestra propuesta 'Escenas para el aula de E/LE', seleccionamos una serie de textos teatrales ligados por tener una voz femenina, es decir, la voz del personaje *dama*, en el género de la Comedia Nueva instaurado por Lope de

---

17   Disponible en Francisco de Quevedo, *Obra poética*, ed. de José Manuel Blecua Teijeiro (Madrid: Castalia, 1969–71), vol. I, 657.
18   Disponible en la Biblioteca Digital ARTELOPE, <https://artelope.uv.es/biblioteca/textosAL/AL0575_LaDamaBoba>, consultado 22 mayo 2019.

Vega. La serie de escenas afines ayuda a los alumnos a detectar convenciones, identificar técnicas y lugares comunes y a apreciar rasgos de género sumamente convencionalizados. Además, el diálogo teatral y la forma discursiva en verso del periodo Barroco nos permiten, de acuerdo con Galván, 'concebir la poesía de forma más pragmática, es decir, más acorde con la semiótica y la teoría literaria actuales, y con el uso comunicativo del lenguaje que se propone en la enseñanza de lenguas.'[19]

Respecto a la afinidad temática de los textos, encontramos en el teatro español del siglo dieciséis, mujeres de toda índole social, de condición trágica o cómica, cuya enorme fuerza dramática hace que destaquen casi como mitos literarios entre las múltiples variantes del arquetipo *dama*. Relacionamos a continuación un grupo de obras que ofrecen una pertinente selección de escenas protagonizadas por el personaje femenino en su vertiente trágica:

1) En *Fuenteovejuna* de Lope, el personaje de Laurencia, víctima del abuso del poderoso, tiene un monólogo memorable en que denuncia y se rebela enfrentándose a su propio padre-alcalde. En dicha escena logra levantar en armas a un amedrentado concejo: 'Dejadme entrar, que bien puedo,/ en consejo de los hombres;/ que bien puede una mujer,/ si no a dar voto, a dar voces' (vv. 1714–1800).

2) En *La vida es sueño*, drama filosófico de Calderón, una osada dama, Rosaura, desafía y logra involucrar al padre pusilánime (Clotaldo), que se debate entre la lealtad al rey y la defensa de su propio honor: 'De ti recibí la vida,/ y tú mismo me dijiste,/ cuando la vida me diste/ que la que estaba ofendida/ no era vida' (vv. 2591–2655).

3) Hallamos mujeres-víctima de una pasión incestuosa en *La devoción de la cruz* (Julia) o en *Los cabellos de Absalón* (Tamar), ambas de Calderón. El personaje de raigambre bíblica también protagoniza *La venganza de Tamar*, de Tirso de Molina. Escogemos un parlamento de Tamar en *Los cabellos de Absalón* en el que pide justicia y reparación a su padre-rey:

---

19   Galván, 'Lectura de poesía en la educación literaria', 70.

'Gran monarca de Israel,/ descendiente del león/ que, para vengar injurias/ dio ayuda al nuevo Jacob' (vv. 1155–1269).[20]

4) Mujer vengadora del agravio masculino es la singular Gila de *La serrana de la Vera* de Vélez de Guevara. Escogemos de la Jornada I el retrato varonil de la serrana que hace Pascuala y una acción posterior de la protagonista que ilustra su fama: 'Gila. ¿Qué dicen en el lugar/ de mí? Pascuala. Que eres Locifer,/ saltabardales, machorra' (vv. 539–696).

Podemos ampliar la serie con textos que provienen de la lírica, pues la mujer como objeto o sujeto poético se encarna en las tablas bajo idénticas máscaras, si bien reformuladas por las convenciones del género teatral. Por ejemplo, en el incipiente teatro renacentista encontramos a una mujer que reivindica su libertad mediante la soltería en el *Auto de la sibila Casandra*, de Gil Vicente, quien compuso para dicho auto una cancioncilla bien conocida: 'Dicen que me case yo, / No quiero marido, no. / Más quiero vivir segura / en esta sierra a mi soltura, / que no estar en ventura / si casaré bien o no' (vv. 294–313).

La voz de la mujer malmaridada, casada con viejo (celoso, tacaño o impotente) también salta de la lírica a las tablas: 'Soy garridilla e pierdo sazón / por malmaridada; / tengo marido en mi corazón / que a mí agrada'. La queja de la mujer malmaridada la entona un abundante y variopinto repertorio de voces dramáticas, desde la comicidad: la Lorenza de *El viejo celoso* de Cervantes, hasta la perspectiva trágica de otra Casandra, la de *El castigo sin venganza* de Lope. En definitiva, nuestro criterio de afinidad coloca el foco sobre el personaje femenino que representa a mujeres en rebeldía ante un destino trágico impuesto, pues reivindican su dignidad (honor) y se enfrentan al tipo varonil opresor que detenta el poder, ya sean padres, hermanos, galanes o maridos de los textos canónicos del Siglo de Oro. No se trata de acumular lecturas fragmentarias, sino de hacer una selección significativa que ayude a mejorar el trabajo con los textos en el aula y que motive al alumno a leer la obra completa.

Proponemos a continuación una secuenciación de actividades a partir de nuestra selección de textos como centro de interés.

---

20 Esta comedia se encuentra disponible en la web TC/12 CANON 60, <https://tc12.uv.es/canon60/C6003_LosCabellosDeAbsalon.php>, consultado 22 mayo 2019.

Sesiones de recepción en el aula

1) Lectura expresiva ante el grupo-clase espectador: el profesor lee un fragmento de la selección ofreciendo un modelo de entonación, ritmo e intención. Si en la programación de las clases se establece una rutina de entrenamiento en la lectura expresiva con escenas o textos teatrales completos, se pueden organizar en el grupo-clase sesiones de lectura en *mesa italiana* (primera lectura de un guión por los actores que van a interpretarlo). Lograr una lectura expresiva requiere no solo un trabajo de dicción, sino de construcción del sentido del texto.[21] Isabel Tejerina adopta como método apropiado para la lectura en el aula la formulación de preguntas sobre la intención del texto. Se trata de una adaptación del método de William Layton para actores:

> No se pretende que los alumnos realicen una interpretación teatral del texto, lo que exigiría traducirlo en toda su significación expresiva y escénica. Pero es importante que en un proceso gradual vayan reflexionando y descubriendo los valores y matices significativos del lenguaje literario y la importancia de la información que lleva oculta el lenguaje verbal, el denominado *subtexto*, el cual es esencial para traducir las intenciones del texto y la auténtica vida de los personajes. Una misma frase puede contener mil maneras distintas y válidas de decirse. Elegir el 'cómo' decir una frase depende al cien por cien del 'qué dices', 'a quién' se lo dices, 'dónde' lo dices y 'para qué' lo dices. También analizar el significado intencional de los diferentes tipos de subtextos escondidos en los puntos suspensivos, los silencios, las acciones, los cambios de tema.[22]

---

[21] Recomendamos dedicar entre diez y quince minutos de cada sesión de lectura a realizar una serie de ejercicios de técnica vocal planificados de forma progresiva. Si bien existen numerosos recursos en la red, resulta muy útil para este cometido el manual de Victoria Blasco, *Manual de técnica vocal. Ejercicios prácticos* (Madrid: Ñaque, 2008). También es muy interesante para este trabajo el análisis del texto dramático que propone Tomás Motos incluido en un libro titulado muy significativamente *Palabras para la acción* (Madrid: Ñaque, 2003).

[22] 'Animación a la lectura con textos teatrales', en Pedro C. Cerrillo, ed., *La motivación a la lectura a través de la literatura infantil* (Madrid: Ministerio de Educación y Ciencia, 2006), 67–88, 72. Conviene señalar que estas técnicas siguen aplicándose en el Laboratorio William Layton, la primera escuela privada de actores que se creó en España.

Escenas para el aula de E/LE

2) Otra modalidad de lectura es la dialógica grupal o, según Caro Valverde y González García, 'lectura comentada por medio del coloquio, donde se promueve la comprensión a partir de las inferencias espontáneas de los lectores y se despliegan con naturalidad las manifestaciones interculturales'.[23]

3) En sesiones de lectura intertextual el profesor introduce los textos afines a las escenas barrocas, como las muestras de lírica popular con voces femeninas, o alguna pieza en tono cómico, como el entremés cervantino *El viejo celoso*. Los alumnos también son receptores activos en este tipo de lectura, pues serán estimulados por el profesor a buscar textos afines de su propia tradición cultural o de cualquier otra fuente que conozcan, para en la siguiente sesión comentar con el grupo los rasgos del texto aportado en relación con la serie. La función del profesor aquí es clave para abordar en este punto el análisis de las características de las obras desde el punto de vista de la historia literaria y de los rasgos del género y del estilo del autor.

4) Con obras teatrales completas, la experiencia óptima de recepción del texto es asistir a una representación interpretada por actores profesionales, pero si no es posible, el Centro de Documentación Teatral tiene un servicio de préstamo de grabaciones audiovisuales *on line* de la cartelera representada en teatros públicos pertenecientes al Instituto Nacional de Artes Escénicas y de la Música, que incluye los montajes de la Compañía Nacional de Teatro Clásico.[24] Comentar la escena vista amplía las perspectivas de los alumnos y dota de significado al texto: el profesor modera y glosa expresiones y términos, al tiempo que aporta algunas claves de semiótica teatral. Fijando de nuevo la atención en el texto, el profesor – en interacción con los alumnos – se aplica al análisis del discurso literario propuesto por *Understanding poetry*: comentario de la situación dramática, de las imágenes y el lenguaje figurado, del estado de ánimo y la actitud de los personajes, del tono o intención de cada uno de ellos en su parlamento y del significado de la escena dentro de la obra completa.

---

23   Teresa Caro Valverde y María González García, 'De la mano de Cervantes: la lectura moderna de los clásicos', *Ocnos* 9 (2013), 89–106, 102.
24   Teatroteca, <http://teatroteca.teatro.es/opac/#indice>, consultado 22 mayo 2019.

Sesiones de re-creación en el aula

Introducimos a continuación algunos ejercicios adicionales que conllevan re-escrituras y nuevas creaciones por parte del estudiante.

1) Se planificarán sesiones-taller de escritura creativa, como explican Caro Valverde y González García 'desde la libre poetización del referente y con el apoyo estratégico de modelos textuales y de organizadores previos para facilitar la redacción o para promocionar la invención', como cartas, canciones, cuentos, cómics, retratos, entrevistas, etc.[25]
2) Ejercicios de improvisación teatral sobre alguna de las escenas leídas con la ayuda de las indicaciones del profesor, que propondrá a los alumnos que reescriban la escena incorporando un personaje nuevo o un contexto espacio-temporal distinto, entre otras posibilidades.

Estas fórmulas de recepción y experimentación del texto teatral allanan el camino para que los alumnos afronten la lectura de obras completas y sirven de estímulo para que ellos mismos indaguen y profundicen en los conocimientos sobre el autor y su obra.

    Nuestra propuesta metodológica combina el análisis con la construcción o, dicho de otro modo, la recepción del *texto dado*, con la producción de un *texto creado*. Las actividades que se proponen para el aula en esta segunda fase provienen de la pedagogía teatral y pueden planificarse con el objetivo de llegar a producir un hipertexto creado por los alumnos, es decir, una nueva dramaturgia inspirada en su hipotexto (una reescritura en prosa, una versión que surja de los materiales producidos en las improvisaciones, o la creación de una *secuela* dramática o poética). La tarea final podría ser la dinamización del texto creado por los alumnos, mediante la técnica teatral que se considere oportuna o que sea viable en el contexto de la programación, desde la dramatización al montaje teatral.[26]

---

25 'De la mano de Cervantes', 102.
26 Tomás Motos Teruel, 'Dramatización y Técnicas Dramáticas en la enseñanza y el aprendizaje', en Víctor García Hoz, ed., *Enseñanzas artísticas y técnicas* (Madrid: Ediciones Rialp, 1996), 113–64.

Creemos que las dificultades de llevar al aula de E/LE en el marco de la educación superior textos literarios clásicos se aminoran con este tratamiento transversal de afinidad temática o de cualquier otro tipo (frente al tradicional historicista) y poniendo en práctica ciertos fundamentos de la educación literaria, como es el acceso directo al texto, el taller de escritura y la dinamización dramática de las propias producciones de los alumnos, creadas a partir de los referentes analizados. Estudiar la literatura de una lengua extranjera no solo tiene como prerrequisitos un nivel avanzado de competencia lingüística, sino una buena dosis de motivación, pues la distancia entre los contextos de producción y de recepción de un clásico en una lengua extranjera puede convertirse en un escollo insalvable si no logramos establecer un vínculo entre el lector y el texto mediante una experiencia intelectual y emocional de las obras. Leer según nuestra propuesta no solo supone comprender mejor, sino experimentar y establecer un vínculo con el texto; de este modo el docente puede optimizar el diálogo entre el lector en formación y el texto literario para su plena apropiación e interpretación.

DUNCAN WHEELER

The pedagogic potential (and limitations) of cinematic adaptations

ABSTRACT

Just like the House of Habsburg, the teaching of the Spanish Golden Age appears to be in perpetual decline. Rather than bemoaning this state of affairs, I would suggest it is our collective responsibility to look for solutions in the context of a post-literary culture. I sketch a history of how and why Golden Age works have been taught in primary and secondary school in Spain, before then analysing the possibilities harboured in audio-visual production to safeguard the presence of Spanish classical theatre as a cornerstone of a holistic democratic education both at home and abroad.[1]

Much like the House of Habsburg, the teaching of the Golden Age often gives the impression of being in perpetual decline. The successive reforms of primary and secondary education in Spain since the first initiatives put in place by Felipe González's Socialist administration (1982–96) have increasingly diminished the space and time allocated to the national classics. The teaching of Spanish in the Anglophone world has experienced a veritable boom over the course of the last three decades: without reaching the levels of the United States – where there are more than double the number of students enrolled in Spanish than of all other modern European tongues combined – the language of Cervantes is the only to be consistently on the rise in the UK.[2] This tendency has not, however, favoured the fortunes of Golden Age studies; quite the contrary. With the exception of the University of Oxford and, to a far lesser degree, Cambridge, undergraduate degrees in

---

[1] This chapter is based on a previous paper in Spanish 'Las adaptaciones cinematográficas como (posible) herramienta pedagógica', published in *Anuario Lope de Vega* 24 (2018), 260–88.

[2] Joan L. Brown, *Confronting our Canons: Spanish and Latin American Studies in the 21st Century* (Lewisburg, PA: Bucknell University Press, 2010), 184.

the British Isles no longer pertain to the ambit of traditional philology. A cause and consequence of the hegemony of Cultural Studies, the replacement of literary by audio-visual texts is a reality.

Unlike in the Spanish higher education system, British academics do not have to follow a national curriculum, but the increased marketization of universities has ensured that student preferences (perceived or real) not only inform but also increasingly determine what is taught. Pedro Almodóvar is by a significant margin the principal protagonist of undergraduate programmes in Hispanic Studies, whilst more UK universities courses feature the films of Iciar Bollaín than the works of Calderón de la Barca, Cervantes, Lope de Vega or Tirso de Molina.[3] On the one hand, disciplinary diversity and a growing reluctance to reify ostensibly 'high' culture (rarely categorized thus at the time of creation) is commendable in many respects.[4] Nonetheless, as I have argued elsewhere: 'me parece más factible defender una tesis sobre Lope de Vega y después hacer investigaciones sobre Isabel Preysler que al revés'.[5] The priorities are other in Spain. Golden Age drama may occupy a relatively privileged place on campus, but it does not fight under the same conditions as Elizabethan theatre in Spanish society more broadly: even leaving aside the hegemony of the English language, the *comedia* has less of a role to play in the school curriculum, whilst Shakespeare occupies a much more central role than any of his autochthonous counterparts in

---

[3] See Stuart Davis, 'The study of the discipline: Hispanic literature and film in UK Spanish degrees', *Journal of Romance Studies* 18/1 (2018), 25–44. I would like to thank Dr Davis for sharing the findings of this article with me prior to publication.

[4] As Jeffrey Knapp argues, this is a good argument for the comparative study of Shakespeare (and, by implication, why not Lope?) and cinema: 'Though few would now scoff at calling Shakespeare's plays art, many would have done so during Shakespeare's lifetime. Associating Renaissance drama with film broadens our conception of the drama, too, by helping us recognize the often self-confessed cheapness and vulgarity in Renaissance plays that their current cultural prestige belies', *Pleasing Everyone: Mass Entertainment in Renaissance London and Golden-Age Hollywood* (Oxford: Oxford University Press), 4–5.

[5] Duncan Wheeler, 'Julio Iglesias, el embajador universal', *JotDown* (August 2014), <http://www.jotdown.es/2014/08/julio-iglesias-el-embajador-universal>, accessed 1 November 2017. A staple of *¡Hola!* magazine, Julio Iglesias's first wife is currently the partner of Nobel-prize laureate Mario Vargas Llosa.

many undergraduate programmes in both Spanish and English literature. The humanities may be increasingly marginalized in Spain as elsewhere but philological degrees continue to be orientated around tradition and the written word despite the fact that it is perfectly possible for 18- and 19-year-olds to embark on an undergraduate degree in their national literature without having read even a fragment from a *comedia*. I have in fact encountered numerous examples of such students in many of the country's most reputable universities.

As opposed to lamenting this state of affairs, it is incumbent upon us to look for a solution within post-literate societies in which, to borrow a phrase from Robert Rosenstone, the 'desire to express our relationship to the past by using contemporary forms of expression, as well as the desire to appeal to a contemporary sensibility, sooner or later has to point us in the direction of the visual media'.[6] In the first part of the chapter, I chart a history of how and why Golden Age drama has been taught in the Spanish school system to argue that pedagogical practice combined with television and cinematic adaptations from the Francoist period have produced a series of prejudices in relation to the national classical theatre that have yet to be dispelled. A comparison of the respective fortunes of Lope and Shakespeare in the classroom and on the silver screen will pave the way for the material covered in the second half, which offers concrete examples to suggest the possibilities afforded by audio-visual production as a means to safeguard Golden Age drama as the cornerstone of a holistic democratic education both at home and abroad. Against the backdrop of a somewhat dispiriting panorama, I attempt to identify glimmers of hope through cinematic Lope adaptations in an attempt to remedy Peter W. Evans's diagnosis from nearly thirty years ago on the pressing need to extirpate 'mummified texts [...] to explicate them and to allow them an integral, front-rank place in the curriculum of civilised establishments of education'.[7]

---

6   Robert A. Rosenstone, *History on Film/Film on History* (Harlow: Longman and Pearson, 2006), 4.
7   Peter William Evans, 'In preface', in Peter William Evans, ed., *Conflicts of Discourse: Spanish Literature in the Golden Age* (Manchester: Manchester University Press, 1990), vi–viii, vii.

The Golden Age in the Spanish school system

A rigorous study of the teaching of the *comedia* during the dictatorship and democracy has yet to be undertaken. For our current purposes, my working hypothesis is that the marginalization of classical texts following the death of General Francisco Franco in 1975 constitutes a paradigmatic example of inheriting the sins of the father. Reacting against the violent didacticism of the dictatorship, changing times gave way to new concepts as regards pedagogical relations: 'En el paradigma LOGSE (Ley de Ordenación General del Sistema Educativo) el currículum no es el espacio para la transmisión de conocimiento, sino el momento de reconstruir el conocimiento de forma democrática'.[8] It does not require subscribing to Javier Orrico's somewhat apocalyptic conclusion – that literature in Spanish secondary schools has 'convertido ahora en un mero registro o lenguaje especializado entre otros muchos' – to acknowledge his premise that in 1990, 'el mismo momento en que se ampliaba la escolarización obligatoria desde los catorce hasta los dieciséis años [...] la denominación de la asignatura pasaba a ser la de lengua castellana y literatura'.[9] When novelist Arturo Pérez-Reverte was asked about the publication of tailored editions of his highly successful *Alatriste* series for school children, he commented that it constituted, 'sin caer en los prejuicios imperiales del franquismo', an attempt 'remediar la desmemoria y la ignorancia que produjo la LOGSE de Maravall [José María] y Solana [Javier]'.[10] It is unlikely a coincidence that the director of the cinematic adaptation of *Alatriste* (Agustín Díaz Yanes, 2006) is a history graduate married to a secondary-school teacher. In his own words: 'España es un país ahistórico que, teniendo una historia riquísima, parece que no interesa a nadie, en

---

8   José Penalva Buitrago, 'El modelo docente en el paradigma LOGSE o de la jibarización del profesor', in Remedios Sánchez García and Ana María Ramos García, eds, *Compromiso docente y realidad educativa: retos para el maestro del siglo xxi* (Madrid: Síntesis, 2012), 45–64, 59.

9   Javier Orrico, 'La lengua y la literatura españolas en la España de la LOGSE', *Claves de la razón práctica* (December 2014), 35–43, 41 and 35.

10 Cited in Miguel Mora, 'Se publica la serie *Alatriste* en edición escolar', *El País* (24 May 2001), 38.

parte porque nadie la conoce [...] Creo que se debe a la Dictadura: creó tal división en el país que todavía es muy pronto para que la gente se reconcilie con su pasado'.[11]

In his overview of teaching practices from the early Franco period, Ángel Luis Abós observes that the 'hombre español del Siglo de Oro es ofrecido como ejemplo: heroico, virtuoso y movido únicamente por causas nobles y espirituales. La escuela es uno de los instrumentos privilegiados para propagar los ideales imperiales del régimen'.[12] As Esther Martínez Tórtola surmises: 'El tema de los Reyes Católicos es una constante en todos los cursos del bachillerato franquista'; with the purported national unity brought about by their dynastic and marital union 'comienza el período hacia el que deben dirigir sus ojos los jóvenes que se están educando en la Nueva España'.[13] As can be gauged from the following description by Fernando Valls, the Golden Age's most prolific writer had a key role to play:

> Por un decreto del 2-IX-1941 el Ministerio de Educación Nacional creaba el Centro de Estudios sobre Lope de Vega, con el fin de 'contribuir a la vulgarización de la obra literaria de Lope de Vega con ediciones manuales, populares y económicas, que pongan al alcance de todos su producción lírica y dramática'. También en la obra de Lope – y concretamente en su teatro – encontraron los ideólogos del franquista materia educativa, en este caso de 'educación femenina': el Hermano Orizana se preguntaba: '¿dónde podría verse expuesto con más galanura el amor conyugal, base de la familia, que en el lindísimo diálogo entre Casilda y Peribáñez?'[14]

With this framework in place, *Fuenteovejuna* and *Peribáñez y el comendador de Ocaña* becoming Lope's most frequently studied plays was entirely lógico, also providing the inspiration for the first post-Civil War cinema adaptations: *Aventura* (Jerónimo Mihura, 1944) and *Fuenteovejuna* (Antonio Román, 1947). Although subversive subtexts can be identified in the latter, the film overall constitutes a paradigmatic example of a didactic form of cinema

---

[11] Cited in Rubén Romero Santos, *La pistola y el corazón: conversaciones con Agustín Díaz Yanes* (Madrid: Tecmerin, 2014), 80–1.

[12] Ángel Luis Abós, *La historia que nos enseñaron (1937–75)* (Madrid: Foca, 2003), 303.

[13] Esther Martínez Tórtola, *La enseñanza de la historia en el primer bachillerato franquista (1938–53)* (Madrid: Tecnos, 1996), 68–9.

[14] Fernando Valls, *La enseñanza de la literatura en el franquismo (1936–51)* (Madrid: Antoni Bosch, 1983), 151.

produced by the regime.[15] Such revisionist appropriation provides a much better fit for the heuristic model, advanced by critics such as José Antonio Maravall and José María Díez Borque, which claims that the *comedia* was a monolithically conservative mode of propaganda than the texts on which they were ostensibly based.[16]

The year after the attempt to hold Spanish democracy to ransom through an unsuccessful coup attempt was thwarted, the PSOE, led by the youthful Felipe González and armed with campaign slogan 'Por el cambio', secured an absolute majority in the 1982 general elections. This was the generation of 1968's first opportunity to govern anywhere in Europe, whilst educational reform was urgently needed if the values enshrined in the 1978 Spanish Constitution were to be put into effect. Secondary school headmaster F. Javier Mestre Marcotegui claims that such transformations '[s]e caracterizan por entender la escuela como un factor de nivelación social y la ven como el lugar para la formación en valores, en actitudes, en procedimientos [...] de modo que los contenidos conceptuales pasen a un segundo plano de importancia'.[17] A boom in teaching English as a foreign language alongside democratic normalization gave rise to an 'identification through Shakespeare with some of the issues (both aesthetic and moral) affecting other citizens of the European Community'.[18] In contrast, the first reform, the LODE (Ley Orgánica del Derecho a la Educación) brought out under the auspices of 1985 by José María Maravall (it is far from coincidental that he was José Antonio's son) almost overnight expelled the Golden Age from the school curriculum.

On the one hand, the creation of the Almagro Theatre Festival and the Compañía Nacional de Teatro Clásico (CNTC) were landmark initiatives. Conversely, however, these new institutions faced ingrained prejudices.

---

15   Duncan Wheeler, *Golden Age Drama in Contemporary Spain: The* Comedia *on Page, Stage and Screen* (Cardiff: University of Wales Press, 2012), 138–43.
16   Duncan Wheeler, 'Contextualising and contesting José Antonio Maravall's theories of baroque culture from the perspective of modern-day performance', *Bulletin of the Comediantes* 65/1 (2013), 15–43.
17   F. Javier Mestre Marcotegui, 'Premisas y antecedentes de la actual revolución educativa: el caso de la Educación Secundaria en España', *Logos: Anales del Seminario de Metafísica*, 38 (2005), 337–49, 341.
18   Keith Gregor, *Shakespeare in the Spanish Theatre: 1772 to the Present* (London: Continuum, 2010), 117.

According to Andrés Amorós's diagnosis: 'desde la escuela nos han presentado a los clásicos como una losa, la gente piensa sólo en el culto a la monarquía, al honor y a la religión, con lo que se ha conseguido una visión tópica del Siglo de Oro'.[19] If there had been a richer tradition in the study of theatrical, television and cinematic adaptations, it would perhaps have been easier to repurpose the study of the *comedia* for new times. As Elaine Showalter remarks on dramatic literature in the classroom, 'of all teaching techniques, performance can be the most active and student-centred, and can lead to engaged intellectual discovery of the text'.[20] It is no mere anecdotal detail to note that the co-ordinators of study-days linked with the principal classical theatre festivals (Felipe Pedraza Jiménez in Almagro and Germán Vega in Olmedo) worked as secondary school teachers before being awarded university chairs. Antonio Serrano, the prime instigator of the Almeria Theatre Festival, staged school productions long before doing so was in fashion.[21]

The general tendency was, however, to dedicate little time to the Golden Age in either history or literary curricula. Student encounters with Lope plays were largely determined by chance, factors such as the enthusiasm of individual teachers or the occasional inclusion of a *comedia* as part of the pre-university exams. Shakespeare at the time occupied a more prominent place in secondary schools in the United Kingdom albeit within an elitist framework.[22] The traditional division between academic education and vocational training was still manifest in the 1980s. Furthermore, there was a clear ideological correlative to the almost exclusively textual mode of study, which reproduced the concept director Jonathan Miller has coined as

19 Cited in José F. Beaumont, 'La escena española, del olvido a la renovación', *El País* (29 September 1979), <https://elpais.com/diario/1979/09/29/cultura/307404016_850215. html>, accessed 1 November 2017.
20 Elaine Showalter, *Teaching Literature* (Oxford: Blackwell, 2003), 87.
21 'Supimos que el teatro es "para verlo" y no solo "para leerlo". Y de esa inquietud y esa premisa nacimos', Antonio Serrano, 'Las jornadas de Almería', in Fernando Doménech Rico and Julio Vélez Sainz, eds, *Arte nuevo de hacer teatro en este tiempo* (Madrid: Ediciones del Otro, 2011), 123–5, 125.
22 To understand the background context, see Oliver Boyd-Barrett, 'Educational reform in Spain and in the UK: a comparative perspective', in Oliver Boyd-Barrett and Pamela O'Malley, eds, *Education Reform in Democratic Spain* (London: Routledge, 1995), 65–78.

'some sort of quantum of intrinsic meaning'.[23] The vagaries of reception and material (pre-)conditions under the reigns of both Elizabeth I and II were generally sidestepped. According to Alan Sinfield's analysis of assessment criteria under Thatcher: 'The combination of cultural deference and cautious questioning promoted around Shakespeare in GCE seems designed to construct a petty bourgeoisie which will strive within limits allocated to it without seeking to disrupt the system'.[24] In 1992, a paradigm shift occurred with the implementation of a national curriculum; for the first time, the Bard's plays became a cornerstone in the education of all children of primary and secondary school age.[25]

The renovation of pedagogical practice in relation to Shakespeare went hand in hand with a new emphasis on performance, the Royal Shakespeare Company (RSC) helping to make fresh educational programmes sustainable through the development of activities aimed at students of all abilities and from different backgrounds. With a combination of civic duty and canny self-preservation, the RSC managed to thrive under a Conservative government loathe to fund the arts at a time when sell-out houses in Stratford were far from the norm. The new pedagogical landscape alongside the invention of VHSs (and later DVDs) also helped to ensure that cinematic adaptations of Shakespeare ceased to be viewed as commercial suicide in the 1990s.[26] The pioneer of this trend was Kenneth Branagh, although *William Shakespeare's Romeo + Juliet* (Baz Luhrmann, 1996) became the first cinematic makeover to deliver a substantial profit.[27] According to James N. Loehlin, the secret of the film's success resided in 'its effective plundering of youth culture and its

---

23 Jonathan Miller, *Subsequent Performances* (London: Faber & Faber, 1986), 20.
24 Alan Sinfield, 'Give an account of Shakespeare and education, showing why you think they are effective and what you have appreciated about them. Support your answers with precise references', in Jonathan Dollimore and Alan Sinfield, eds, *Political Shakespeare: Essays in Cultural Materialism* (Manchester: Manchester University Press, 1994), 158–81, 168.
25 Maurice Gilmour, 'Shakespeare in the secondary school', in Maurice Gilmour, ed., *Shakespeare for All in Secondary Schools* (London: Cassell, 1996), 5–8.
26 Daniel Rosenthal, *100 Shakespeare Films (BFI Film Guides)* (London: British Film Institute, 2007), xxi.
27 Peter Holland, 'Foreward', in Mark Thornton Burnett, ed., *Shakespeare, Film, Fin de Siècle* (Houndmills: Macmillan Press, 2000), xii–xiv.

aggressive marketing toward a teenage audience'.²⁸ The critical reaction was mixed. To quote an apt summation from Robert Nery: '*William Shakespeare's Romeo + Juliet* is high energy, triumphantly vulgar, a gaudy bricolage. If you seek earnest reserve or understatement, you won't find it here. The film is as far from the beige good taste of Kenneth Branagh's *Much Ado about Nothing* (1993) as Memphis furniture from Ikea'.²⁹ In Spain, reviews tended to lambast the adolescent nature of the film starring Claire Danes and Leonardo DiCaprio.³⁰ Audiences also revealed a clear preference for the reputedly good taste of Emma Thompson's husband, the homeland of Lope de Vega being one of the few territories where more cinemagoers purchased a ticket to see *Much Ado about Nothing* than *Romeo + Juliet*. This, I would suggest, was symptomatic of a largely uncritical veneration of classical theatre, the cause and consequence of teenagers being less entranced by Shakespeare's suicidal lovers being given a postmodern makeover.³¹

Said preferences need to be situated within a broader habitus described by Sally Faulkner as follows: 'The Spanish middlebrow film, dating from 1970s on, responds to social mobility off screen through the advent of a socially- and culturally-aspirant middle-class audience'.³² The chief institutional architect of this parvenu cinema had been Pilar Miró in her capacity as Director-General of Cinematography (1982–5). She subsequently became

28   James N. Loehlin, '"These violent delights have violent ends": Baz Luhrmann's millennial Shakespeare', in Mark Thornton Burnett, ed., *Shakespeare, Film, Fin de Siècle* (Houndmills: Macmillan Press, 2000), 121–36, 121.
29   Robert Nery, '*William Shakespeare's Romeo + Juliet*', *Cinema Papers* (February 1997), 36–8, 36.
30   Hence, for example, in a disgruntled report from the Berlin Film Festival, Ángel Fernández-Santos observed how '[c]ompletó la jornada una ridícula versión californiana, de las llamadas de estilo *mariachi*, de *Romeo y Julieta*, de William Shakespeare', 'Tim Burton ataca con una divertida pandilla de marcianos completamente terrestres', *El País* (23 February 1997), <https://elpais.com/diario/1997/02/23/cultura/856652401_850215.html>, accessed 1 November 2017.
31   Statistics taken from the database of Spain's Filmoteca, <https://www.mecd.gob.es/cultura-mecd/areas-cultura/cine/industria-cine/base-datos-peliculas-calificadas.html>, accessed 11 November 2017, alongside the EDI database available in the reading room of the BFI in London.
32   Sally Faulkner, *A History of Spanish Film: Cinema and Society (1910–2010)* (London: Continuum, 2013), 278.

the first filmmaker to make the *comedia* legible to a mainstream film-going audience in Spain: *El perro del hortelano* (Pilar Miró, 1996), marketed as the Spanish equivalent to Branagh's *Much Ado about Nothing* and *Cyrano de Bergerac* (Jean-Paul Rappeneaut, 1990) starring Gerard Depardieu, became Lope's first major success at the domestic box office.

According to Miró's lament: 'En España [...] estamos muy mal educados y tendemos a despreciar nuestra cultura. Como forma de expresión universal, el cine es el vehículo perfecto para dar a conocer nuestro patrimonio cultural'.[33] *El perro del hortelano* has had some repercussion in foreign university classrooms, but the lack of an international marketplace for films based on Lope's plays – or, more generally, about the Spanish Golden Age – constitutes a major obstacle.[34] Period films tend to be very costly, unlikely to recoup investment at the domestic box office whatever their success amongst local audiences. At the time it was made, *Alatriste* had the highest budget ever in Spanish cinema history and starred a bankable Hollywood star in the guise of Viggo Mortensen. The producers were however unable to sell the film to as many markets as they had predicted. In a national industry in which all films tend to be subsidized in one form of another, *Alatriste* proved to be the most commercially and critically successful example of a passing trend by which producers from private television channels (obliged by law to invest in cinema) privileged period dramas.[35]

Lope (Andrucha Waddington, 2010), a Spanish variation on *Shakespeare in Love* (John Madden, 1998), was beset with production problems, and the Brazilian director could not presume the same cultural familiarity that his English predecessor was able to largely take for

33 Cited in Pedro Costa, 'Pilar Miró obtiene el máximo premio en el festival de Mar del Plata', *El País* (17 November 1996), 34.
34 Carmen García de la Rasilla, 'Teaching Golden Age theater through filmic adaptations', in Laura R. Bass and Margaret R. Greer, eds, *Approaches to Teaching Early Modern Spanish Drama* (New York: MLA, 2006), 69–75.
35 Duncan Wheeler, 'Back to the future: repackaging Spain's troublesome past for local and global audiences', in Duncan Wheeler and Fernando Canet, eds, *(Re)viewing Creative, Critical and Commercial Practices in Contemporary Spanish Cinema* (Bristol: Intellect, 2014), 205–33, 217–26.

granted. According to co-scriptwriter Ignacio del Moral, Waddington underplayed the humour – reinstated to a certain extent in a book based on the film written by Verónica Fernández – underpinning the original proposal: 'El resultado fue una película demasiado solemne, oscura y sin magia que, además, dio unos rendimientos de taquilla más bien modestos, muy por debajo de las expectativas que el proyecto había despertado'.[36] The biopic focused on the experiences of the 'primer Lope', the denouement set up for continuation in a sequel that never materialized due to the film's disappointing box-office performance and the end of the passing fad for high-budget national period dramas.[37] Cultural production in Spain suffered the fallout of the financial crash in particularly acute fashion. It is unlikely a film of the calibre of *El perro del hortelano* will come to a cinema near you anytime soon.

Distribution and exhibition are at least as important as production, a fact that raises its own challenges and opportunities in relation to teaching and promoting the classics. The historical monopoly of state television ensured that up to seven million viewers turned into Lope adaptations such as *La dama boba*, *Peribáñez* or *La viuda valenciana* broadcast as part of the *Estudio 1* theatrical slot in the 1960s and 1970s.[38] The segmentation of audiences that has resulted from the liberalization of the media-scape and increased competition ensures that, even with the presence of a popular star such Aitana Sánchez Gijón, it would have been quixotic to hope for similar viewing figures when *Estudio 1* returned to Spanish screens in 2010 with a new adaptation of *La viuda valenciana*. That said, free online access to classic broadcasts facilitates the revitalization of pedagogical practice. We have at our fingertips a remarkable archive of audio-visual resources unthinkable even a decade ago. The next section will use a case-study from an undergraduate module at the University of Leeds to suggest that we have yet to take full advantage of this audio-visual heritage in the classroom.

36 Verónica Fernández, *Lope* (Madrid: Temas de Hoy, 2010) and e-mail from Ignacio del Moral sent to the author on 27 April 2013.
37 Alba Carmona, '*Lope* de Andrucha Waddington: una biografía del Fénix para el lienzo de plata', *Hipogrifo* 4/2 (2016), 123–34.
38 Manuel Palacio, *Historia de la televisión en España* (Barcelona: Gedisa, 2005), 14, 70.

Correction or collaboration? Academia, pedagogy and the media

In his memoires, Adolfo Marsillach, the CNTC's first artistic director, wrote that 'preferíamos que se escandalizase Domingo Ynduráin a que bostezara un estudiante'.[39] Manuel Iborra observed with feigned perplexity how university lecturers complained at the premiere of his 2006 film adaptation of *La dama boba* that they were unable to fathom out some of what was being said when 11-year-old pupils from humble backgrounds at a school in Chiclana (Cádiz) experienced no such difficulties.[40] Mutual hostility between academics and theatrical practitioners in Spain has abated to some extent in recent years, but relations too often remain an uncomfortable marriage of convenience, reticence and self-defensiveness by both factions not always yielding the best results as regards the creation of pedagogical tools. Much ink has been spilled on the question of fidelity, academics having an unfortunate tendency to be self-appointed custodians when philological correctness is just one and not always the most important consideration at play when it comes to appraising a theatrical staging or film adaptation. This discussion is underpinned by the conviction that a spirt of collaboration as opposed to correction is a vital prerequisite for the Golden Age to have a greater role to play in both contemporary society and specific learning environments.

I will begin with a brief overview of pedagogical initiatives already in place in relation to the *comedia* before going on to suggest how and why the educational possibilities of cinematic and television adaptations could be better utilized. In a context where there are, for example, multiple introductions to Picasso designed for children and adolescents, the relative absence of

---

39 Adolfo Marsillach, *Tan lejos, tan cerca: mi vida* (Barcelona: Tusquets, 2002), 465.
40 Manuel Iborra, 'Lope y el cine', in Fernando Doménech Rico and Julio Vélez Sainz, eds, *Arte nuevo de hacer teatro en este tiempo* (Madrid: Ediciones del Otro, 2011), 135–40, 139–40. For a rigorous and comprehensive overview of the changes undertaken by Iborra, see Oliver Noble-Wood, 'A silly little thing called love: foolishness, farce, and fancy in Manuel Iborra's *La dama boba* (2006)', in Aaron M. Kahn, ed., *Connecting Past and Present: Exploring the Influence of the Spanish Golden Age in the Twentieth and Twenty-First Centuries* (Newcastle: Cambridge Scholars Publishing, 2015), 187–209.

The pedagogic potential (and limitations) of cinematic adaptations 239

similar initiatives in relation to Golden Age authors is striking. Rosa Navarro Durán, who has adapted texts such as *Don Quijote* and *Lazarillo de Tormes* within a series called 'Clásicos contados a los niños', is something of a voice in the wilderness. The University of Barcelona Professor characterizes her labour as follows: 'Quiero acercar a los niños a nuestra gran literatura que ahora no está a su alcance. Además como no está como lectura obligatoria en los planes de estudio, la única forma para que no se pierda nuestro patrimonio cultural es hacer que los niños puedan leer estas obras maravillosas'.[41]

At the time of writing, 'Clásicos contados a los niños' has yet to feature any works by Lope. Honourable exceptions aside (see, for example, a production of *La dama boba* by the Compañía Pie Izquierdo) relatively little has been done to foster interest in Golden Age dramatists amongst the young. Shakespeare consequently has an unfair advantage with multiple adaptations (both in Castilian and in English) alongside countless initiatives to stimulate curiosity amongst future audiences in the United Kingdom. In an introductory guide titled *What's so Special about Shakespeare*, author Michael Rosen recommends that:

> If any part of this book has grabbed your attention, if there's anything about Shakespeare and what he wrote that has made you stop and wonder, then don't leave it at that. You could hire a video of one of the Shakespeare films. Perhaps a theatre near you is putting on one of the plays. Why not go? But before you do, you could find one of those books that tell the story of the play. If you read it before you go, it might help you to concentrate. If you're studying Shakespeare at school, it's great to get a chance to act out some of it – even just one short scene.[42]

Preparing the terrain with cultural publicity of this kind helps to nurture future audience(s) for plays and films. Cinematic adaptations constituted a key component of *Shakespeare Lives* – a British Council initiative designed to promote the genius of English letters within and beyond the United Kingdom – which included recommendations on how best to implement pedagogical exercises based, for example, on the honing of listening skills

---

41 This quotation is taken from the following interview, available on YouTube: <https://www.youtube.com/watch?v=z-QR0AU7f8Q>, accessed 11 November 2017.
42 Michael Rosen, *What's so Special about Shakespeare* (London: Walter Books, 2016), 131–2.

through the use of film.⁴³ That the commercial DVD release of *La dama boba* did not include any subtitles is symptomatic of a lack of engagement with potential non-native learners. A specially produced school edition of *Lope* limited its tailoring to eschewing a few sex scenes as opposed to including any pedagogical activities or guidelines, although the producers did to be fair organize some activities and events within individual Spanish secondary schools.⁴⁴

Schools groups have priority access to the Madrid home of the CNTC on both Tuesdays and Wednesdays. Unfortunately, not all students outside of the capital have equal opportunities when it comes to watching the National Company perform, a postcode lottery exacerbated by a lack of funding for streaming of professional recordings – audiences in, say, Malaga or Oviedo can watch operas direct from New York or Shakespeare from Stratford but not Lope from Madrid. However, the multimedia content of the CNTC's website has improved greatly in recent years. This is now complemented by a YouTube channel in which it is, for example, possible to watch a trailer of a production of *Fuenteovejuna* staged by the Joven Compañía de Teatro Clásico – comprised of actors under the age of 30 – shot on a terrace.⁴⁵ On the one hand, a directorial style redolent of advertising runs the risk of offending purists but it does undoubtedly employ an audio-visual vernacular familiar to young people. In recent years, television programmes such as *Águila roja* (2009–16), *Isabel* (2011–14) and *El Ministerio del Tiempo* (2015–) have performed a more instrumental role than cinema or theatre in introducing adolescents to the Golden Age.

An episode from the first series of *El Ministerio del Tiempo* dedicated to Lope is predicated on the conceit of civil-servants returning to Spain's imperial past in order to avert the dramatist setting sail on a doomed boat in the purportedly Invincible Armada. The narrative 'emphasizes the need to read "*our* classics" and justifies the need to prevent the writer's premature death (the central conflict of that episode) to avoid the devaluation of the

---

43   See <https://www.britishcouncil.org/voices-magazine/ideas-using-shakespeare-film-practise-listening>, accessed 11 November 2017.
44   E-mail from the film's producer Edmon Roch sent to the author on 2 August 2017.
45   See <https://www.youtube.com/watch?v=kM3MktEcuYk>, accessed 11 November 2017.

Spanish cultural icon'.[46] Popularity was such that 'Lope de Vega se convirtió en *trending topic* en Twitter durante 24 horas, algo más común para comentar las últimas acciones de las estrellas de fútbol'.[47] Audio-visual productions of this kind constitute a veritable goldmine for secondary-school teachers, but optimizing didactic potential requires an 'interpretation of the formal curriculum into a form suitable for the design of programmes and schemes of work, textbooks and teaching materials and lesson plans'.[48] The need to develop schema of this kind alongside the accessibility of screen adaptations inspired an initiative at the University of Leeds, grounded in a recognition of what Laura R. Bass and Margaret R. Greer term as 'the prevailing presentism of today's students and the linguistic and cultural difficulties of comprehending the *comedia*'.[49]

In 2013, I began co-ordinating two different second-year undergraduate modules on Spanish cinema and literature respectively. The gulf between the numbers who enrolled was substantial: I have taught 245 students *Te doy mis ojos* (Iciar Bollaín, 2003) and ninety-nine (and it would have been far less if not for Erasmus students) about the Golden Age. The 'Spanish Theatre and Literature' module begins in the contemporary period with a play (usually José Luis Alonso de Santos's *La estanquera de Vallecas*) before embarking on a literary journey in reverse chronological order to end with *Rinconete y Cortadillo*. In the classes on Cervantes's *novela ejemplar*, I employ audio-visual materials ranging from clips from *Cervantina* (a co-production between the CNTC and Ron Lalá) to an emblematic television biopic of the author of *Don Quijote* from 1981. In 2015, the first year a new assessment component was introduced, I invited Noelia Iglesias Iglesias to deliver a talk to the students titled 'Las posibilidades pedagógicas de los clásicos del Siglo

---

46 José Carlos Rueda Laffond and Carlota Coronado Ruiz, 'Historical science fiction: from television memory to transmedia memory in *El Ministerio del Tiempo*', *Journal of Spanish Cultural Studies* 17/1 (2016), 87–101, 91–2.
47 Simon Breden, 'El Lope era un figura: fingiendo la verdadero', in Concepción Cascajosa, ed., *Dentro de* El Ministerio del Tiempo (Madrid: Léeme Libros, 2015), 107–14, 114.
48 Christopher Winch, *Teachers' Know-How: A Philosophical Investigation* (Oxford: Wiley-Blackwell, 2017), 154.
49 Laura R. Bass and Margaret R. Greer, 'Preface to the volume', in Laura R. Bass and Margaret R. Greer, eds, *Approaches to Teaching Early Modern Spanish Drama* (New York: MLA, 2006), xi–xii, xii.

de Oro'. In addition to having worked as an actress and being the incumbent co-ordinator of the Jornadas de Teatro Clásico de Almería, she has vast experience in teaching Golden Age texts to secondary school, university and mature students. Dr Iglesias prepared a comprehensive PowerPoint with interactive resources (which I have lay recourse to in subsequent years by making the presentation available on the module's on-line platform), and outlined the presence (or lack thereof) of classical works in the Spanish school system alongside the challenges teachers and students face. Specific case-studies of good didactic practice were highlighted.

The CNTC and the Fundación Siglo de Oro both complement videos on their respective webpages with teaching guides. These can perform an important function for teachers and students wanting to become better informed before or after watching a production. There is, however, also an additional need to offer concrete lesson plans and exercises that teachers could employ in the classroom given a context in which the amalgamation of literature and language has too often resulted to the marginalization of classical drama *qua* theatre.[50] This backdrop provides the rationale for the task undergraduate students at Leeds are asked to complete: they study independently a play of their choice and, after consulting the RSC schools resources, prepare a hypothetical lesson plan that could be delivered in a real-life classroom based around a specific theatrical production or cinematic adaptation (the marking criteria and feedback sheet is included as an appendix).[51] To support them in this endeavour, I run seminars in which Cervantes's defence of fiction-making alongside the Aristotelian distinction between poetic and historical are employed as starting points to critically interrogate the extent to which they believe it legitimate for the *Lope* biopic to prioritize 'el objetivo de trasladar al público no tanto la biografía del dramaturgo como la leyenda que le envuelve'.[52] This debate is framed in

---

50   For a discussion of how and why this phenomenon has, for example, affected the edition of classical texts, see Antonio Rey Hazas, '*El caballero es sueño* o el futuro de nuestros clásicos', *Revista de libros* (September 1998), <http://www.revistadelibros.com/articulos/el-teatro-barroco-el-caballero-de-olmedo-y-lavida-es-sueno>, accessed 1 November 2017.

51   See <https://www.rsc.org.uk/education>, accessed 11 November 2017.

52   Carmona, '*Lope*', 125.

relation to such contemporary concerns as how and why audio-visual media and literature might constitute distinct regimes of knowledge. The presence of Erasmus students in the Leeds lecture theatre broadens the scope, facilitating the inclusion of diverse examples and interpretative communities.

In terms of assessment, the quality of submissions has been highly variable. Most of the higher marks have gone to students who have implicitly or explicitly followed a model proposed by Rex Gibson through which the study of Shakespeare adaptations is orientated around the comparison of different versions, a consideration of what has been lost (and gained) in relation to the play-text and the fostering of original thought by asking for alternative ways in which individual scenes might have been shot or staged.[53] Many encompassed prior research mediated by the Spanish state television's online archive ('a la carta'), with two of the most accomplished featuring a link to a five minute discussion as part of the programme *Historia de nuestro cine*, in which the presenter discussed with an invited guest the tendentious nature of the Francoist adaptation of *Fuenteovejuna*.[54] Against this backdrop, one project then explored the ambivalent nature of a play variously characterized as conservative and/or revolutionary; the other offered different hypothetical scenarios for filming Laurencia's return to the village after possibly being raped. Another accomplished submission drew on a comparison of the two *Estudio 1* productions of *La viuda valenciana* from 1975 and 2010 respectively to develop multiple activities with a common focus on academic Lisa Vollendorf's claim that 'Spain's long seventeenth century (1580–1700) should be recognised as a foundational period for women's intellectual and educational history'.[55]

Although some individual submissions lacked rigour (incorrect dates, the repetition of clichés surrounding the black legend, etc.), a more general fault has been taking insufficient account of the intended audience(s). In

---

53 Rex Gibson, *Teaching Shakespeare* (Cambridge: Cambridge University Press, 1998), 149.
54 The discussion about Antonio Román's cinematic adaptation of *Fuenteovejuna* is available at <http://www.rtve.es/alacarta/videos/historia-de-nuestro-cine/historia-nuestro-cine-fuenteovejuna-presentacion/3585194>, accessed 11 November 2017.
55 Lisa Vollendorf, *The Lives of Women: A New History of Inquisitorial Spain* (Nashville, TN: Vanderbilt University Press, 2007), 3.

one project, for example, a dense academic quote by feminist theorist Toril Moi – which might have functioned well in a traditional essay, but less so in a PowerPoint designed for use with secondary school students – provided a somewhat obtuse gateway to Manuel Iborra's fairly accessible cinematic adaptation of *La dama boba*.[56] Given that many of the Leeds second-year undergraduates enrolled on the 'Spanish Theatre and Literature' module spend the following year as British Council language assistants in Spain, it is especially vital that they learn to gauge the importance of the receiver in any act of communication. In relation to our role as educators concerned with the Golden Age, I have sought throughout this chapter to use empirical class practice to demonstrate how and why we should identify parameters that extend beyond philological correctness to critically assess how and why audio-visual materials might be best exploited in order to bring students into closer contact with the period's cultural production and, at the same time, to improve critical thinking and to nurture transferable communication skills.

Conclusion

I am hardly the first to point out that traditional models of humanist education are in crisis, quite possibly on the brink of extinction. This is an age in which we teach as well as live in a society of the spectacle. The existence of compulsory reading lists in which Lope still enjoys a certain prominence for Hispanic studies post-graduates in the United States ensures the survival of the literature of the Golden Age amongst the academic community the other side of the Atlantic, but an increased emphasis on specialisms in doctoral study in the United Kingdom has already produced a generation of young scholars and educators whose versing in the Spanish classics is minimal or non-existent.[57] On the one hand, certain traditional universities continue to offer specialist modules dedicated to the Golden Age (Oxbridge aside, Durham, Nottingham and Queen's University Belfast are distinguished

---

56 Toril Moi, *Sexual/Textual Politics* (New York: Routledge, 2002), 64.
57 Brown, *Confronting*, 77.

examples). This is, however, increasingly the exception as opposed to the rule. Many British undergraduates will have their first and sometimes only encounter with the Golden Age in modules dedicated to cinema. At the University of Exeter, Sally Faulkner's 'Volver: Screening the Past in Spanish Cinema', which provides scope for both Miró's *El perro del hortelano* and Bollaín's *También la lluvia* (2010), is evidence of this evolving paradigm. Cinematic and television adaptations are neither panaceas nor betrayals in and of themselves.

In theory, I occupy a privileged space within the British higher education system: my doctorate was awarded by Oxford, and I currently hold a chair in the country's largest unit of Hispanic Studies. My teaching is nevertheless still dictated in no small measure by the demands of an increasingly cutthroat market for students. UK universities have created a series of structures by which it is increasingly difficult to provide a rationale for teaching the Golden Age according to traditional paradigms. Rather than merely lament the fact, however terrible we may feel it to be, we need to look for solutions and new pedagogical models in a pro-active as opposed to reactive manner. In Spain, the implementation of the Bologna Plan within a culture in which the traditional centrality of the written word is in decline ensures the heavily didactic model of a university curriculum orientated around reading huge tomes associated with degrees in Spanish Philology is fast becoming obsolete. It is not necessary to fall into the trap of eulogizing false Arcadias, more redolent of Don Quijote than Cervantes, to recognize that if not the primary obstacle militating against the ostensible modernization of the school education system was the rushed, unreflective and anachronistic importation of foreign didactic models.[58] This error ought not to be replicated in the beleaguered public university system at a time when departments of Education are about the only to be expanding.[59]

---

58 For examples of this tendency, see Jesús López Medel, *Libertad de enseñanza, derecho a la educación y autogestión* (Zaragoza: Fragua, 1984) and Gregorio Salvador, *El destrozo educativo* (Madrid: Unisón, 2012).

59 At least one doctoral thesis has now been completed that studies pedagogy in relation to the cultural production of the Golden Age. See Julián Jesús Pérez Fernández, *La motivación en la educación secundaria obligatoria: estudio y tratamiento interdisciplinar a partir de una obra teatral española del Siglo de Oro* (La Coruña: Universidade da Coruña, unpublished thesis, 2009).

The migration (sometimes voluntary, sometimes forced) of many talented young philologists to Education bodes well; in order that this potential be fulfilled, collaborative dialogue between all stakeholders is required with the common aim of renovating pedagogical practice in relation to Lope and his contemporaries, to optimize profit and pleasure through the implementation of a genuine as opposed to a simulacrum of education.

Appendix

SPPO2690: Spanish Literature and Theatre

School Resource Marksheet

Student number:

First marker: First marker's grade score:

Moderator: Agreed grade score:

Resource topic:	

A 1st class resource (70–75) will meet all of the following criteria:	
It will show a comprehensive understanding of the chosen text, as well as of appropriate modern-day iterations (e.g. in film, television or theatre) in their corresponding socio-historical contexts.	
Its understanding of the text will be informed by academic research, drawing critically on a range of appropriate sources and links to where both students and teachers can find more information.	
The classroom activities will show an awareness of the demands of the Spanish curriculum, will be appropriate for a single class period, and will display the creativity necessary to appeal to students.	
It will be presented professionally and with a bibliography. It needs to be 1,000 words long (bibliography excluded). You can choose the format you feel is best, but you might want to keep the RSC Schools' resources discussed in class in mind as an appropriate model.	

A high 1st class presentation (76+) will meet one or more of the criteria particularly well.
A high 2:1 class presentation (65–69) will meet three of the criteria and one partially.
A low 2:1 class presentation (60–64) will meet two of the criteria and two partially.
A 2:2 class Presentation (50–59) will fail to meet three of the criteria.
A 3rd class Presentation (40–49) will be characterised by poor research, a failure to assist teachers in the use of primary materials in class, poor classroom activities, and will be characterised by poor and/or incomplete presentation.

Comments:

The best features of this presentation:

To improve in the future:

Notes on contributors

AROA ALGABA GRANERO is a predoctoral fellow and assistant lecturer in Spanish Golden Age Drama at the University of Salamanca, where she earned her undergraduate degree in Spanish Language and Literature (2011–15), for which she received the Graduation Award for Achievement. Her research centres on contemporary stagings of Cervantes's plays. She has contributed extensively to conferences in Spain and abroad and has had her work published in various academic journals (*Anagnórisis* and *Siglo XXI. Literatura y cultura españolas*) and collaborative books (*Topografías literarias: el espacio en la literatura hispánica de la Edad Media al siglo XXI*, *El teatro de Cervantes y el nacimiento de la comedia española* and *Cervantes, Shakespeare y la Edad de Oro en la escena*). She spent three months as a visiting researcher at the University of Oxford (September–December 2018).

TED BERGMAN is lecturer in Spanish at the University of St Andrews in Scotland. He holds a PhD in Romance Languages from Princeton University and has published widely on early modern Spanish theatre, mainly focusing on humour and criminality. He is currently expanding his research area into popular medicine, charlatans, and performance. His book *The Art of Humour in the Teatro Breve and Comedias of Calderón de la Barca* (Tamesis, 2003) explores the mixing of high and low forms of theatre. He is currently working on a monograph that examines lawbreaking, peacekeeping and theatricality. His published articles on humour cover such themes as metadiscourse and language games, voyeurism and the *pecado nefando*, and self-censorship. Articles on criminality have focused on themes such as gypsies and transversality, *jácaras* – seventeenth-century gangster ballads, including their connection to modern *narco-corridos* – and graphic criminal violence in *La Celestina* (1499).

ANTONIO CARREÑO-RODRÍGUEZ is associate professor of Spanish at George Mason University. He completed his undergraduate work at Trinity College in Hartford, Connecticut (BA in French Studies and Political

Science, 1997) and his graduate work at Middlebury College (MA, 1998) and Yale University (MA, 2001, MPhil 2001, PhD 2005). His scholarly and teaching interests lie mainly in the areas of Medieval and Early Modern Spain, cultural studies, comparative literature, literary theory, performance studies, and popular culture. He is the author of the monograph *Alegorías del poder: crisis imperial y comedia nueva, 1598–1659* (Tamesis, 2009) and co-editor of *Corona trágica*, Lope de Vega's epic poem on the ill-fated Mary Queen of Scots (Cátedra, 2014).

GEMA CIENFUEGOS ANTELO teaches Didactics of Language and Literature at the University of Valladolid in Spain. She is a graduate in Hispanic Philology from the Universidad Complutense in Madrid, where she earned her doctorate in 2004. She also holds an MA in Theatre and the Performing Arts from the same university (2011). She has taught Spanish and Spanish as a Foreign Language for over fifteen years at universities in Spain and Canada, as well as for IES Abroad. Her research focuses primarily on classical Spanish theatre, including aspects such as censorship, and she has published three books and over thirty articles in specialist journals in her field of expertise. She has recently expanded her lines of enquiry to include modern-day stagings of classical plays and the teaching of Golden Age theatre to young learners.

RUBÉN CRISTÓBAL HORNILLOS is an associate lecturer of the Faculty of Education at the University of Zaragoza, Spain, where he has taught since 2015. He holds undergraduate degrees in Spanish Philology, Journalism and Advanced Spanish Literature Studies, as well as an MA in Teaching Spanish as a Foreign Language. He was awarded his PhD in the Didactics of Spanish Language and Literature by the University of Granada in 2017. He taught Spanish Language and Literature at secondary-school level in Zaragoza (2011–12) and at the Liceo José Martí in Warsaw (2012–15). A member of the scientific boards of a number of journals, he has published several books and articles in his field of expertise and delivered papers at conferences in Spain and abroad.

STUART DAVIS is College senior lecturer in Spanish at Girton College and an affiliated lecturer in the Department of Spanish and Portuguese, University of Cambridge. Stuart has particular research interests in memory, shame and other emotions in Hispanic literature, film and visual cultures, as well as long-standing interests in canon theory, metacriticism, museum studies and representations of gender and sexuality. He is the author of *Writing and Heritage in Contemporary Spain: The Imaginary Museum of Literature* (Tamesis, 2012) and co-editor of *The Modern Spanish Canon. Visibility, Cultural Capital and the Academy* (Legenda, 2018). As well as lecturing, he is Admissions Tutor for Arts subjects at Girton College.

ALMUDENA GARCÍA GONZÁLEZ is an assistant professor of the Faculty of Education at the University of Castilla La Mancha (UCLM) in Ciudad Real, where she teaches Spanish Language and Literature. She earned her undergraduate degree in Spanish Language and Literature at the University of Valladolid, where she also completed her PhD. From 2005 to 2015, she worked at the Almagro Institute for Golden Age Theatre, a research centre belonging to UCLM. Her research works focus on two main areas: Spanish Golden Age theatre (with particular emphasis on the work of Vélez de Guevara, Rojas Zorrilla and Enríquez Gómez) and adaptations of Golden Age literature (especially theatre) for children and young people. She is the author of one monograph and various articles and book chapters and has also edited a total of nine books.

JEREMY LAWRANCE is an honorary research fellow, Faculty of Medieval and Modern Languages, at the University of Oxford and Emeritus Professor at the University of Nottingham. He earned his MA and DPhil at Oxford, where he later taught before taking up posts at the University of Manchester and Nottingham. A philologist and literary scholar, he is the highly respected author of approximately sixty studies on the cultural history of late medieval and early modern Spain, with special emphasis on the impact of the classical Renaissance on art and the history of ideas. He was elected to the British Academy in 2011 and is also a past president of the Association of Hispanists of Great Britain and Ireland (2004–6).

COLLIN MCKINNEY is an associate professor in the Department of Spanish at Bucknell University. He is the author of *Mapping the Social Body: Urbanisation, the Gaze, and the Novels of Galdós* (2010), as well as articles on the cultural production of masculinity in the nineteenth century and the novelistic works of Leopoldo Alas and Benito Pérez Galdós. He also studies the links between Spanish masculinity and football, as well as representations of gender in Spanish graphic novels.

KARL MCLAUGHLIN is senior lecturer in Spanish at Manchester Metropolitan University, with a focus on Translation and Interpreting. He spent his undergraduate years at Queen's University Belfast before embarking on career as a professional conference interpreter. He holds a PhD in Golden Age literature and is the co-author of a modern edition of the poetry of Catalina Clara Ramírez de Guzmán (1618–c. 1684), as well as the author of various articles on the work of this little-known writer from Extremadura. In addition to seventeenth-century literature and aspects of Inquisition work, his research interests include the relationship between English author Anthony Burgess and the translations/translators of his works.

IDOYA PUIG is a senior lecturer at Manchester Metropolitan University. She completed her PhD on Cervantes and the *Novelas ejemplares* at Westfield College, University of London. She has published a number of articles on Cervantes and sixteenth-century Spanish culture and society and edited *Tradition and Modernity: Cervantes's Presence in Spanish Contemporary Literature* (Oxford: Peter Lang, 2009), which explores Cervantes's influence in contemporary literature. She is currently working on exploring new media to teach literary classics and ways to bring literature back into the language class. She is also working on the *Litinclass* project (<https://litinclass.wordpress.com>).

SARA SÁNCHEZ HERNÁNDEZ is a lecturer at the University of Salamanca, where she earned her undergraduate degree in Hispanic and English Philology and her MA in Spanish and Hispano-American Literature. She is a member of the *TESAL 16* project and the Institute of Medieval and Renaissance Studies and Digital Humanities (*IEMYRhd*). Her research focuses on theatrical aspects of the Spanish Renaissance playwrights Juan del Encina, Lucas Fernández, Gil Vicente and Torres Naharro. She has collaborated with the Biblioteca Virtual Miguel de Cervantes in the *Lucas Fernández* and *Juan del Encina* web portals and has delivered papers at numerous international conferences. Editor of the monographic volume *Topografías literarias: el espacio en la literatura hispánica de la Edad Media al siglo XXI* (Biblioteca Nueva, 2017), she has published approximately forty papers in specialized research journals and monographs on theatricality in Spanish Renaissance playwrights and on the teaching of their works on university programmes.

DUNCAN WHEELER is Professor of Spanish Studies at the University of Leeds and Editor (Hispanic Studies) of *Modern Language Review*. In 2016, he was inducted into the Spanish Academy of Stage Arts in recognition of his research into and teaching of Hispanic Theatres. A published translator, he is the author *Golden Age Drama in Contemporary Spain: The Comedia on Page, Stage and Screen* (Cardiff: University of Wales Press, 2012) and *Art, Power and Governance: The Cultural Politics of Spain's Transition to Democracy* (Manchester: Manchester University Press, 2019) as well as over fifty journal articles and book chapters. He regularly writes journalistic pieces in both Spain and the UK for outlets such as *The London Review of Books, The Guardian, The Times Literary Supplement, Prospect, JotDown* and *La Revista de Libros*.

JULES WHICKER is a senior teaching fellow at the University of Birmingham, where he has taught since 1996. He completed his BA in English and Spanish at Christ Church, Oxford, where he went on to complete his doctorate on the seventeenth-century playwright Juan Ruiz de Alarcón. His interests lie principally in the field of the Golden Age *comedia*, as well as writing and teaching on the development of drama in early modern Spain and on controversies surrounding the moral status of theatre in the Golden Age. Other interests include the intellectual history and wider cultural background to Golden Age literature, English and French drama in performance, and early music in Spain and Latin America. He has a long-standing interest in translation, having translated (independently and in collaboration) several Golden-Age *comedias*, a number of previously unpublished Latin American Baroque lyrics, and a novel – *La sonrisa etrusca*, by José Luis Sampedro.

Index

2Pac *see* Tupac Shakur
50 Cent 71, 82–3, 84, 173
80 *veces* 185, 186

Abadía, La 202
Abós, Ángel Luis 231
academies 145–9, 156, 157
academy verse 148
Acevedo, Doña Victoria (anti-heroine) 78, 79
action heroes 74–5
   see also heroes
Action Heroes and Anti-Heroes in Early Modern Spain 74–5
adaptations *see* cinematic adaptations; graphic novels; television; theatre
aemulatio 173
AICLE 188
Alarcos, Emilio 212
Alonso, Dámaso 212
Alonso Maluenda, Jacinto 155
Alonso-Arévalo, Julio 105
alter egos 168
Amorós, Andrés 212, 233
analogy 73, 74–5, 78–9, 80–2, 84–5, 118
Ángel Garrido, Miguel 214
anti-heroes 74–5, 76–7, 79–80, 82
   see also action heroes; heroes
Anti-Heroes: Is There a Goodness of Purpose? (Kinnaird) 76
anti-heroines 78
   see also heroines
anti-Semitism 153, 161, 165
Aprendizaje Integrado de Contenidos y Lenguas Extranjeras (AICLE) 188

aprendizaje significativo 179, 180, 189
Apter, Emily 18
Aravamudan, Srinivas 17
archivos del Ministerio, Los 67
Arellano, Ignacio 82, 165
Arens, Katherine 110–11
Armada Invencible 58, 60, 240
Arte nuevo de hacer comedias 68, 127, 204
artworks 125
audio-visual production 229, 241, 242–4
audio-visual resources 237, 240–1
authenticity 110, 115
Auto de la sibila Casandra 221
Avilés, Luis F. 72

'Bad Blood' Video (Swift) 78–9
Baena, Julio 74
ballads 78, 80, 81, 85, 162, 171
baños de Argel, Los 62, 68
Barón, Emilio 212
Bass, Laura R. 241
Becker-Cantarino, Barbara 35–6
beefs (rap wars) 160–1, 163–4, 170
Benjamin, Walter 12–14, 15, 20, 30
Biblioteca Digital Hispánica 68, 131
Biblioteca Nacional de España 68, 131
Bieito, Calixto 206
biografía de los autores 67
Blecua, José Manuel 164
'Blood Hound' (50 Cent) 82–3
Borgia, Los 200
Bouterwek, Friedrich 35
Breden, Simon 60, 63, 69
Bridge Wars 170

Brookman, Helen 123–4, 125
Brooks, Cleanth 217
burlador de Sevilla, El 42, 205, 206

caballero de Olmedo, El 205, 206, 209
cabellos de Absalón, Los (Tamar) 220–1
Calderón de la Barca, Pedro 38, 127, 128, 194, 196, 220
Campbell, Joseph 75, 76
canciones 68, 162, 174, 178, 179, 181–7
Canseco, Manuel 201
Canvas Virtual Learning Environment (VLE) 132
carátula, La 201
cárcel de amor, La 218
Cardenio 70, 101
Cary, Stephen 95
castigo sin venganza, El 69, 221
celebrity feuds 149–52
Celestina, La 38, 195, 219, 249
Centro de Documentación Teatral del INAEM 197
Centro de Documentación Teatral Teatroteca 195
cerco de Numancia, El 201
Cervantes, Miguel de *see individual works*
cinematic adaptations 229, 230, 231–2, 235–7, 239–40, 243, 245
  Lope de Vega 23, 25–6, 28–9, 30, 238
  Shakespeare 23–4, 25, 75, 234–5
Cirrus 134
Clásicos contados a los niños 239
CNTC (Compañía Nacional de Teatro Clásico) 195, 205, 206, 207, 232, 238, 240, 242
Colbert Cairns, Emily 117
collaboration 109, 135, 136, 238
Coloquio de Selvagia 201
comedia 199–200, 204, 228–9, 230, 232–3, 236, 241
comic books 92, 95, 96–7

  see also Complete Don Quixote, The (Davis); graphic novels
communication, channels of 105, 109
Compañía de Titiriteros UNSAM 206
Compañía Nacional de Teatro Clásico *see* CNTC
competencia lectora 180, 193, 213
Competencias para el siglo XXI 194
competitions 141, 145–8, 149, 154, 156, 157
Complete Don Quixote, The (Davis) 88, 92, 93–5, 96, 98–9, 101–4
contagio de la literatura 214–16
Cope, Bill 109
Corbett, John 114
Cordón-García, José-Antonio 105
Cornudo y contento 201
Coronado Ruiz, Carlota 241
corral de comedias de Almagro 69
critical framing 111, 116, 117, 119, 120
Crystal, David 141
Cueva, Juan de la 194, 201
cueva de Salamanca, La 201
Culler, Jonathan 18, 21–2, 23, 25
cultural contexts 32, 39, 114, 141, 144, 160, 161
Cutchins, Dennis 116

dama 219, 220
dama boba, La (Iborra) 23, 25–6, 28–9, 30, 237, 238
dama boba, La (Lope de Vega) 64, 68, 219, 238, 239
dama duende, La 196
Damrosch, David 17
Dent-Young, John 135
desengaño 15, 22–3
devoción de la cruz, La (Julia) 220
Dieze, Johann Andreas 33–4
digital literacy 108
digital media 105, 108
dime 184, 185, 218
Dirty Harry (film) 77, 78

Index

diss tracks 160–1, 165–6, 170, 172–3
Don Quijote (Cervantes) 87–104, 107, 112, 113, 219
Donnell, Sidney 3–4, 120
Dragontea, La 64, 169
Dupuy, Beatrice 111, 120
Durán, Agustín 77, 78, 80

East Coast–West Coast feud 163–4, 172–3
Eisenberg, Daniel 96, 98
embustes de Fabia, Los 64
'En un pastoral albergue' (Góngora) 128–9
Encina, Juan del 127, 194, 200, 201
'Ensíllenme el asno rucio' (Góngora) 151, 171, 172
Entremeses 196, 201, 202
Entrerríos, Alonso de 59
epitaphs 154–5, 157
'Escápate conmigo' 185
escenografía 204, 206
española inglesa, La (Cervantes) 111, 112, 113, 114–15, 116–18, 119
Espiral Teatro, La 202
Evans, Colin 42

Facal, Darío 206
Farndon, John 27–8
Faulkner, Sally 235, 245
female characters 25–7, 211
Fénix de los Ingenios 63
Fernández, Esther 60
Fernández, Lucas 127, 194, 200, 201
feuds *see* rivalries
film adaptations *see* cinematic adaptations
Folch, Amelia 59
Friedman, Edward 72–3, 89
Fuenteovejuna 127, 205, 220, 231, 240, 243
Fuentes, Carlos 101

Galatea, La 68
Galván, Luis 217–18, 220

gangsta genre 82–3, 84, 163–4, 173
García Lorca, Federico 43, 159, 175–6
Garcilaso de la Vega 178
Gaunt, Simon 129
germanía (criminal jargon) 81, 82
gifs, canal de 67
Goethe's Elective Affinities 14, 20, 30
Golden Age, origins of the term 33–5
Gómez-Díaz, Raquel 105
Góngora, Luis de 20–3, 128–9, 161–2
    Lope rivalry 150, 151, 162, 166–8, 169–71, 173
    Quevedo rivalry 67–8, 152–3, 155, 164–5, 169
Google Books 131
Google Earth 125
graphic novels 88, 92, 93–100, 101–4
    see also comic books
Greer, Margaret R. 241
Gutiérrez, Carlos 146

Hegstrom, Valerie 196
hermosura de Angélica, La 61, 64
Hero With a Thousand Faces (Campbell) 75
heroes 25, 75, 76
    see also action heroes; anti-heroes
heroines 25
    see also anti-heroines
hip-hop 72, 74, 172, 174, 175
    rap wars 160–1, 163–4, 170
Historia de nuestro cine 243
homophobia 161, 165, 170
humanidades digitales 195

Iborra, Manuel 238
Ice Cube 165–6, 172
Ife, Barry, W. 114
Iglesias, Noelia 241–2
images, power of 108
imitatio 21, 173
improvisación teatral 224

Inés de la Cruz, Juana 38, 43, 178, 185, 186
information and communications media 109
information mining 131
intercultural skills 112–15
internet 41, 66, 108, 124–5, 131
intertextuality 161, 172, 177
Iser, Wolfgang 144
Isidro, el 64

Ja Rule 173
jácaras 71, 77, 81, 82
Jay-Z 172
Jemmet, Dan 206
Jenkins, Henry 108, 109
Johnson, Carroll 99
juez de los divorcios, El 92, 201

Kalantzis, Mary 109
King, Willard F. 145–6
Kinnaird, Brian A. 76–7
Ksec Act 205

'LA, LA' (Capone-N-Noreaga) 172
Laboratorio Escénico Univalle 201
Lalá, Ron 205, 207, 241
Lamar, Kendrick 74
Landero, Luis 215
Lathrop, Tom 91
Lauer, Robert 196
Lazarillo de Tormes 11, 53, 58, 65, 127, 239
Lázaro, Fernando 212
lectura dramatizada 201
Leño 68
Lerma, Duque de 63
libro de buen amor, El 218
Lil Wayne 168
lindo don Diego, El 205
literary communities 145, 146
locus amoenus 185
LOGSE 230
Lope de Rueda 127, 194, 201

Lope de Vega 174, 200, 228, 231, 235, 241
    Cervantes rivalry 151–2
    Góngora rivalry 150, 151, 162, 166–8, 169–71, 173
    Ministerio del Tiempo 57–70
López Bueno, Begoña 36, 53

machine translation (MT) 131, 133
    see also translation
Manning, Patricia 90, 92, 95
Manrique, Jorge 178
Manuel Rozas, Juan 34, 36, 212
Martínez Tórtola, Esther 231
meaning, patterns of 109
meaningful parallels 144–8, 149–52, 153, 155, 156, 157
media literacies 108, 109, 110
Méndez, Jesús 'Pacino' 59, 61, 62, 66, 67
Mestre Marcotegui, F. Javier 232
metaphors 22, 75, 118, 149
metre/*métrica* 78, 85, 177, 178, 184, 187
Ministerio del Tiempo, El (TV series) 57–70, 240
Mira, Magüi 205, 206
Miró, Pilar 205, 235, 236
misogyny 161
Morfeo Teatro 201
movies *see* cinematic adaptations
Mujica, Barbara 73, 74
multiliteracies 108–11, 112, 113, 115–19, 120
multimodality 109, 110
Muñoz Molina, Antonio 212
music *see* diss tracks; hip-hop; rap; reggae; reggaetón

Nao d'amores 201
Narros, Miguel 206
Navarro Durán, Rosa 239
Nelson, Bradley J. 72, 73–4
Nery, Robert 235
New Criticism 217

'New York, New York' (Tha Dogg
    Pounds) 172
'Noche oscura del alma' 185
Notorious B. I. G. 163
Novelas ejemplares (Cervantes) 41, 53,
    107, 113, 114
NWA 164, 165–6, 172–3

*Ocho comedias y ocho entremeses
    nuevos* 68
Oliva, César 196
Olivares, Javier 60, 61, 63, 65
Orlando furioso 61, 132
Orozco Díaz, Emilio 150, 167, 168
Orrico, Javier 230
overt instruction 111, 116

Pacino *see* Méndez, Jesús 'Pacino'
Padlet 132, 133, 134
Paesani, Kate 111, 120
parallels *see* meaningful parallels
Parker, Stephen 106
parody 84–5, 98, 151, 161, 166, 171–2, 173
Parr, James, A. 88, 89, 90
pedagogía del teatro áureo 196
Pedro de Urdemalas 195
Penalva Buitrago, José 230
Penn Warren, Roben 217
Pérez, Gil 59–60, 62
Pérez-Reverte, Arturo 230
Performance Studies 195
Peribáñez 65, 231, 237
perro del hortelano, El 205, 206, 209
Perry, Imani 168
Pimenta, Helena 205, 206
plays *see* theatre
poesía clásica 177–89
poesía mística 185
poetry 33, 34, 72, 74, 145, 157
    competitions 145–6, 154, 156
polemic 150, 161–2, 163–8, 169–75
    rivalries 152–5

rivalry 161–2, 164–5, 166–8, 169–70,
    175
translation 124, 126, 134
popular culture 72, 73, 77, 82
'Por tu vida, Lopillo, que me borres'
    (Góngora) 170–1
Pratt, Dale J. 196
pseudonyms 168
puertas del tiempo, Las 57, 58, 67

quarrels *see* rivalries
'Que contiene una fantasía contenta con
    amor decente' 185
Quevedo, Francisco de 81, 82, 83–4, 85
    Góngora rivalry 67–8, 152–3, 155,
    164–5, 169

Ramírez de Guzmán, Catalina
    Clara 153–4, 252
Ramos, Julián 59
rap 164, 168
rap wars (beefs) 160–1, 163–4, 170
Raw, Laurence 116
recursos literarios 184, 186–7
reggae 177, 185–7
reggaetón 177, 185
Restrepo, Luis Fernando 52
retablo de las maravillas, El 92, 201
revenge 78, 79
rhyme/*rima* 85, 134, 146, 172, 178, 184,
    187
Richard III (Coursen) 75
Rico, Francisco 212
ritmo 184, 222
rivalries 78–9, 149–56, 160–1, 163–4
    see also Góngora; Lope; Quevedo
Robbins, Jeremy 37, 145–6
Robinson, Olivia 124, 125
romance genre 77, 78, 81, 85
romancero 78, 81, 175
Romeo and Juliet (Zeffirelli) 23
Rosen, Michael 239

Rosenstone, Robert 229
Rozalén 185, 186
Rozas, Juan Manuel 34, 36, 212
Rueda Laffond, José Carlos 241

Sampson, Fiona 126
San Juan de la Cruz 39, 178, 185
Sánchez Corral, Luis 215–16
Santa Hermandad 69
satire 85, 156, 157, 161, 171
search engines 112, 131
Secuencia 3 205
Seliten@t 195
serrana de la Vera, La 221
Sessa, Duque de 63
Shakespeare, William 2, 64, 69, 113, 141–2, 233–4, 239
    adaptations 23–4, 25, 75, 234–5
Shangay 186
Showalter, Elaine 233
Sieber, Diane E. 196
Sinfield, Alan 234
situated practice 111, 116–17, 119
Sobre ruedas 201
social media 142, 144, 145, 149, 152, 153
spats 151
social networks 109, 146
social skills 109
songs *see* ballads; diss tracks; hip-hop; rap; reggae; reggaetón
Sons of Anarchy (TV programme) 79, 80
Stafford, Barbara 92
Star Wars (film) 76
street cred 82
Sturm, Jessica 115
subcultures 82, 176
Swaffer, Janet 110–11
Swift, Taylor 78–9, 149
symbolic images 168

TAAULA (Teaching Innovation Project) 193–210

talent shows 144–7, 156, 174
Tato, Álvaro 207, 209
TC/12 195
Teatro Clásico Español 204
Teatro Corsario 201, 205
Teatro de la Comedia de Madrid 206
Teatroteca 197, 205
technologies 108–9, 112–13, 131–5
técnica vocal 222
television 240, 241
    adaptations 116, 237, 239
    anti-heroes 79–80
    online archive 243
    talent shows 144–5, 146, 147, 156
    see also Ministerio del Tiempo
TESAL16 195
textos dramáticos españoles 193
Th3atre Mad 202
Thacker, Jonathan 27
theatre 193–208, 211–24
theatre festivals 232, 233
Ticknor, George 33–4
TICs 194, 208
'Tierra de Jauja, La' 201
Tirso de Molina 194, 205, 212, 220, 228
Todo Góngora project 131, 132
Torres Naharro, Bartolomé de 127, 200
transformed practice 111, 116, 117, 119, 120
translation 125–6
    collaborative 134–5
    comparison 135–6
    individual 136
    induction 131
    lexical analysis 132–4
    machine 131, 133
    reflective essay 136
    research 132
    visualization 125
transmedia 66, 120
Triunfo de amor 201, 202
Tudor, Los 200
Tupac Shakur (2Pac) 163, 168–9, 172, 173

Index

TV *see* television
Twitter 60, 152, 241

Understanding Poetry (Brooks & Penn Warren) 217–18, 223
Urzáiz, Héctor 60

Valls, Fernando 231
Vasco, Eduardo 205, 206
vejamen 156
Velázquez, Luis José 33
Vélez de Guevara 221
venganza de Tamar, La 220
Vergara, Juan de 194, 201
verse portraits 147, 149
Vicente, Gil 127, 194, 200, 221
vida es sueño, La (Calderón) 14, 53, 127, 196, 205, 206, 220
videos clips 73, 75, 76, 77, 80, 85
   50 Cent 83, 84
   Taylor Swift 78–9
viejo celoso, El 201, 221, 223
VLE (Canvas Virtual Learning Environment) 132

Vollendorf, Lisa 88, 89, 90, 243
Voyant Tools 133

Wagner, Lloyd S. 95, 98
Welsh, James M. 116
Western Canon, The (Bloom) 31
Wheeler, Duncan 65, 116
White, E. B. 84
Wicks, Ulrich 99, 101
William Shakespeare's Romeo + Juliet (Luhrmann) 23–4, 25, 234, 235
Williams, Claire Bryony 155
Willis Allen, Heather 111, 120
Winch, Christopher 48
Wisin y Ozuna 178, 185
Woolsey, Gamel 135
word clouds 133, 134
World Economic Forum 194

Yahr, Emily 79
youth culture 25, 234
YouTube 72, 74, 83, 197, 205, 206, 240

SPANISH GOLDEN AGE STUDIES

Series Editor: Duncan Wheeler, University of Leeds

This series publishes titles on the Golden Age, including but not limited to studies on the New World, the imperial wars, internal strife, visual arts, the popular theatre and prose fiction. Our remit is to provide an outlet for new socio-historical and cultural research on the Early-Modern period, a time when Spain could for the first and last time lay claim to being the world's leading military, economic and political power. The series is particularly interested in reflections on how cultural production both reflected and shaped the age that ostensibly brought it forth. We welcome both monographs and edited collections in English or Spanish.

Idoya Puig and Karl McLaughlin (eds):
Spanish Golden Age Texts in the Twenty-First Century:
Teaching the Old Through the New.
ISBN 978-1-78874-635-9. 2019.